HISTORY OF LINCOLNSHIRE

Edited by
MAURICE BARLEY

VOLUME X

RURAL SOCIETY AND COUNTY GOVERNMENT IN NINETEENTH-CENTURY LINCOLNSHIRE

by
R. J. OLNEY

PREFACE

THIS volume marks the halfway point in the publication of what is projected as a twelve-volumed series on the history of the historic county of Lincolnshire. Lincolnshire is not one of the favoured regions of England. Unlike many other counties it has never had its own history produced by an industrious eighteenth or nineteenth century antiquary. It is not that there have been few students of history within the county. Rather the size of the county, among other factors, has presented problems in bringing together all this material into a comprehensive historical and topographical account of Lincolnshire, a basis for all future work; and the Victoria County History proceeded no further than one volume.

Conscious of this lack, the Lincolnshire Local History Society (now the Society for Lincolnshire History and Archaeology) took the first steps in 1965 towards a new county history, and in the following year the History of Lincolnshire Committee was born. The aim was to publish a series of volumes which would be at the same time both scholarly and of general interest, written by specialists already engaged in work on particular periods and subjects, and yet in their summaries of recent work aimed at the general reader as well as the scholar.

The Committee has thus planned a series of twelve volumes to provide a more or less comprehensive account of the region from prehistoric times until the middle of the twentieth century. The series benefited immensely from the wisdom and hard work of the first General Editor, Dr Joan Thirsk of St Hilda's College, Oxford, but commitments necessitated that she should relinquish this task. This volume has been edited by Maurice Barley, Professor Emeritus of Archaeology in the University of Nottingham. The Committee is deeply indebted to Professor Barley for all his work.

An initial financial basis for the Committee's work was provided by the Pilgrim Trust, the Seven Pillars of Wisdom Trust, the Marc Fitch Fund, the Lincolnshire Association and the Willoughby Memorial Trust. Help in other ways has been given to the project by the Lincolnshire Association, the Lincoln City and County Library and Museum Services, the Society for Lincolnshire History and Archaeology, the Community Council of Lincolnshire and the Department of Adult Education of the University of Nottingham.

This volume could not have been published without a financial guarantee generously offered by the Lincolnshire County Council; and we are most thankful to them for this help. It has materially advanced the whole project.

Other help must also be acknowledged; of Ted Hulatt of Fakenham Press Limited who has gone beyond his official duties in helping on the production of this series, and Mrs Elizabeth Everson and her helpers in the office at 86 Newland. To all these and to many others who have assisted in so many ways, we are very grateful. It is with their help that the Committee presents the tenth volume in

THE HISTORY OF LINCOLNSHIRE

ALAN ROGERS
Chairman, History of Lincolnshire Committee

The Burton Hunt. Painting by John Ferneley, 1830. The central figures are Sir Richard Sutton, M.F.H., and Charles Chaplin. Usher Gallery, Lincoln.

HISTORY OF LINCOLNSHIRE

X

Rural Society and County Government in Nineteenth-Century Lincolnshire

by

R. J. OLNEY

LINCOLN

HISTORY OF LINCOLNSHIRE COMMITTEE
for the Society for Lincolnshire History and Archaeology
1979

PUBLISHED BY
THE HISTORY OF LINCOLNSHIRE COMMITTEE
86 NEWLAND, LINCOLN

© THE HISTORY OF LINCOLNSHIRE COMMITTEE
ISBN 0 902668 09 9

SET, PRINTED AND BOUND IN GREAT BRITAIN BY
FAKENHAM PRESS LIMITED, FAKENHAM, NORFOLK

FOR RUTH

CONTENTS

LIST OF PLATES

LIST OF TEXT FIGURES

ACKNOWLEDGEMENTS

For permission to reproduce plates and figures I am grateful to Lincolnshire Museums: the Usher Gallery, Lincoln (jacket and frontispiece), Lincolnshire Library Service: Lincoln Central Library, Local Collection (plates I, II, III, and XII), Lincolnshire Archives Office (plates IV, V, VI, and VII, and figures 3, 4, and 7), Lincolnshire County Council (plates VI and VII), W. E. R. Hallgarth, Esq. (plate IX), Lt-Col R. Sutton-Nelthorpe (plate X), Professor and Mrs John Barron (plate XI), and the Royal Commission on Historical Monuments (England): National Monuments Record (plate XIII).

In connection with research and photography help was most kindly given by Mr R. H. Wood (Keeper of Art, the Usher Gallery), Mr E. H. Roberts (County Librarian), Miss Susan Gates (Lincoln Central Library), Mr C. M. Lloyd (County Archivist), to whom I was already indebted in many other ways, Mr N. F. French (Lincolnshire Archives Office), who took photographs of material in the Archives Office and also for plates VI, VII and VIII, Mrs C. M. Wilson (Keeper of Lincolnshire History, the Museum of Lincolnshire Life), and Mr G. Tokarski, the owner of the negative of plate X. Plate VIII was made from a printed book kindly lent for the purpose by Lincolnshire Library Service.

Identification of figures in the frontispiece and in plates XI and XII is based on information in two Museum of Lincolnshire Life exhibition catalogues, *Three Hundred Years of the Burton Hunt*, 1973, and *The Curious World of Charles Uppleby*, n.d.

The maps (figures 1, 2, 5 and 6) were very professionally drawn from my sketches by the Department of Geography of the University of Nottingham.

My other debts are acknowledged in the Introduction.

R.J.O.

INTRODUCTION

Most people feel a close attachment to the town or village where they live and work, but have a much vaguer sense of belonging to a county. Communities may regard other communities within the same county as rivals, and anybody involved in local government or voluntary organizations at county level soon becomes aware of the strength of these local prejudices. But county feeling does exist today, and it is one of the tasks of the local historian to assess its importance in the past. What did the county mean to the average squire, parson, farmer, or labourer in nineteenth-century Lincolnshire? On what occasions did the county leaders meet together? How cohesive was the county as a geographical, social, and administrative unit? How was it affected by the changes that took place in the nineteenth century—improved communications, urban growth, increased middle-class participation in politics and local government, boundary changes, the growing power of central government in London? These are some of the questions raised in this book.

The reader may also like to consider how the county worked, in other words who got things done and how. Many features of Lincolnshire a hundred years ago, from its courts of sewers to its flourishing country house life, now seem remote, yet other features are strangely familiar. The county magistrates of today, for instance, are a different body of people, and their duties are different in many ways, but the processes by which they are selected remain fundamentally the same.

This volume is concerned with rural society, county government, and county politics. Other aspects of nineteenth-century Lincolnshire, such as its agriculture, towns, transport and religious life, are touched on where necessary, but their detailed consideration is left for other volumes in the series. Even within the scope of this volume there are some largely uncharted territories. The rural middle class, for instance, is a neglected topic, and local government records are still much under-used. But where possible I have gratefully relied on the published work and generous help of Lincolnshire historians.

Sir Francis Hill's volumes on *Georgian* and *Victorian Lincoln* have proved a great inspiration, and a mine of information about the county as well as the city. In common with many others I have benefited from Mr Rex Russell's unrivalled knowledge of rural life in nineteenth-century Lindsey. To Mrs Joan Varley I owe much in many ways. Her *Parts of Kesteven* is the only study to date of a major administrative division of the county. Among others to whom I am particularly indebted are Mr R. W. Ambler, Miss Judith Cripps, Mr Norman Leveritt, Mr Michael Lloyd, and Professor James Obelkevich.

Mrs Esther de Waal was to have collaborated with me in a volume covering both the eighteenth and nineteenth centuries. That, alas, was not to be. But the present volume owes a great deal to her influence. She made me think about the relations between central and local government, and generously allowed me to make use of her own drafts on aspects of local government in the county.

During six years at the Lincolnshire Archives Office I had the opportunity to familiarize myself with a great range of nineteenth-century manuscript sources, some as yet little explored. This book could not have been written had not so many owners of records, both public and private, deposited them for the use of students. My colleagues, too, contributed a great deal, and I hope that they will find these pages, however inadequate, of some use in return.

For permission to make use of manuscript material in their possession I am grateful to the Rt Hon. the Earl of Ancaster, Professor and Mrs J. Barron, the Rt Hon. the Lord Brownlow, the Rt Hon. the Earl of Feversham, Philip Gibbons, Esq., J. N. Heneage, Esq., the Rt Hon. the Lord Monson, Mrs H. N. Nevile, R. Fenwick Owen, Esq., and the Rt Hon. the Earl of Yarborough.

Dr Alan Rogers and his committee, for publishing this volume, and for exercising so much patience during its long gestation, deserve my grateful thanks. Professor Maurice Barley gave me the full benefit of his editorial advice and expertise.

My wife is the dedicatee of this volume. Her name might with greater justice have appeared with mine on the title page, but it would have been unfair to associate her with those faults and inadequacies that remain, despite the many improvements adopted on her suggestion.

CHAPTER I

THE COUNTY IN 1800

THE CHARACTER OF THE COUNTY

LINCOLNSHIRE has never been a county popular with the tourist, but perhaps at no time did it seem so unattractive as in the late eighteenth century. George Byng, later Viscount Torrington, who visited it in the 1790s, thought it squalid in its contemporary aspect and unmindful of its more glorious past. Wild-looking villagers might be able to sell the inquisitive stranger a handful of Roman coins from a nearby site, but they were often unable to direct him to an inn with decent food or a comfortable bed. Even a town such as Louth, by no means bereft of polite society, could not boast a tolerable inn. Elsewhere even society was lacking. 'Not only gentility have fled the county,' wrote Byng, 'but the race of yeomanry is extinguished.'[1] Lincolnshire's human population was in fact less impressive than its vast numbers of sheep. Flocks grazed on the rich coastal marshes and roamed the partly unenclosed uplands. But the undrained lowlands of Lincolnshire hampered the progress of agriculture just as they hampered the traveller. Many thousands of acres were still under water for part of the year, and the effective drainage of the fens had by 1800 scarcely got under way.[2]

Although many Lincolnshire villagers in 1800 had never seen the sea, the county's long coastline, from the Wash to the Humber, had a greater effect on its character then than it has now. Skegness and Cleethorpes, as large seaside resorts, were yet to be, but small bathing places were springing up at Freiston Shore, near Boston, and at Mablethorpe. The ancient ports of Boston and Grimsby were much in need of improvement, but there was a flourishing coastal trade. Cockle gathering was reported to be very profitable at Fulstow and Marshchapel in 1791, and smuggling was carried on with some vigour.[3] The Jolly Bacchus hotel at Sutton-on-Sea was at one time a favourite haunt of the 'free traders'.[4]

The typical Lincolnshire village of 1800 was neither picturesque nor imposing. The ruinous profile of its parish church reflected the

[1] *Torrington Diaries*, ii. 371.
[2] W. H. Wheeler, *A History of the Fens of South Lincolnshire*, 2nd edn., p. 106.
[3] LAO, HILL 22/1/9/3/40; 22/2/2/14.   [4] EXLEY 16/9.

low state of the Church in the county, and the parsonage house was likely to be of 'small size and mean construction'. Aisthorpe rectory, fit only for conversion into two labourers' tenements, was no worse than many others. At Digby near Sleaford, surveyed for Lord Harrowby in 1801, the larger farm houses were of stone construction, one of the cottages had walls of cob (clay mixed with gravel and straw), and thatch was still preferred to tiles for roofing.[5]

Lincolnshire's smaller market towns were little different in appearance and population from its villages. The great gulf between town and country, so prominent a feature of modern Lincolnshire, was much less pronounced in the pre-railway age. Only Boston and Lincoln had populations of as much as 10,000. Stamford and Louth were half that size, and towns such as Horncastle and Barton had well under 3,000 people. Cottage and workshop industry rather than factory production went on in these places. A woollen manufactory at Louth, paper mills at Tealby, and a spinning mill at Claypole were not enough to convince contemporaries that the industrial revolution had reached Lincolnshire. Even when Lincoln, and to a lesser extent Grantham and Gainsborough, became foundry towns in the mid century, they concentrated on the manufacture of farm machinery. An early nineteenth-century attempt to find coal was a failure, although it led eventually to the development of Woodhall Spa; and it was not until the 1860s that iron ore was exploited in any quantity.

To some extent, therefore, the Lincolnshire of 1800 presented a homogeneous character; but differences within the county did much to counteract any superficial impression of unity. It was partly a matter of sheer size. Coming from London, a stage coach traveller could reach Stamford in a day; but only after another day, more bumpy than the first, could he reach the waterside at Barton. Barton still seems at least three counties farther north than Stamford, and the contrast in 1800 must have been even more striking. East, moreover, contrasted with west. What could a fenman have to say to an inhabitant of Gainsborough? The townspeople of Gainsborough had little enough to say to much nearer Lincolnshire neighbours: they belonged to the Midlands rather than the eastern seaboard.

Apart from Lincoln, which lacked the size to assume a dominant county rôle, the major towns of Lincolnshire were centrifugal forces. Stamford belonged more to Rutland and Northamptonshire than to Lincolnshire. Grantham looked west to Nottingham and the

[5] W. H. Hosford, 'Digby in 1801, The Anatomy of a Lincolnshire Village', *Lincs. Historian*, vol. 2 no. 3 (1955–6), p. 26.

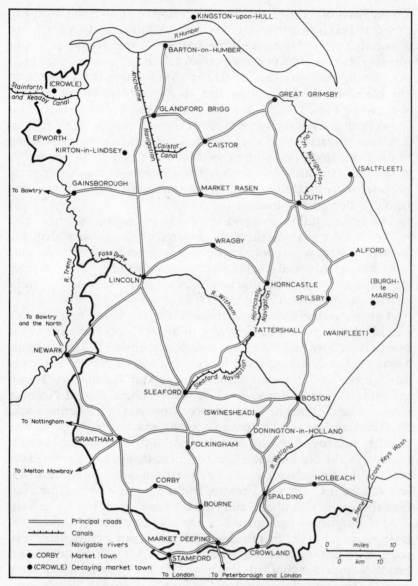

Figure 1 *Lincolnshire in 1800, showing market towns and communications*

Trent. Ports like Boston tended to develop their own characters, to the virtual exclusion of county loyalties; and Louth, though more of a 'county' place, lay beyond the barrier of the Wolds. It is also remarkable how the most distinctive regions of the county lay at its periphery—the Fens, the coastal Marsh stretching from Boston to the Humber, the little ports and villages of the Humber bank, looking to Hull as their nearest large town, and the settlements lining both sides of the Trent north of Gainsborough. These regions had their characteristic local industries, such as fishing and fowling in the Fens, stock fattening in the Marsh, and boatbuilding and its attendant crafts along the Trent. They were also regions of small proprietors and smallholders, in contrast with some of the more landlord-dominated areas of the county.

The great landlords were also widely scattered, but they were more characteristic of the upland parts of the county than the lowland. There were concentrations of large squires around Grantham, for instance, and smaller squires around Spilsby. In both cases the pattern of landownership produced a distinctive landscape and a characteristic form of local society.

A glance at road communications in 1800 serves to bring out both Lincolnshire's isolation and its lack of internal cohesion. The Great North Road virtually by-passed the county, although it did provide a way for Londoners to reach Lincoln by way of Newark. A more direct route from London to Lincoln and Hull led the traveller up the middle of the county. Turning off the north road at Norman Cross, near Stilton, he could proceed by way of Peterborough, Market Deeping, Folkingham (with its unexpectedly good inn, recently improved by the Heathcotes), and Sleaford, to Lincoln; then on by the old Ermine Street to Spital, Brigg, and Barton. This was never a first-class road. The major town on the route, Lincoln, was not itself a very good centre, and the roads leading from it to Gainsborough, Grantham, and Market Rasen were not turnpiked.

More important for Lincolnshire as road centres were Stamford, Boston, and Louth. In the case of Boston and Louth there was southward communication with London through Spalding and Peterborough or Stamford. But of greater commercial importance were the cross-roads running east and west, Boston to Sleaford and Newark, and Louth to Gainsborough and Bawtry. These routes brought the agricultural regions of the Fens and Wolds into closer touch with the consuming and manufacturing districts of the Midlands and South Yorkshire. Neither of these cross-routes went through Lincoln, which was not particularly easy of access either from Louth or from Boston. In certain districts, therefore, the canals and turnpike roads of the mid- and late eighteenth century had quickened the movement of goods and people, but elsewhere the difference in pace had not been enough to disturb the static life and narrow outlook of the rural population.

THE MACHINERY OF GOVERNMENT

Externally, or from the national point of view, Lincolnshire was one county. It had one lord lieutenant, differing in this respect from its northern neighbour Yorkshire, which had a lieutenant for each riding. Internally, however, Lincolnshire functioned for many administrative purposes not as one county but as three. Its divisions, Lindsey, Kesteven, and Holland, had their own commissions of the peace and held their own courts of quarter sessions. Other counties—Suffolk, Sussex—were divided, but their divisions lacked the strong territorial identities to be found in Lincolnshire. Lindsey, its largest division, was larger than many whole counties. It had once, indeed, been a kingdom, and at the time of Domesday had been divided into three ridings. The origins of Kesteven and Holland are less clear, but by the early nineteenth century they had developed very distinct, and at times antagonistic, characters.

The magistrates in quarter sessions dealt with those criminal cases too serious to be tried by two magistrates in petty sessions, but not serious enough to go before the judges of assize. In practice, and later in the century by law, offences carrying the death penalty, such as murder, arson, and sheep stealing, were tried at assizes, not at quarter sessions. But the magistrates in quarter sessions were also the predecessors of the county councils, regulating by quasi-judicial process such important matters of county administration as prisons (or 'houses of correction'), roads and bridges, lunatics and vagrants, and the policing of the county. Quarter sessions supervised parochial administration, particularly in connection with poor law matters, and also acted as agents of the central government in implementing legislation. The magistrates were supported by no staff of full-time salaried officials: even the clerks of the peace were remunerated by fees, not paid a regular salary by the county, and they were also in private practice. Nothing resembling the modern county seats of government, with their imposing buildings and armies of bureaucrats, existed in the Lincolnshire of 1800. Locally the magistrates were dependent for the implementation of their orders on the high constables of the wapentakes and the annually appointed parish constables. Yet they managed to affect the life of the county at many points, in fixing carriers' rates, for instance, registering friendly society rules, or compelling millers to display tables of prices in their mills.

The situation in Lincolnshire was further complicated by the fact that the divisions were themselves subdivided. That is to say, the magistrates meeting at a certain town did not deal with the whole business of the division, but as a rule only with the cases arising in that part to which the town belonged. In Holland, for instance, the sessions held at Boston were for the northern subdivision, which consisted of the hundreds of Kirton and Skirbeck. For the southern division, consisting of the single large hundred of Elloe, quarter sessions were held at Spalding. As their name implies the sessions were held four times a year, following the feasts of Epiphany, Easter, St Thomas Becket (midsummer), and Michaelmas. Since only one session could be originated each quarter, the problem of subdivisions was solved by making adjournments. The Holland quarter sessions for Epiphany 1800 were opened in the Cross Chamber at Boston on 14 January, and adjourned to Spalding Town Hall on 15 January.[6] If the business at one town lasted more than one day, as it often did in Lindsey and Kesteven even at this date, then the adjournment to the next town would be delayed until all the cases had been dealt with.

Although there was a single commission of the peace for each division, and nothing to prevent magistrates from attending in both subdivisions, they normally confined their activities to one bench. It was very rare, though not unknown, for a Spalding magistrate to appear at Boston or vice versa. Each division had a single clerk of the peace, but the situation with regard to county treasurers, who accounted for the product of the county rate, was not so clear-cut. Lindsey had had a single treasurer since 1750. Kesteven had one treasurer by 1800, but he continued to account separately for both subdivisions. Holland in the early nineteenth century still had two treasurers, one for each subdivision.[7]

The towns at which sessions were held were chosen partly because they were populous or important, but mainly for reasons of administrative convenience. In local affairs one town's convenience is another's inconvenience, and many were the struggles for precedence among the market towns of Lincolnshire. In Lindsey the two subdivisions were divided by a line running roughly north-east from Lincoln to the coast beyond Marshchapel. The western (or north-western) subdivision consisted of the wapentakes of Bradley Haverstoe, Yarborough, Manley, Walshcroft, Aslacoe, Lawress,

[6] Holland Quarter Sessions (HQS), minutes 1800.
[7] Lincolnshire Archives Committee, *Archivists' Report* 5 (1953–4), p. 6.

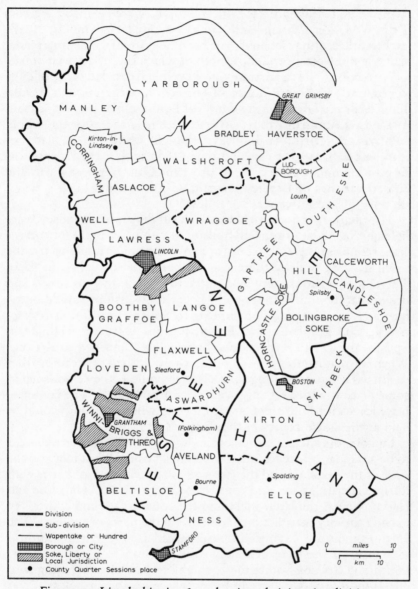

Figure 2 *Lincolnshire in 1830, showing administrative divisions*

Well, and Corringham. Its principal towns were Grimsby, Barton, Brigg, Market Rasen, and Gainsborough. For much of the eighteenth century sessions had been held in alternate quarters at Caistor and Gainsborough, at both of which there had been houses of correction. The magistrates, however, had decided on a policy of centralization. A new house of correction, large enough to take long-term prisoners for the whole of Lindsey, was built at Kirton-in-Lindsey, and from 1791 sessions were held there for the whole subdivision. Kirton-in-Lindsey, though anciently a place of importance, was a very small town in 1800, and its chief virtue was its position mid-way between Caistor and Gainsborough. From the coastal parishes of Bradley wapentake on the other hand it was a distance of some twenty-five miles.

The quarter sessions for the eastern subdivision of Lindsey were held alternately at Louth and Spilsby. Louth had a house of correction, rebuilt in the 1780s, but for a sessions house it had to use the town hall. At Spilsby there was no house of correction in 1800. There, too, sessions were held in the town hall. In 1791 it was laid down that the midsummer and Michaelmas sessions should originate at Kirton, with adjournments to Spilsby and Louth respectively. The Epiphany and Easter sessions were to originate at Spilsby and Louth respectively, both being adjourned to Kirton.[8] When the magistrates of both subdivisions wished to meet together to discuss a matter relating to Lindsey as a whole, they adjourned to some place at which sessions were not normally held. The favourite place for such adjournments was Lincoln, where meetings could be held at the assize courts in the Castle Yard.

Lincoln, the ancient capital of Lindsey, might have been expected to be a regular centre for quarter sessions business; but it lay on the edge of the division, and the city was in fact a county of itself, with its own sheriff, assize, and court of quarter sessions. The close and bail, however, the latter including the county gaol and courts, lay outside the city jurisdiction and hence in the parts of Lindsey. The Kirton subdivision, lying closer to Lincoln itself, and being slightly the larger of the two, generally took the lead in Lindsey affairs, Louth and Spilsby sometimes grumbling but usually falling into line. If the division had an administrative centre, nevertheless, it was at Spilsby, where the clerk of the peace, Joseph Brackenbury, had his office. Spilsby was largely the property of the dukes of Ancaster, to whom the Brackenbury family mainly owed its rise.

Kesteven was subdivided by a line running east and west, passing to the south of Sleaford but north of Grantham. The northern

[8] LQS, minutes 7 May 1791.

subdivision comprised the wapentakes of Boothby Graffoe, Lan-
goe, Loveden, Flaxwell, and Aswardhun, and its sessions place was
Sleaford. The Sleaford bench was more numerously and influen-
tially attended than that for the southern subdivision, and its chairman was well-placed to be the most powerful magistrate in Kesteven, just as the chairman of the Kirton bench had considerable
sway in Lindsey. The southern subdivision met alternately at
Bourne and Folkingham, places which had had sessions since at
least the seventeenth century. Folkingham was the site of the house
of correction for the whole division, a distinction it owed to its
central position rather than to its commercial importance. The clerk
of the peace for Kesteven, Benjamin Cheales, was in legal practice at
Sleaford, a small but rapidly improving town, conveniently placed
not just for its own division but also for other parts of Lincolnshire.
It was about equidistant from Lincoln and Boston, and was connected by a turnpiked road across the Witham fens with Tattershall,
Horncastle, and Spilsby. This was at least partly why Cheales was
exalted over his colleagues at Spilsby and Boston and given clerkly
responsibilities for the business of the county at large.

In Holland the ancient seats of justice had been Kirton-in-
Holland for the northern subdivision and Spalding for the south,
but by 1800 Boston was the northern capital, and carried more
influence in the division than Spalding. The clerk of the peace,
Francis Thirkill senior, was also town clerk of Boston, and the
county bench was dominated by such influential Bostonians as the
Revd Samuel Partridge and members of the Fydell family. The
division's house of correction, however, was at Spalding, on a site
acquired by the county magistrates as far back as 1619.

The county magistrates were not the only justices empowered to
hold quarter sessions in Lincolnshire. That privilege had also been
granted to six corporate towns—Lincoln, Grimsby, and Louth in
Lindsey; Stamford and Grantham in Kesteven; and Boston in Holland. In Louth the county magistrates exercised a concurrent jurisdiction with the borough justices, but elsewhere the boroughs were
beyond their authority. Boston and Louth were the only boroughs
to act as hosts to county quarter sessions. Elsewhere the county
magistrates enjoyed the less fettered situations of the non-corporate
towns. The City of Lincoln, with its own assizes, was a special case.
The other 'local jurisdictions' sent prisoners to the county assizes at
Lincoln and lodged them in the county gaol, but in the early
nineteenth century there was no means of getting them to make an
appropriate contribution to county funds. This helped to foster
antagonism between the county and the boroughs, exacerbated by

the fact that the borough magistrates, though respectable townsmen, were not generally of the same social class as the rural justices.

Where borough jurisdictions extended to outlying rural parishes, thus further reducing the county's rateable value, the grievance was especially strongly felt. The county of the city of Lincoln stretched into Kesteven on its southern side, embracing the townships of Bracebridge, Branston, Waddington, and Canwick. The Grimsby justices had some jurisdiction over Clee and Wellow with Weelsby. The worst case was Grantham, whose soke extended to fourteen parishes or townships, some of them detached and lying at some distance from the borough itself. Several prominent country gentlemen with seats near Grantham found themselves as justices without jurisdiction over their own front doorsteps, and cases were not infrequently dismissed because of uncertainty over the precise spot on the Great North Road at which an offence had occurred.[9]

Thus Lincolnshire in the early nineteenth century had nine separate commissions of the peace, and quarter sessions were regularly held in thirteen towns. As regards administration it could hardly have presented a greater contrast with a county such as Gloucestershire, where the county quarter sessions were confined to the county town.[10] The Lincolnshire benches varied in size. Some, like Kirton and Sleaford, were often attended by six or eight magistrates. Two or three was a more usual number at Bourne or Spalding. Such arrangements were a convenience in their localities, where jurors, witnesses, and parish officers naturally wished to avoid long journeys over bad roads in order to attend court, but over the county as a whole magisterial talents were dissipated and vigorous and united action inhibited. The benches, moreover, were not regularly attended by the uppermost rank of the county. The small squires and clergymen who conducted most of Lincolnshire's business around 1800 were diligent, but their outlook was too narrow to embrace the whole county.

The one permanent representative of the county was its lord lieutenant. Only he could co-ordinate the three divisions in a common policy, and without his support and influence county projects were liable to fall to the ground. The lieutenancy was a military office, the lord lieutenant being responsible to the Crown for the raising of the armed force of the county. This responsibility was a heavy one during the Napoleonic war period, and in Lincolnshire it fell upon the feeble shoulders of the last duke of Ancaster. The

[9] 2 BNL 29.
[10] Esther Moir, *Local Government in Gloucestershire 1775–1800, A Study of the Justices of the Peace*, Bristol and Gloucs. Arch. Soc., Record Section vol. 8, 1969.

THE COUNTY IN 1800

county had two old militia battalions, the North Lincoln recruited from Lindsey and the South Lincoln from Kesteven and Holland. During the French wars further balloted forces—a supplementary and a local militia—had to be raised. In this the lord lieutenant had the assistance of deputy lieutenants, who met in general meetings for the whole county and then began the work of enlistment in their respective subdivisions. Benjamin Cheales, clerk of the peace for Kesteven, also acted as clerk of lieutenancy, drawing up returns, advising the lord lieutenant on appointments, and communicating with the subdivision clerks.[11]

It was in his capacity as custos rotulorum, keeper of the rolls or records of the county, that the lord lieutenant exercised his civil powers, recommending county magistrates to the lord chancellor for appointment under the great seal. The duke of Ancaster was generally content to pass on from the acting magistrates the names of those they wished to add to their number, but his successor, as we shall see, was much more self-assertive. The lord lieutenant also appointed the clerks of the peace, who by 1800 were all practising solicitors acting for themselves rather than as deputies to sinecure holders of the post.[12]

The high sheriff also served for the whole county, but only for one year. His office was anciently one of great importance, and he was still responsible for serving the king's writs and preserving the rights and franchises of the Crown within the county. He had charge of the county gaol, whose keeper he appointed, and whose inmates he had to deliver to the king's judges at the assizes. He also held the county court, whose main function by 1800 was to return two knights of the shire to serve in parliament. Lincolnshire was still at this date a single county constituency.

By 1800 the office had long since become one of honour rather than administrative importance, and the routine work connected with holding assizes and passing accounts was done by deputy. But the sheriff was expected to uphold the dignity of the county, by entertaining the assize judges and making a public show on those occasions. Matthew Bancroft Lister of Burwell was high sheriff in 1800, and his expenses at the Lent assizes included the payment of trumpeters and ringers, and the purchase of green cloth for the court room. His year of office cost him £307 3s. 6d., a large sum for a country gentleman of moderate fortune. Even if the sheriff kept his private expenditure to a minimum by cutting back on entertaining, he could not avoid being left out of pocket when it came to settling his official accounts. W. A. Johnson found in 1830 that he had to

[11] KQS, militia papers.   [12] *Archivists' Report* 7 (1955–6), p. 17.

account for fee-farm rents from persons such as Simon the Jew of Lincoln and Deborah the Jewess of Stamford, who had been dead some hundreds of years. Passing the accounts cost him £113 8s. 7d., including fees to such quaint officials as the Cursitor Baron and the Controller of the Pipe.[13]

In the early nineteenth century the assizes were held twice a year, at Lent and midsummer. The county magistrates came to Lincoln to hear what the judges had to say to them, and they were also frequently involved in the proceedings as members of the grand jury. This body was chosen by the high sheriff, and in Lincolnshire usually included a few men of slightly less than gentry status. Among the jurors in 1798 were J. W. Yorke of Wyberton and Francis Otter of Stainton, both on their way to becoming gentry but not yet there. The grand jury was a jury of presentment: if after a preliminary hearing it found a true bill in a particular case, the case then went forward to be tried before a petit jury consisting of farmers, tradesmen, and the like. The grand jury also had power to inspect the structure of the county gaol, and to present the necessary repairs.

The magistrates of the county were associated with the high sheriff and grand jury in matters concerning the county buildings and county gaol. Only the magistrates, by means of county rates, could raise the funds necessary to pay the gaoler, look after the prisoners, and keep the prison buildings in good repair. This was where Lincolnshire presented problems of peculiar difficulty, because the county gaol was situated in the parts of Lindsey, and the Kesteven and Holland magistrates had therefore no jurisdiction over it. Before 1788 the magistrates attending the assizes met with the grand jury to consider the upkeep of the gaol, and to recommend to the three divisions that the contingency and repair bills should be met by a levy on the county rates. By the late eighteenth century it was established that Lindsey should meet half, or seven-fourteenths, of this shared expenditure, Kesteven contributing four-fourteenths and Holland the remaining three-fourteenths. But Kesteven and Holland could not be compelled to contribute: the system rested on custom, not on law.

In 1788 the *ad hoc* meetings at the assizes were replaced by more formal meetings of the justices of all three divisions of the county, held during Lincoln race week in September. This was largely the idea of Sir Joseph Banks, the most influential individual in the county at that time. The new gaol in Lincoln Castle had just been finished; the first task of the magistrates was to draw up regulations

[13] 3 FALK 1; CoC 2/1, pp. 311 ff.

for its management and rules for the prisoners. For a time the annual meetings were well attended, but the change marked more the declining importance of the grand jury than a real increase in the powers of the county magistrates acting as one body. After a time the Holland magistrates ceased to attend regularly, and in 1819 they refused to make their contribution to an increase in the gaoler's salary. Only a large magistrates' meeting at Lincoln attended by the lord lieutenant himself persuaded them to change their minds. The rules of the gaol had been approved by the Lindsey magistrates but not submitted as they should have been to the assize judges. Discipline grew lax, and there was no adequate system of inspection by visiting justices.[14]

Finally in this survey of county administration in 1800 we come to the Church. Lincolnshire belonged to one diocese, although it was split into the two archdeaconries of Lincoln and Stow. The diocese extended southwards, however, through several other counties, and the bishop resided not at Lincoln but at Buckden in Huntingdonshire. The cathedral was Lincolnshire's outstanding architectural monument but not much more. The dean and chapter played very little part in county affairs, although they were sometimes called on for charitable subscriptions. The archdeacons were potentially men of some influence. The crusty Archdeacon Illingworth, for instance, was a leading magistrate, and concerned himself particularly with the county gaol; but Bishop Pretyman-Tomline did little for the county, earning himself a reputation for meanness and nepotism.

COUNTY GATHERINGS

The nobility and gentry of the county gathered in Lincoln only at certain times of the year. The assizes were 'county' occasions, but they took place at somewhat inconvenient seasons, and it came increasingly to be felt that they were not entirely suitable occasions for carefree jollity.[15] It was for a few weeks in the autumn that the best society was to be seen in the county town. The great landowners were then generally in residence on their estates in the county: even Sir Joseph Banks laid aside his other multifarious pursuits in the autumn, and devoted himself to local matters.

The short county season began with the Lincoln races, perhaps at the zenith of their popularity in the early nineteenth century. The

[14] CoC 2/1–2.
[15] Cf. the Revd Richard Cobbold's description of the Bury St Edmunds' assizes in *Margaret Catchpole*.

leading gentlemen acted as stewards and subscribed to the various purses offered. Plays, balls, and assemblies occupied the evenings of race week. The Monsons, especially in the days of the fourth baron, took a lead in giving entertainments, and the officials and support-ers of the Burton hunt were much in evidence; but the Monson interest declined after the death of the fourth baron in 1809, the mastership of the hunt passed into the hands of outsiders, and the races began their fall from fashion.

The high point of the social year was a comparatively recent tradition, the stuff or colour ball. Held originally at Alford from 1785, it took place for the first time in Lincoln in 1789, at the county assembly rooms above hill. The date, in late October or early November, was fixed to give parties returning homewards the benefit of a full moon. The patroness, always a lady of high standing in the county, chose the colour of the year, and the purchase of woollen ball dresses was supposed to encourage the manufacture of cloth in the county. Round the ball a pattern of subsidiary events grew up. In 1828, for instance, there was a play to attend before the ball started and a meeting of the Burton hounds the following day. That evening the annual ball in aid of the Horncastle Dispensary was generally held. The afternoon before the stuff ball was a good chance to hold meetings on county matters, the theme in 1825 being the appropriate one of improving the assembly rooms. In 1811 meetings in connection with the projected county asylum were arranged to coincide with the assizes, the races, and the stuff ball. Even the stuff ball, though, was not a representative or unadulter-ated gathering of pure county society. The majority of parties from the country came from houses no more than fifteen miles from Lincoln, and they mingled with the upper crust of Lincoln society, mainly the clerico-medico-legal denizens of the cathedral precincts. In the pre-Macadam era bad weather could decimate such gather-ings, and a journey of thirty miles was not lightly to be attempted. In February 1799 a party from Brocklesby was unable to reach Lincoln for a ball given by the Thirty-fourth Regiment.[16]

The stuff ball was not the only institution to blend town and country. The Lincoln News Room, which held its annual dinner in the White Hart in October, had forty-five country members, including the leading nobility and gentry, and twenty-two town members. The Lincoln Monthly Dinner Book Club, established in 1792, had a similar social range, but with a greater clerical bias.[17] But perhaps the finest concentration of great Lincolnshire landowners was to be encountered not in Lincoln but in London, where the

[16] *Stamford Mercury* 22 Feb. 1799.   [17] 3 ANC 9/5/10; AND 6/2 pp. 147 ff.

London Lincolnshire Society met at the Thatched House tavern on the first Friday of each month from February to May. Already meeting in the early 1720s, the society was re-constituted in 1770, and given a new lease of life in the 1790s, at the time of the meetings to organize the defence of the county.[18]

The county liked to feel that some altruistic purpose was mingled with its amusements, the stuff ball and its encouragement to native manufacture being a case in point. The very first scheme for establishing county assembly rooms in 1737 had one eye on raising funds for a county hospital, and once the hospital was established, in 1768, it became the county's favourite charity. A county lunatic asylum (now the Lawn Hospital) followed, although it was not opened until 1820. In November 1818 the newly elected county members, rather than hold an extravagant election ball, gave £100 each to the hospital and asylum funds.

The professions followed the aristocracy in establishing county bodies. A fund to succour clergy widows and orphans was launched in 1797. In 1804 the Lincolnshire Medical Benevolent Society, set up to provide similar help to distressed doctors and their families, held its first annual meeting at Horncastle.[19] A few years later the solicitors and attorneys followed suit with the Lincolnshire Law Society, and after an abortive start around the turn of the century an agricultural society for the county was established in 1819.

TOWN AND COUNTRY SOCIETY

In the market towns of Lincolnshire, as in the county capital, the favourite amusements were assemblies, theatregoing, and (where they existed) race meetings. Only at Stamford were the balls and races really fashionable affairs, and there the gentry were drawn from Rutland, Northamptonshire, and even Leicestershire as well as Lincolnshire. Elsewhere in the county assemblies varied in their social character with the towns in which they were held, but they were in the main middle-class affairs. At Grantham, Spalding, or Boston the commercial element was probably uppermost. Even very small market towns had a public social life during the winter, and at these places the tone was set by a mixture of town and country. At places like Folkingham and Caistor the minimal ranks of the urban middle class—clergymen, doctors, attorneys, and the odd merchant or two—were heavily supplemented by the well-to-do farmers of the neighbourhood. At Caistor the assemblies were held in the principal room of the George inn, and run, as

[18] ASW 10/24/1; TDE H/2/6.   [19] LMBS 1.

BY DESIRE OF THE SPALDING TROOP OF
GENTLEMEN YEOMENRY CAVALRY.

Meſſrs. Robertſon and Franklin's Company.

THEATRE, SPALDING.

On FRIDAY EVENING the 29th of JULY, 1796,

Will be preſented, a new COMEDY, called, The

WHEEL of FORTUNE.

Penruddock,	Mr.	R A C K H A M.
Governor Tempeſt,	Mr.	G R A H A M.
Henry Woodville,	Mr.	P R A T T.
(From the Theatre-Royal, Norwich.)		
Weazle,	Mr.	H E M L E Y.
Sir David Daw,	by A	G E N T L E M A N.
Woodville,	Mr.	E L L I O T T.
Jenkins,	Mr.	Q U A N T R E L L.
And Sydenham,	Mr.	R O B E R T S O N.
Mrs. Woodville,	Mrs.	M I L L E R.
Dame Dunkley,	Mrs.	R A C K H A M.
Maid,	Miſs	H E M L E Y.
And Emily Tempeſt,	Mrs.	T. R O B E R T S O N.

Preceding the Play, " GOD ſave the KING," in full Chorus.

End of the Play, The FEMALE VOLUNTEER, written and to be ſpoken
By Mrs. T. ROBERTSON.

CONCLUDING with " RULE BRITANNIA," in FULL CHORUS.

To which will be added, a MUICAL FARCE, called,

No SONG, no SUPPER!

Frederick,	Mr.	D A R L E Y.
Farmer Crop,	Mr.	H E M L E Y.
Lawyer Endleſs,	Mr.	G R A H A M.
William,	Mr.	Q U A N T R E L L.
Thomas,	Mr.	W R I G H T.
Sailors by others	of the Company.	
And Robin,	by A	G E N T L E M A N.
Dorothy,	Mrs.	D A R L E Y.
Louiſa Miſs H E M L E Y.	Nelly, Mrs.	E L L I O T T.
And Margaretta,	Miſs	V A L E N T I N E.

The Spalding Cavalry Band will, during the Evening, play ſeveral
ſelect Pieces of Martial Muſic.

⁂ Doors opened at Six and to begin at Seven o'Clock.—Boxes 3s. Pit 2s. Gallery 1s.
‡§‡ Places for the Boxes to be taken at Mr. *Taylor's.*
†‡† Tickets to be had at the Printing-Office, the Inns, and of Mr. *Robertſon,* at Mr.
Dalton's, Baker, Double-ſtreet.

PRINTED BY J. L. & T. ALBIN.

Figure 3   *A Spalding playbill, 1796* (Lincolnshire Archives Office MISC DON
94/6/3)

elsewhere, on a subscription basis. For an assembly on 27 February 1797 there was to be dancing from seven till one, and there were no doubt card tables as well. Non-subscribers were to pay half-a-crown. By 1802, to judge from newspaper advertisements, most of the market towns held monthly assemblies from November to April.[20]

With the exception of Stamford and Lincoln the most popular race meetings were in the north of the county. Regular spring meetings were held in the early nineteenth century at Barton and Caistor, the latter supported by the farmers who hunted with the Brocklesby hounds. Grimsby too had meetings for a few years, and in 1810 or 1811 George Chaplin started a coursing meeting at Louth that rapidly became a popular three-day event.

Most of the market towns were visited periodically and for short seasons by travelling theatre companies. For much of the early nineteenth century the county was virtually divided between two theatrical families, the Robertsons of Lincoln and the Smedleys of Sleaford. Smedley's company played regularly at Barton, Brigg, Grimsby, Alford, and Sleaford, with less frequent visits to other places inside and outside the county, from March in the south to Wakefield in the north. After some thirty-five years on the boards Joseph Smedley retired in 1841 to Sleaford, where he set up as a printer, stationer, and bookseller. These travelling companies performed under middle-class patronage, but gallery prices were sometimes low enough to admit apprentices and servants, and at Lincoln upper-class approval was not withheld. The programmes were appropriately eclectic. They might begin with Shakespeare, continue with a comic song, and end with a farce.[21]

Purely musical events were rare, and so were the public lectures that became such a feature of the winter season in market towns towards the middle of the century. Eating and drinking, however, were never so much in vogue as in 1800. Ordinaries, or cheap set meals, could precede a ball, follow a race meeting, or even provide the climax to a school speech-day gathering of old boys. Eating and dancing took place at inns: there were as yet no Mechanics Institutes or Temperance Halls to provide alternative if less cheerful rooms for public functions.

In 1800 dispensaries and 'societies of industry' were among the most popular of the more formal institutions in the market towns. These were succeeded in middle-class favour by schools, especially after the meeting in support of the National Society chaired by Lord

[20] *Stamford Mercury* 17 Feb. 1797; LAMB 1/10.
[21] *Archivists' Report* 25 (1973–5), p. 76.

SHEEP SLAUGHTERING.

15 Guineas

REWARD.

Wragby New Association for the Prosecution of Felons.

Whereas on the Night of Thursday the 8th, or early in the Morning of Friday the 9th instant, a

TUP HOG SHEEP,

THE PROPERTY OF

Messrs. WILLIAM & JOHN GHEST,

OF BARLINGS,

in the County of Lincoln, was stolen from a Field in their occupation, and slaughtered in a Turnip Field near thereto, and adjoining the road leading from Langworth to Barlings, and the Skin and Carcase taken away ;—

The Skin is branded on the side of the near Hip with a deep red mark.

Notice is hereby given, that whoever will give such information of the offender or offenders, so that he or they may be brought to justice, shall, on conviction, receive a reward of Five Guineas from the Treasurer of the above Association, and a further reward of Ten Guineas from the said William and John Ghest.

BY ORDER,

DUDDING & DANBY,

SOLICITORS.

Lincoln, 10th January, 1846.

W. AND B. BROOKE, PRINTERS, HIGH-STREET, LINCOLN.

Figure 4   *Sheep stealing at Barlings, 1846: a reward offered by the Wragby New Association for the Prosecution of Felons* (Lincolnshire Archives Office 4 DEG 2/4/2/4)

Brownlow in 1812. The early 1820s saw a craze for missionary meetings. The clergy of course were active in promoting such causes, especially by sermons; and the gentry were expected to subscribe to them and chair the occasional meeting. Farmers whose minds dwelt on philanthropic matters were a rarity, their favourite organizations being mutual benefit and protection societies. Of these by far the most popular were associations for the prosecution of felons, their proliferation in the years around 1800 reflecting both the totally inadequate policing of the countryside and also the closing of ranks among the propertied classes against horse stealers, sheep stealers, and petty thieves. By 1810 every market town had an association, and so had villages such as Swineshead, Heckington, Hogsthorpe, and Long Bennington. The large associations based on Grantham and Sleaford were under aristocratic patronage, whilst Holland tended to organize itself by hundreds rather than by market towns.

The amusements of the ordinary people of the county were more often village affairs, and their social institutions lacked the publicity and formality of the middle and upper classes. The characteristic annual entertainment was still the village feast, although voices were already being raised against drunkenness and riotous profanation of the Sabbath. Some of the larger village feasts grew into unpoliced fairs, with stalls, races, and much tippling in public houses. Sibsey feast, held on the first Sunday in August and frequented by merrymakers from Boston, was causing dissension in the parish in 1803, but not until 1825 did the vicar and church-wardens succeed in quelling the drunkenness and riotousness of the proceedings.[22]

For many people the most exciting event of the year was the fair. More people assembled at the greatest of them—the Boston sheep or the Horncastle horse fairs—than at any other event within the county. All classes were represented, from gentlemen farmers to thimble-riggers and pickpockets, and there was an influx of strangers from well beyond the confines of Lincolnshire. Country cousins would come in to stay a night or two with town cousins, and business would be combined with pleasure.[23]

Some country pleasures would not appear pleasant to modern eyes. Cockfighting was prevalent in 1800, and was known in villages in the Lincoln (Lindsey) petty sessional division as late as 1840. Bull running at Lincoln and Stamford had not yet called upon itself the wrath of the R.S.P.C.A. And fisticuffs were popular. Of a

[22] *SM* 1 July 1803; 29 July 1825.
[23] For Horncastle Fair see George Borrow, *Romany Rye*.

pugilistic match at Coningsby in 1807 it was reported that at the end the contestants 'could hardly be recognised by their friends'. Forty years earlier the champion wrestler of Lincolnshire had been Bill Scrimshaw of Claypole, whose exploits were recorded in popular song.[24]

LINCOLNSHIRE AT WAR

The way the county worked, the balance of influences within it, the stratification of its society—all these are illustrated by the way in which it reacted to the threat of French invasion in the late eighteenth and early nineteenth century. In 1794 there was a movement to raise and equip a volunteer defence force. Following a resolution of the grand jury at the Lent Assizes, the lord lieutenant called a meeting of Lincolnshire proprietors in London. At this and subsequent meetings a fund was launched, and a committee of gentlemen was appointed to encourage the flow of subscriptions in different parts of the county. It was agreed that volunteer bodies of infantry should be raised in towns near the coast and that the gentry and farmers should be organized into corps of rural yeomanry. In June the high sheriff (Sir Joseph Banks) called a county meeting at Lincoln, which endorsed the plan and created a general committee of expenditure open to subscribers of twenty pounds and upwards. The London committee met for the last time in July. It re-assembled in Lincoln at the summer assizes and met again the day after the stuff ball.[25]

Lindsey was slow to form troops of yeomanry, leaving the initiative to Holland and Kesteven. The young and wealthy Sir Gilbert Heathcote took the lead at Bourne and Folkingham. Sir John Trollope and Sir Thomas Whichcote formed a troop at Market Deeping for the wapentake of Ness, and a body of cavalry was formed for South Holland which proved useful in helping to suppress local disturbances such as the anti-militia riots of 1796. The ranks in these cavalry bodies corresponded to the ranks of society. The captains were esquires, the lieutenants and cornets were usually 'gentlemen', and the other ranks were plain tenant or yeoman farmers. It took the invasion alarms of 1797–8 to get the urban infantry troops started, and they lacked the social tone of the mounted volunteers.

[24] R. W. Malcolmson, *Popular Recreations in English Society 1700–1850*, 1973, pp 127–34; *SM* 3 April 1807; M. W. Barley, 'A Lincolnshire Ballad', *Lincs. Historian* vol. 1 no. 2 (1948), pp. 69–70, and 'Another Scrimshaw Ballad', *ibid.* vol. 2 no. 5 (1958), pp. 42–5, where a tune is also given.
[25] *SM* 1794 *passim*; Lincolnshire County Library, Banks papers.

These bodies were disbanded in 1802, but when the war was renewed the following year a new and more extensive volunteer movement began. Even villages formed little armies, to avoid a ballot for the Local Militia. Most of the south Lincolnshire units re-formed, but the most noticeable feature was an impetus from Brocklesby that had been lacking in the 1790s. Lord Yarborough subscribed a thousand guineas to launch a cavalry and infantry body covering the lieutenancy subdivisions of Brigg and Caistor. The gentry followed his lead and about three thousand men enrolled, almost half the entire voluntary force of the county. It was probably fortunate that these amateur soldiers were never called on to defend their country. Their military experience extended only to a little drilling, some parading, and a great deal of dancing and drinking, but they were a lesson in patriotism as well as hard drinking for many a young farmer. When the Barton infantry was disbanded in 1813 Captain Hesleden described the volunteers as 'the best *national school* that was ever brought forward in this country'.[26]

Just as a man's standing in society determined whether he was offered a commission or not, so the different social grades were reflected in the amounts subscribed for the defence of the country. In 1794 the duke of Ancaster and Lord Brownlow headed the list with £500 each. The county members, Charles Pelham and Sir John Thorold, put their names down for £500 and £300 respectively, and other subscribers of £300 were Banks, Heathcote, and Sir Peter Burrell (later Lord Gwydir). Other leading gentlemen subscribed £100 or £200, smaller squires £50, and upper middle-class people £20, thereby just qualifying for membership of the committee. The defence subscription of 1798 is even more revealing. Parish collections were made, and for several weeks the local newspaper carried summaries of the results, sometimes giving individual contributions. At South Ormsby, for instance, W. B. and C. B. Massingberd gave £30 each, the Revd W. B. Massingberd five guineas, female members of the Massingberd family three to five guineas, the butler one guinea, the farmers one or two guineas, and the farm servants an average of 1s. 6d.[27]

The difference between 1s. 6d. and £30, and again between £30 and £500, is some measure of the social inequalities present in a county that drew a large proportion of its wealth directly or indirectly from land. The next three chapters will discuss the distances that separated the magnate from the squire, the gentleman farmer from the smallholder, and both landowners and farmers from the men who tilled the soil.

[26] *SM* 16 April 1813.   [27] *SM* 1798 *passim.*

CHAPTER II

LANDED SOCIETY

THE NOBILITY

I N 1800 there were an estimated sixty-six landowners who owned estates of 3,000 acres or more in Lincolnshire. Together they owned about 570,000 acres, or a quarter of the county.[1] Within this group there were seventeen owners of 10,000 acres and upwards, whose total holding amounted to nearly 300,000 acres. Compared with other counties (and the comparison can be made only for the much later date of 1873) Lincolnshire had a higher than average proportion of great estates exceeding 10,000 acres, but was a little short of owners in the 3,000 to 10,000 acre range.[2]

With this concentration of land into a handful of great estates went a concentration of power and influence into the hands of a small and partially inter-related group of families. Provided that a great landowner was periodically resident and not of very recent origin, he could hardly avoid at least nominal involvement with the major political and social enterprises going forward in the county. If in addition he was a keen sportsman and generous with subscriptions, he would soon find himself a popular figure and possibly a member of parliament for the county. Within this small circle, however, there were important gradations. A squire of 3,000 acres could not expect more than local influence in a county the size of Lincolnshire. Even an estate of 10,000 acres, which would confer a leading rôle in some smaller counties, was not enough to secure automatic pre-eminence in Lincolnshire. In 1800 the six largest owners each had an estate of over 19,000 acres. The greatest magnate was Lord Yarborough, with around 50,000 acres, a remarkable concentration for any English county and exceeded only by the duke of Northumberland's estate in the county of his title, the duke of Devonshire's in Derbyshire, and possibly the earl of Darlington's in County Durham. Even Yarborough had no great pull in Kest-

[1] Calculation based on land tax returns, county directories, and the parliamentary *Return of Owners of Land 1873*.
[2] F. M. L. Thompson, *English Landed Society in the Nineteenth Century*, 1963, pp. 32, 114.

even and Holland, his vast interests being concentrated in northern Lindsey. The other five magnates were all in the 20,000 acre bracket—the duke of Ancaster, Lord Monson, Lord Brownlow, Sir Gilbert Heathcote, and Charles Chaplin. Two of these owners were commoners: Lincolnshire continued throughout the nineteenth century to be conspicuous for its untitled aristocracy.

The peers were set apart by their position as a separate estate of the realm. The dukes of Ancaster, the county's only ducal family in 1800, had monopolized the lord lieutenancy in the eighteenth century, but by the early nineteenth century their interest was in decline. The estates had been divided on the death of the fourth duke in 1779. They were mostly re-united on the death of the fifth duke in 1809, but in the female line. He died without issue and the dukedom became extinct, but the barony of Willoughby de Eresby continued through his sister and her issue. Her son, the nineteenth baron Willoughby de Eresby, married a Scottish heiress and never became very prominent in Lincolnshire affairs. On the death of his son in 1870 the estates again passed in the female line, this time to the Heathcotes. That family had long held large estates in Lincolnshire, although their principal seat was Normanton in Rutland. Sir Gilbert John Heathcote, fifth baronet, had been raised to the peerage as baron Aveland and was lord lieutenant of Lincolnshire from 1862 to 1867. It was his widow who became baroness Willoughby and their son who eventually united the Heathcote and Willoughby estates, being created earl of Ancaster in 1892. By the end of the century these dynastic changes had produced an estate in Lincolnshire of about 40,000 acres, almost rivalling that of the earl of Yarborough.

When the last duke of Ancaster died in 1809 he was succeeded in the lord lieutenancy not by Lord Yarborough but by the second baron Brownlow. Neither claimant had an old peerage. The Custs of Belton near Grantham had been ennobled as barons Brownlow in 1776 and the Anderson Pelhams as barons Yarborough as recently as 1794. Yarborough had the larger estate and the greater wealth, but Brownlow had compensating claims. His estates lay in all three divisions of the county and were soon to be swelled through a substantial inheritance from the Hume family. He was also politically the stronger candidate in the eyes of the tory government of the day. Brownlow was promoted to an earldom in 1815 and held the lord lieutenancy until 1852. After his death in 1853 the Lincolnshire estates were divided. His grandson, the third earl, held the lord lieutenancy from 1867 until the end of the century, but he owned more land in Shropshire than he did in Lincolnshire, having come into part of the immense Bridgewater property.

Meanwhile the Anderson Pelhams had been making progress up the ladder of aristocratic prestige. The second baron Yarborough was made an earl by the whigs in 1837, and was commodore of the Royal Yacht Squadron. His son, the second earl, conscientiously devoted himself to the furtherance of the family's political and local interests, and might have achieved more had his health not given way. He was passed over for the lord lieutenancy in 1852 when the post was given to the marquis of Granby, a leading Conservative. On Granby's succession to the dukedom of Rutland in 1857 Yarborough finally attained the lieutenancy, but he died five years later.

Despite occasional sales or purchases, the Brocklesby estates remained roughly the same size during the nineteenth century. The Cust estates were reduced through inheritance rather than by sale. In the case of the Monsons of Burton-by-Lincoln, however, an estate of the first consequence in the county in 1800 was reduced by large sales to the second or third rank. The fifth baron Monson, who died in 1841, sold off over 12,000 acres, leaving his cousin to inherit an encumbered property of under 7,000 acres. The chief purchaser of Monson land was John Angerstein (d. 1858), the last London plutocrat to buy Lincolnshire land on a grand scale. Had Burton itself been for sale Angerstein might have settled there, but as it turned out the family made Norfolk their home county. Their Lincolnshire properties were sold up by 1900.[3]

Although the nobility were the official leaders of the county, their links with it were not of the strongest. In the case of the Custs and the Willoughbys the acquisition of estates in other counties reduced the importance for them of their Lincolnshire interests, and hence the amount of time they spent in the county. Among the greater nobility the calls of London society and the demands of court and parliamentary duties militated against any long periods of rustication. The post of hereditary lord great chamberlain may not have involved the barons Willoughby de Eresby in much official work, but the duties of Lady Brownlow (third wife of the first earl) as a lady of the bedchamber to Queen Adelaide for nearly twenty years were a little more demanding.[4] For much of the year houses like Belton and Grimsthorpe were shut up, their furniture under dust covers and the servants on board wages. Poor health might keep

[3] Suffolk Record Office, Barne MSS, HA 53/359/42, A. Boucherett to J. Angerstein, 2 Aug. 1830. In his will Angerstein's father had directed the investment of his personal fortune in land.

[4] Cust, Emma Sophia, Countess Brownlow, *The Eve of Victorianism: Reminiscences of the Years 1802 to 1834*, 1940.

their owners away from the county even during the traditional winter season of rural hospitality. The first earl Brownlow and the second earl of Yarborough transacted part of the county business from south coast watering places.

In the eighteenth century the houses of Grimsthorpe, Belton, and Brocklesby had all made important alliances within the county, daughters and younger sons intermarrying with neighbouring gentry. The first baron Yarborough, for instance, was connected through the marriages of his daughters with the Elwes, Heneage, and Dashwood (of Well) families. During the nineteenth century these local connections weakened, although the Heathcote-Willoughby alliance and the later marriage of the seventh baron Monson to the second earl of Yarborough's widow were important exceptions. After 1810 the Custs made no important Lincolnshire marriage.

'To be Member for the County is a road to a Peerage etc', wrote Charles Tennyson to his father in 1828.[5] Only a magnate could hope for an earldom, but Lincolnshire politicians were not unsuccessful in securing lesser honours. Sir John Trollope, Conservative member for South Lincolnshire from 1841 to 1868 and a junior minister in the short Derby government of 1852, was created baron Kesteven by Disraeli in 1868. He was an obvious candidate, respected both in parliament and in the county, and having sufficient income—£10,000 a year from land—to support the dignity of a peerage. Likewise Rowland Winn, member for North Lincolnshire and a tory whip, was made baron St Oswald in 1885. Two Liberals were also rewarded for party services: the seventh baron Monson became Viscount Oxenbridge in 1886, and Edward Heneage, by then a unionist, received a barony in 1894. For men of less political weight and smaller means, however, to sit for the county was by no means the automatic prelude to ennoblement. G. H. Packe and Weston Cracroft Amcotts were both passed over for political honours.

THE SQUIRES

In his *Great Landowners of Great Britain and Ireland*, first published in 1876, John Bateman defined squires as owners of estates between 1,000 and 3,000 acres, reserving the term great landowner for owners of over 3,000 acres.[6] As a squire himself, he should have known. But in Lincolnshire the term was much more loosely

[5] TDE H/104/5.   [6] 1883 edn., repr. 1971, p. 501.

applied—to 'Squire' Chaplin with his 23,000 acres at one end of the scale, and at the other to occupiers of land who were no more than substitute squires. In Lincolnshire it was possible to live as a gentleman on a thousand acres or even less. Around Spilsby, for instance, there were families like the Maddisons of Partney and Brackenburys of Scremby and Skendleby who were undeniably gentry, although their estates were very small by county standards. At this level, however, there was more movement in and out of the gentry class. An estate of a few hundred acres was not beyond the dreams of avarice, and families not infrequently sold up after a generation or two. What distinguished the owners of over 3,000 acres (although the figure should not be taken too rigorously) was firstly that they could play a more prominent part in county society, and secondly that they formed a remarkably stable element in that society. Of the sixty-eight owners of over 3,000 acres in Lincolnshire in 1900, as many as fifty-five were lineally descended from the sixty-six similar owners of a hundred years before.

The estates in existence in 1800 were mostly kept together by strict settlements, and the high price of land, at least between 1800 and 1875, made it hard to accumulate or buy outright a substantial property. In 1860, for instance, the parish of Worlaby, an estate of just over 3,000 acres near Brigg, was sold for £160,000, a price of £55 an acre.[7] There was some movement into the gentry class between 1800 and 1840, and several families, mostly from within the county, raised their estates over the 3,000 acre mark by piecemeal purchases. At the same time some of the larger gentry extended their holdings still further, as if to show that it was vain for the newcomers to hope to catch them up. For the rest of the century there was little change, although the economic reasons for stability changed completely after 1875. With the onset of agricultural depression land prices slumped, and owners held on only because they could find no purchasers.

The land market had a somewhat different character in each of the three divisions of the county. It was comparatively open in Lindsey, providing more scope for the rising gentry of the early nineteenth century. Kesteven saw the consolidation of great estates, whilst in Holland the break-up of the estates of absentee landlords increased the number of small owner-occupied farms.

It was the seeming permanence of the squirearchy and the depth of their local roots which enabled them to claim the deference of a tradition-bound rural society. Their virtues in local eyes were exemplified by Charles Chaplin (1786–1859), the leading Lincoln-

[7] *SM* 3 Aug. 1860.

shire squire of his time. He had both great wealth and aristocratic connections, but he preferred country life and local business to the fashionable world. Although a county member for thirteen years he left parliamentary politics in 1831 without regrets, and was too independent of party to set his sights on a peerage. In the county his popularity rested mainly on his devotion to hunting, and his reputation among his equals owed much to his attention to local business. His rigid cast of mind made him an unbending landlord and a sometimes terrifying magistrate; but he liked things done in style, both on his own estate and in county affairs. Although never master of the Burton hounds, he subscribed £1,200 a year to their expenses.[8]

Sir Robert Sheffield (1786–1862) of Normanby Park followed not far behind Chaplin in popularity and influence. His estate of 9,300 acres was concentrated in north-west Lindsey and he therefore lacked the territorial range enjoyed by Chaplin, but when his daughter married Sir John Trollope in 1847 he established a useful connection with the south of the county. He was for a few years M.P. for North Lincolnshire, but his influence rested mainly on his long tenure, from 1827 to 1856, of the chair at Kirton quarter sessions. Chaplin was chairman at Sleaford for a similar period, and Trollope was a leading magistrate both at Bourne and in the soke of Peterborough. All three had the political, sporting, and local interests of the typical early Victorian country gentleman. In their very appearance, their burly figures and ruddy complexions, they contrasted with highly bred and thin-faced peers such as the first earl Brownlow and the second earl of Yarborough.[9]

Men such as Chaplin and Sheffield could not be described as earnest, but they had a seriousness lacking in some of the next generation of Lincolnshire squires. Henry Chaplin, nephew of Charles, succeeded to Blankney in 1859, and soon became even more popular in the county than his uncle had been, due mainly to his exploits on the turf and in the hunting field. Prisons, poor law administration, and drainage matters had scant attraction for him. At Oxford he got into undesirable company, including the prince of Wales, and once in the Commons he essayed the heights of Disraelian oratory. The end was almost inevitable—ruin and a viscountcy. But even when his neglected estate was sinking into mud and debt he continued to receive the adulation of his native

[8] *Henry Chaplin, a Memoir, prepared by his daughter the Marchioness of Londonderry*, 1926, p. 11; Lord Henry Bentinck, *Foxhounds, and their Handling in the Field*, 1922, p. 7 (introduction by Viscount Chaplin).
[9] See plates VI and VII.

county, and it was said that he could have returned his footman to parliament had he tried.[10]

There was only one truly gentrified region in Lincolnshire, and that was the neighbourhood of Grantham. The combination of pleasant country and comparatively easy communication with London had long made it a favoured region for big houses. The Welbys, Thorolds, and Cholmeleys were among the most ancient families in the county, and the Custs and Turnors were well established. None of them, however, owned more than one or two parishes in the immediate vicinity of their principal seats, and their close proximity to one another, combined with the near presence of the great ducal domain of Belvoir, just across the Leicestershire border, tended to diminish the individual importance of their interests. Turnor and Cholmeley in fact had more land in Lindsey than in Kesteven.

In contrast the neighbourhood of Spilsby, Spilsbyshire as it was sometimes called, was a region of small squires. The southern Wolds is a picturesque region of small parishes, and in the nineteenth century it contained several country houses whose modest estates did not stretch very far beyond their park palings. Here too were to be found ancient families such as the Langtons of Langton-by-Spilsby as well as more recent arrivals such as the various branches of the Brackenbury family. Spilsbyshire was not dominated by any strong aristocratic presence, the Willoughbys being non-resident on their Lindsey coast estates. But elsewhere, particularly in the early nineteenth century, squires tended to look to more powerful neighbours for leadership and patronage. The pull of the dukes of Rutland, as already mentioned, was strong in the Grantham area. In the far south of the county the Cecils of Burghley, marquises of Exeter, were a considerable presence. In northern Lindsey the first baron Yarborough cultivated such lesser neighbours as the Upplebys of Wootton and Barrow and the Revd John Parkinson of Ravendale, and through them strengthened his links with the upper middle class of clergymen and leading farmers. Yarborough even erected a memorial to a 'tenant and friend' who had left him a small estate.[11] Such condescension was not to be found at Brocklesby in later generations, and it can hardly be imagined at Belton at any date.

How did the smaller squires preserve the social distinction between themselves and their non-gentle neighbours? The basic

[10] Sir Francis Hill, *Victorian Lincoln*, Cambridge, 1975, p. 191.
[11] DIXON 16/3, diary of the Revd John Parkinson 1804–27; Pevsner and Harris, *The Buildings of England: Lincolnshire, sub* Brocklesby.

qualification for gentry status was of course to have a sizeable house situated within partly ornamental grounds, and removed some little distance from the public gaze. A squire could farm: at Casewick, the Trollope seat near Stamford, farm buildings lay virtually at the back door of the house. But the squire farmed by choice and not as his main means of livelihood. For this reason it is hard to decide whether some of the leading residents of Holland, the Everards of Gosberton or the Gleeds of Donnington, were genuine squires or just prosperous farmers living in some style. The difficulty arose partly from the pattern of landownership in Holland. Parishes were very large, and estates within them were often scattered.

Families arriving in the county from other parts of England—the Liveseys of Stourton, the Foxes of Girsby, or the Bartons of Saxby—found little difficulty in gaining *local* acceptance, but it took time, perhaps two generations, for them to be fully accepted into *county* society. During that time the formation of marriage connections was the most important social determinant. Thomas Coltman (d. 1826) was only the third generation of his family to reside in Lincolnshire, and his estate at Hagnaby near Spilsby was under 2,000 acres. But his marriage into the Burtons of Somersby and through them his connection with the Langtons and Massingberds secured him a place in Spilsbyshire society. He was a frequent chairman of quarter sessions for the Louth and Spilsby subdivision of Lindsey between the 1790s and the early 1820s.[12]

At a higher social level marriages were equally significant in defining the extent of one's influence in the county. Charles Chaplin married a Fane of Fulbeck, a family of no great territorial power but one that throughout the century carried social weight in Kesteven. The Cracrofts of Hackthorn also made local marriages, inheriting the Kettlethorpe estate from the Amcotts family. Weston Cracroft Amcotts (1815–83) was connected through the marriages of his sisters with two other gentry families near Lincoln, the Jarvises of Doddington and the Sibthorps of Canwick. He once described a meeting of magistrates at Lincoln, probably a gaol sessions, as resembling a 'family party'.[13] Though liberal and even nonconformist in his private opinions, he had a strong sense of belonging to the gentry class, and this meant conforming to some extent to its conservative and establishment ethos. He was active as a magistrate and militia officer, and sat as a Liberal member for Mid Lincolnshire in the parliament of 1868, though before his death he had become a Conservative in party allegiance.

[12] LQS, minutes; *Archivists' Report* 19 (1967–8), p. 11.
[13] Quoted in Hill, *Victorian Lincoln*, p. 75.

The family background, the 'breeding', and the life-style of the Lincolnshire squire of the early nineteenth century all helped to preserve his social status and distinguish him from the farmers and business people. His appearance, his dress, his manner, and his way of speech were characteristic of his class, and owed much to a style of education beyond the means of most middle-class people. It was supposed to cost £200 a year to send a young man to university: if he ran up debts, as many did, it cost much more. If he was intended for the Church, this expenditure could be looked on as an investment, but to educate him for the life of a gentleman of no fixed occupation was a luxury indeed. Of the sixty-six great landowners of Lincolnshire in 1800, thirty-nine had received university educations, Cambridge being favoured over Oxford by a proportion of more than two to one. The preferred colleges were St John's and Trinity at Cambridge and Christ Church Oxford. As Charles Tennyson wrote to his father in 1828, there was a waiting list for the larger and more fashionable colleges, the smaller ones being less socially desirable.[14]

With the larger squires a formal public education was not essential to gentility, and uncouthness could be affected without much risk of losing caste. Later in the century it became fashionable to pass from Eton straight into a regiment of Guards. With the small squires, however, lineage and education were the two main bulwarks against incursions from the lower orders. It was important for a newly arrived landowner to send his son to college, as Philip Skipworth sent his son George to Wadham as part of his training for squiredom. At this level of society rising standards of education among the clergy and lesser gentry probably contributed to the widening of social rifts in the countryside during the early nineteenth century.

THE BIG HOUSE

'This county,' wrote John Britton of Lincolnshire in 1806, 'is more noted for its religious than for its civil architecture. Though an extensive district, it contains but few mansions of consequence, grandeur, or elegance, and those that are standing are chiefly of modern erection.' A county seat may be defined as a large house standing in its own grounds, owned by a gentleman with a thousand or more acres in the county, and occupied either by himself or by a close relative. This definition excludes houses let to tenants such as Gunby and Culverthorpe, and secondary seats such as Well Vale and Norton Place. Even so Lincolnshire had seventy-

[14] TDE H/104/42.

nine country seats in 1872–3, or one for every six parishes. Of these only about sixteen dated substantially from before 1700, and thirty-three from before 1780. The period of greatest building activity was 1790–1845, with a peak during the Tudor-Gothic vogue of the early 1840s. This pattern contrasts with Hertfordshire, where there had been much more building in the sixteenth and seventeenth centuries and consequently less need for drastic rebuilding in the nineteenth. Despite the passion of some Lincolnshire squires for bricks and mortar, however, the county remained relatively speaking one of non-resident landowners. Even among the resident gentry as many as a quarter had a second seat in another county, compared with only 13 per cent of the Hertfordshire gentry.[15]

The early years of the century saw a few essays in late Georgian classicism: Sudbrooke Holme (c. 1800) and Easton (1805) were followed by Normanby and Syston in the 1820s. Of these four houses only Normanby survives. Its architect was Sir Robert Smirke, who shortly afterwards designed the assize courts at Lincoln. The rate of building increased in the 1830s, which witnessed the two most adventurous domestic building projects of any period of Lincolnshire's history, Harlaxton and Bayons Manor. Harlaxton was the grandiose conception of Gregory Gregory, a bachelor squire of some £12,000 a year, who spoke of his house as his hobby just as his neighbours might speak of hunting, shooting, or feasting. Designed by Anthony Salvin and completed by William Burn, a former pupil of Smirke's, it was in a flamboyant Elizabethan style, with a great hall, a long gallery, and huge kitchen and stable wings. It took twenty years to complete, and was said to have cost £200,000. Bayons Manor was a Gothic extravaganza, designed by its owner Charles Tennyson D'Eyncourt with the assistance of the Lincoln architect William Nicholson. Interestingly enough neither of these landowners began as leading county figures, and their mansions, though marvelled at, did not make them so.[16]

It was the early 1840s, however, that marked the peak of house building by the gentry, as it may also have marked the peak of their social influence. Stoke Rochford (begun in 1841 and completed at a cost of £60,000), South Rauceby (1842–5), and Revesby (1845) were

[15] *The Beauties of England and Wales*, vol. 7 (1806), p. 542; Lawrence Stone and Jeanne C. Fawtier Stone, 'Country Houses and their Owners in Hertfordshire, 1540–1879', in *The Dimensions of Quantitative Research in History*, ed. William O. Aydelotte and Others, 1972, pp. 56–123.

[16] Charles C. F. Greville, *The Greville Memoirs*, ed. Henry Reeve, 1909, iv. 44; Russell Read, *Harlaxton*, pr. Horsfall Davenport Ltd., Grantham, 1978; Mark Girouard, *The Victorian Country House*, 1971, pp. 57–9.

all from the drawing-board of William Burn, and all built for prominent Conservative squires. Their style, approximately Tudor, certainly seems to give them a Conservative rather than a whig atmosphere. Lincolnshire has no important examples of the high Victorian period, but there was a resumption of activity towards the end of the century, showing that at least some landowners had not lost confidence in country life. Sir Arthur Blomfield and his nephew Sir Reginald Blomfield were responsible for Denton (1883) and Caythorpe Court (1899, for Edgar Lubbock), whilst J. MacVicar Anderson continued the Burn tradition at Branston (1884).

The Victorian country house was intended for comfortable family occupation, supported by increasingly large numbers of servants, but there can be little doubt that it was also meant to impress visiting neighbours and support its owner's position in county society. The combination of comfort and ostentation sometimes produced houses of gargantuan proportions. It is said that Christopher Turnor specified the sizes of the rooms he required at Stoke Rochford without realizing what the total size of the house would be. The Welby-Gregorys were less casual, to judge from a painting of them studying the architect's model for Denton Manor. Houses were often given one particularly striking feature, such as the baronial hall of Bayons Manor, or the library at Syston, from whose gallery George Fieschi Heneage was overheard proposing to his future wife.[17]

A big house, filled with family guests and servants, might be as populous as a small village. Servants, and particularly male servants, were engaged for reasons of social prestige as much as household management. By 1851 Heneage was a widower, although he had a fourteen-year-old daughter and two other relatives living with him at Hainton. His dignity as a great landowner, with a rental of nearly £18,000 a year, was upheld by a bevy of male servants comprising a butler, an under butler, an usher, a valet, a footman, two grooms, and a coachman. The female staff was headed by a housekeeper, and included a cook, lady's maid, nurse, two housemaids, kitchen maid, scullery maid, dairy maid, stillroom maid, and laundry maid.[18]

These were just the indoor servants. When the establishment at Grimsthorpe was looked into following Lady Willoughby's death

[17] Sir Francis Hill, 'Squire and Parson in Early Victorian Lincolnshire', *History*, vol. 58 no. 194 (Oct. 1973), p. 338; Hill, *Victorian Lincoln*, p. 16n.; Mark Girouard, *The Victorian Country House*, 1971, plate 11.

[18] 2 HEN 1/1/18; 1851 census, enumerator's return for Hainton.

in 1828 there were ten male servants about the house and stables but a further sixteen on the estate and plantations, ten in the gardens, and ten looking after the park and the game preserves, making a grand total of forty-six.[19] At Brocklesby a number of employees lived in cottages near the house, especially those involved in the stables and kennels and those who patrolled and maintained Lord Yarborough's vast and gloomy plantations.

Lesser gentry such as George Marmaduke Alington of Swinhope contented themselves with one or two indoor male servants and no more than half a dozen female domestics. To have a footman in livery to open the front door to callers and ride behind the carriage was the great thing, even if the footman was at other times to be found mucking out the stable. At Fulbeck around 1900 there were a footman and a groom clad in green and white livery, and a coach-man in charge of the stable of five horses—two carriage horses, two hunters, and a cob. Before the days of the motor car the family means of transport consisted of a landau, a double brougham, a dogcart, a market cart, and a battlesdon car drawn by the cob. Among the conveniences of the brougham was a cord attached to the footman's arm and pulled to attract his attention. In the days of higher taxation and the welfare state after 1918 the Fulbeck estab-lishment was halved, although no saving was achieved since wages had doubled since pre-war days.[20]

The influence of the great house was most powerful in the village or villages immediately adjacent to it, where a high proportion of the population was directly dependent on it for employment. Even the most testy of squires, such as James Banks Stanhope, were adulated. 'How we here love the name of Stanhope!' wrote one of the Revesby tenants around 1916; 'it rolls round our tongues with such a rich loving flavour as no other name has ever done or ever will.'[21] It was the villages at the heart of the great estates—Brock-lesby, Revesby, Blankney, Belton—which were rebuilt as Gothic showpieces in the 1840s, visible testimonies of the wealth and benevolence of their owners. Outlying parishes, even on the most highly capitalized estates, bore less outward evidence of paternal landlordism, and the personal influence of the landowner was cor-respondingly weaker.[22]

Beyond the confines of the estate itself, the creation or

[19] 3 ANC 7/23/20/86.   [20] FANE 6/11/1/7,

[21] T. Kime, *Some Reminiscences of the Stanhopes of Revesby Abbey, about 1855 to 1914*, n.d.

[22] Heather Fuller, 'Landownership in Lindsey *c.* 1800–1860', Hull M.A. thesis, 1974.

maintenance of a local interest depended more on money than on deference. Apart from patronage, to be discussed in a later chapter, the influence of the great landowners was largely determined by the extent of their local bounty and charitable subscriptions. G. F. Heneage, well-known as an improving landlord, ploughed back nearly £4,000 of his rental in 1851 into estate buildings and improvements, but he also spent nearly £550 on subscriptions. By far the largest item was his £300 subvention of the South Wold hunt, but he also supported educational, medical, and other causes in the districts in which he had property. The Grimsby and Market Rasen races benefited from his patronage, as did the Caistor and Donington-on-Bain ploughing societies.[23] Presents of game were a more discriminating means of preserving useful connections, although offence could be caused among those who considered themselves neglected by their exclusion from the list. In the 1820s thirty-eight people annually received half a buck every season from the Grimsthorpe estate, and they included not only aristocratic neighbours but local props of the Willoughby interest such as William Garfit of Boston and the Revd Thomas Hardwicke Rawnsley of Halton Holegate.[24] Only in exceptional cases did a magnate's influence extend into parts of the county where he had no property at all. It was a sign of a powerful Brocklesby interest when, in 1857, Yarborough received from towns as far distant as Epworth and Horncastle addresses of congratulation on his escape from shipwreck. 'Though Horncastle is some distance from Brocklesby,' wrote its local correspondent for the *Stamford Mercury*, 'we are assured that in no community in the county is his Lordship's benevolent disposition more appreciated.'[25]

HUNTING COUNTRIES

Lord Willoughby de Broke, in a well-known passage in his book *The Passing Years*, describes what 'the County' meant in mid-nineteenth century Warwickshire. It was composed of certain personages arranged in descending order of importance, beginning with the lord lieutenant. Next to him, and above the agricultural landlords, the bishop, and the chairman of quarter sessions, Willoughby placed the master of fox hounds—understandably, since he himself was master of the Warwickshire hounds.[26] In Lincoln-

[23] 2 HEN 1/1/18, rental and account 1851–2.
[24] 3 ANC 7/23/20/88.
[25] *SM* 26 June 1857.
[26] R. G. Verney (Lord Willoughby de Broke), *The Passing Years*, 1924, p. 57.

shire matters were more complicated. There were several hunting countries, and not all had such aristocratic masters as Lord Willoughby de Broke.

The north-west part of Lincolnshire was shooting country, and the fenlands were too much intersected with wide dykes to be good for hunting. The rest of the county in 1800 belonged mostly to the Brocklesby, the Burton, and the Belvoir hunts. The Brocklesby was divided in 1823, with the formation of the South Wold. In 1871 Henry Chaplin, finding that hunting six days a week interfered somewhat with his parliamentary duties, gave up the northern part of the Burton country and started the Blankney hunt. The southern part of Kesteven belonged to the Cottesmore, hunted at one period by Sir John Trollope.

The Brocklesby hounds had been maintained by the Pelhams from the early eighteenth century, and the family retained the mastership throughout the nineteenth century. The first earl was not as active a sportsman as his father, and the second earl did not appear often in the field; but the third earl was a popular master, and when he died his widow carried on the hunt at her own expense until her son the fourth earl came of age. Apart from a few years of retrenchment at the end of the century, the country was hunted five days a week, excellent sport was shown, and much entertaining was done at Brocklesby. The chief feature of the hunt, however, was the support it received from the farmers of the district, who provided a well-mounted and immaculately turned out field. Even at the end of the century, when some of the old farming families had died out, as many as eighty tenants might muster at a meet. The fourth earl paid tribute to 'the cheerful and cordial co-operation on the part of the occupiers of land with the owner of the pack. . . . There are no better puppy-walkers,' he wrote, 'no keener fox preservers, and no finer sportsmen than the tenant farmers in North Lincolnshire.'[27]

The Burton hunt passed out of the direct control of the Monson family after 1809, and had a succession of masters in the next few years. Sir Richard Sutton, master from 1824 to 1842, was succeeded by the strange figure of Lord Henry Bentinck, who erected a Turkish bath for his horses at Reepham but lived unhospitably in rooms in the White Hart in Lincoln. He was succeeded in 1862 by Lord Doneraile. Then in 1865 Henry Chaplin took over, having acquired the hounds the previous year. After 1871 the reduced Burton country was hunted for nine years by F. J. S. Foljambe, who built Monks Tower as his Lincoln residence.

The Belvoir, like the other two, began the century as a family

[27] G. E. Collins, *History of the Brocklesby Hounds, 1700–1901*, 1902, p. viii.

concern; but in 1829 the fifth duke of Rutland handed over the mastership to Lord Forester, who took a subscription of £1,000 per annum from the Grantham side of the country. (More of the Belvoir country lay in Lincolnshire than in Leicestershire.) A subscription list of 1847 included several of the leading squires of the Grantham and Folkingham neighbourhoods, headed by Lord Brownlow (£100), Sir Thomas Whichcote (£100), and General Reeve, whose seat at Leadenham was on the northern boundary of the hunt (£80). The field included also a number of farmers and not a few hard-riding parsons, although towards the end of the century the local people were diluted by devotees who came down by rail and stayed in Grantham. The sixth duke was master from 1858 to 1888, but had to ask for another subscription from the Lincolnshire side in 1881. In 1896 the seventh duke resigned the mastership to Sir Gilbert Greenall.

At the beginning of the century, 'to say that you were hunting with the duke's hounds was a passport all over the district. The state and splendour of the Castle seemed natural and proper to the neighbourhood, which felt that the lavish expenditure was a benefit by causing the circulation of money.'[28] Money must indeed have circulated when by the middle of the century it cost more than £4,000 a year to hunt the (admittedly large) Belvoir country during the winter season. The owners of packs and hunt subscribers were naturally brought into close contact with each other, and owners of coverts were expected to co-operate in the preservation of foxes. The landlords met their tenants in the hunting field, where social distinctions disappeared in the excitement of the chase. Tenants were supposed either to hunt themselves, if they could afford it, or at least to regard with cheerful equanimity the occasional cavalry charge across their newly ploughed fields or through their yards. Farmers were generally offered compensation for damage done, but some even refused it. ('"On no account, my lord," replied this true specimen of an English farmer....')[29] But there was always an undercurrent of bad feeling, coming to the surface when a hostile landowner excluded the hounds from his coverts or when a farmer outraged his neighbours by shooting a fox.

TWO LINCOLNSHIRE ARISTOCRATS

The culture that revolved around horses and dogs tended to produce a stereotyped rural upper class. It is easy to assume that all

[28] T. F. Dale, *The History of the Belvoir Hunt*, 1899, p. 108.
[29] Collins, *Brocklesby Hounds*, pp. 306–7.

country gentlemen devoted themselves to hunting and shooting, confining their intellectual exercise to after-dinner conversation with the ladies, or, less pleasantly, the chores of estate and local business. In reality there were innumerable variations in tastes, interests, philosophy, and behaviour. The sixth baron Monson (1796–1862) and Sir Charles Anderson (1804–91) are good examples of the way landowners could differ in their attitudes to religion, politics, estate management, country pursuits, and county affairs.

William Monson was the son of the fourth son of the second baron Monson. In 1828 he married Eliza Larken, the daughter of a London merchant, and they raised a family of eight children on £700 a year. Then in 1841 his cousin the fifth baron died without issue. William Monson succeeded to the title, and to a much reduced and encumbered estate. There were two country houses to maintain, Burton-by-Lincoln and Gatton in Surrey, and as a peer he was now expected to make an appearance in society and play some part in public life. His net income in the early 1840s was, however, probably less than £3,000 a year. Fortunately he had no craving to cut a figure in society, and the retired life that he continued to live at Chart Lodge near Sevenoaks suited his inclinations as well as his purse. He did without a town house: he even did without a carriage. He let Gatton, and kept away from Burton as much as possible lest he should be pounced on by tenants demanding improvements or clergy begging for subscriptions. His chief pleasure was in antiquarian pursuits, and he cared little for hunting or shooting.

He was nevertheless anxious to restore the fortunes of the family, and he hoped by scraping and saving to enable his eldest son eventually to enjoy a decent income. He also wished to see his son launched into the right circles. 'I have always endeavoured . . .', he once wrote to him, 'to put you forward instead of myself. I think the first time you ever went to Lord Yarborough's this was the case.'[30] It was Yarborough, the recognized head of the whig interest in Lincolnshire, who was to take young William Monson under his wing. But other county families were not to be neglected even though they differed in politics. 'I am very glad that you are going to the Chaplins,' the father wrote to the son in 1850. 'There is no family in Lincolnshire I could wish you to be more intimate with as they are among the oldest friends of the Monson family though in politics we have always split.' The Dymokes too were people to visit. 'I should like much to hear about Scrivelsby when you go there. We once intermarried with the Dymokes but it was two

[30] MON 25/10/3/4/56.

centuries and a half ago and I suppose little recollection exists of this alliance. . . .'[31]

William Monson junior was duly launched on his political career, helping Yarborough with an electoral registration society for North Lincolnshire and later (despite his father's groans about election expenses) becoming M.P. for Reigate, their nearest borough in Surrey. But his father was also anxious about his marriage, and was disturbed by William's hints that he preferred a bachelor's life. 'It is really a duty you owe the name, at least to look forward to the possibility nay the hope of finding one worthy of sharing it, and perpetuating the owners of Burton.'[32] Monson did not want his son to marry entirely for money: indeed, a good housekeeper was even better than an heiress. But William remained single during his father's lifetime. Afterwards he married the dowager Lady Yarborough, but there were no children.

Scraping and saving was no way to become a popular landlord. The low lands on the Burton estate needed draining, and there was a shortage of buildings, especially on the Cliff. But the progress of improvement was very slow when extra capital had to come from the sales of outlying properties, or from yet further economies in personal expenditure. Monson and his man of business regarded the Lincolnshire tenants as a slow, poor lot, unwilling to change their old-fashioned ways. The tenants for their part resented being told that they lacked the capital to farm their holdings and that their faith in a return to Protection was nonsense. The depression of 1849–52 led to demands for rent reductions and a deterioration in relations on the estate.

Despite the largely absentee régime of the sixth lord, his attention to business and passion for correspondence enabled him to exercise a surprisingly tight control over the estate, but it was control of a largely negative kind. Political conformity was expected, although not always achieved; and in the matter of schools both the sixth and seventh lords liked to keep them as much under their own control as possible. This was partly due to their dislike of parsons, a feeling especially strong in the sixth lord. In 1855 the question of the endowment of South Carlton school from a charitable fund arose, and at one point it looked as though Monson would lose his right to appoint the schoolmaster. 'I do not know that Kaye (the incumbent) has had a hand in this,' wrote Monson, 'but it is monstrous like *Parson's work*.'[33] Dislike of the interference of parsons in local affairs was not accompanied by any love of nonconformity. 'As for Dis-

[31] MON 25/10/2/4/10, 12.
[32] MON 25/10/4/1/118.   [33] MON 25/10/4/1/49.

senters', wrote the sixth lord to his son in 1850, 'I agree in the main with you. I detest them all, Catholics included, but if there is an excuse anywhere it is under our Rector who does no parochial duty and never sees any of them. It is thoroughly disgusting.'[34]

Subscriptions were kept to a necessary minimum. No shortage of cash, however, could prevent the acquisition of land when the purchase was considered necessary in the interests of the estate. Even the sixth lord made small purchases to consolidate the home estate around Burton. His son managed in 1876 to raise £95,000 to buy back North Carlton, which had gone out of the family in 1838.

Although he did not live to see much result of his solicitude, the efforts of the sixth lord, continued faithfully by his heir, did eventually pull the estate round. Dowagers died off, rents could be raised in better times, and the Gatton estate proved to be less of a dead weight than had once been feared. The seventh lord became a politician of national standing and an important figure in the county, being elected first chairman of Lindsey County Council in 1889. Just as he had been brought out into political life by the second earl of Yarborough, so he fulfilled the same rôle for the young fourth earl thirty years later. Yarborough left the Liberals over Home Rule, but Monson, increasingly old-fashioned in his old age, remained faithful to the party of his youth, becoming a whip in the House of Lords and taking the title of Viscount Oxenbridge in 1886. He died in 1897, being succeeded by his brother Debonnaire.

Sir Charles Anderson was in some ways similar in background and outlook to the sixth baron Monson. Both came from old-established Lindsey families, and the Andersons had in the past been on good terms with both the Monsons and the Anderson Pelhams of Brocklesby, who represented the older line of the Anderson family. Both Anderson and Monson were keen antiquarians. They went round the county together in 1835 when Monson was compiling his *Church Notes*;[35] and when in 1841 Monson succeeded to the Burton estate Anderson advised him on its management.

But by this time they were diverging in politics. Anderson, though brought up a whig, had come down from Oriel a strong high churchman, and by 1837 was already writing to his friend Samuel Wilberforce that he put 'the necessity of adhering more closely to the Church' above his whig allegiance.[36] Although

---

[34] MON 25/10/2/4/5.

[35] Published by the Lincoln Record Society, 1936.

[36] Bodleian Library Oxford, MS Dep. c. 190, Anderson to Wilberforce, 15 April 1837.

reluctant to oppose the Yarborough interest openly during his father's lifetime, he refrained from supporting Lord Worsley in 1841. In later years he became one of the leading Conservative country gentlemen in North Lincolnshire, supporting R. A. Christopher, of whom he thought very highly.

This meant something of a break with traditional family friends. Indeed, there is no more bitter enemy than a former friend: his comments on the second earl of Yarborough ranged from the sorrowful to the angry. In sorrowful mood he regretted that the earl had not 'a little more of the needful in his noddle'. In his anger he accused him of a misuse of patronage, by making brokendown tenants into stationmasters on the Manchester, Sheffield, and Lincolnshire Railway. The feeling was reciprocated from Brocklesby. Lady Yarborough complained in 1862 that during her husband's illness everybody was considerate except Anderson, who sent letters complaining that the business of the county was being neglected. Monson came to detest the meddlesome ways of his former friend, ending by referring to 'those horrid Andersons'.[37] Anderson had transferred his allegiance to what might be called the other half of the county leadership. Brownlow was his model lord lieutenant, a staunch churchman and 'ever at his post'. As a local administrator his mentor was Sheffield, whom he eventually succeeded as chairman of Kirton quarter sessions.

In his letters to Wilberforce Anderson often deprecated the prevalence of 'party spirit'. For many years he preferred his acquaintance Gladstone's politics to those of Disraeli, and he often expressed the hope that there would be a union of moderate men against the radicals. In this, and in his occasional outbursts against the high-handedness of political peers, he was expressing the age-old feelings of the independent country gentleman. Yet it is noticeable how strongly his judgments of men were coloured by politics. His political views reflected his social attitudes. He was a small squire by Lincolnshire standards, owning merely the parish of Lea near Gainsborough where he lived, although there was another estate in Yorkshire. He was therefore vulnerable to social pressures from below, and accordingly tenacious of the privileges of his own class. Hence the bitterness of his observations on a rising family such as that of the Tennysons. Charles Tennyson D'Eyncourt of Bayons Manor, with his mediaeval folly of a house and vaunted Norman ancestry, was a fair target for satire, but Anderson went beyond good taste when he designed a coat of arms for 'Baron

[37] *Ibid*, Anderson to Wilberforce, 14 Feb. 1853; Anderson (Helmsley) MSS, diary 1849; MON 25/13/8.

Dungcart of Bayons Manure'. With younger sons of attorneys acquiring fair-sized estates no wonder Anderson considered that 'the squirearchy are going downhill'. When he looked about him in Lincolnshire he could see dissent and republicanism growing on every side. He was 'not sanguine in his views', recorded Sir George Prevost, and he regretted the worsening relationship between the classes.[38]

Although he could assume a haughty aspect with dependants and inferiors, nobody could deny that he set his neighbours a good example in attending to local business. He sat on the bench for sixty years, and he last took the chair at Gainsborough petty sessions only a fortnight before his death. He was near enough to Lincoln to take a regular part in gaol sessions and was for many years foreman of the grand jury at the assizes. He chaired the Gainsborough board of guardians and even exerted himself as a commissioner of sewers, a job country gentlemen usually left to the farmers. He was concerned in the formation of the Diocesan Board of Education in 1839, and in later years was looked to as a leading layman in the diocese. To complete this picture of the model squire, he was fond in his younger days of hunting and shooting. In all this he was typical of those gentry who guided the day-to-day business of the county. Despite his friends in high places and his connections with Nottinghamshire and Yorkshire he was first and foremost a Lincolnshire, or perhaps one should say a Lindsey, gentleman.

In many ways Anderson and Monson were contrasting figures—one a country gentleman, the other a peer; one a high churchman, the other an anti-clericalist; one a tory, the other a whig. Most of all they differed in the parts they played in the life of the county. But the similarities went deeper. They were both representatives of families that had once been richer and more prominent in public life. Their antiquarian interests and their great consciousness of rank and social position sprang at least in part from their comparatively straitened circumstances. Despite their political differences they shared fundamentally conservative attitudes. For them the future, if it had any function, was to conserve the past.

NEW WEALTH

County society was difficult to penetrate, but it was not totally exclusive. Compared with the sixteenth or even the early eighteenth century, the nineteenth century saw little movement of

[38] AND 5/2/2, p. 283v.; Anderson to Wilberforce, April 1853; Sir C. H. J. Anderson, *The Lincoln Pocket Guide*, preface to 3rd edn., 1892.

new families into the higher strata of Lincolnshire society; but the recruitment of successful businessmen and professional people into the ranks of the smaller gentry was not entirely halted by the high price of land in the period 1800 to 1870.

Unlike some counties, Lincolnshire in the early and mid-nineteenth century could boast no spectacular accession of financiers, brewers, or cotton spinners. The county was saved from that fate by its comparative remoteness and lack of the picturesque. Its rising families, few though they were, came from within its borders. The most important group were the bankers, who did not have to struggle against the social disadvantage of having made their money in trade. In 1800 the leading bank in the county was Smith, Ellison and Co. Richard Ellison of Sudbrooke (d. 1828) became an M.P. for Lincoln and a chairman of Lindsey quarter sessions, though he did not achieve his ambition to represent the county in parliament. His illegitimate son was established as a landed proprietor at Boultham. The Sleaford banking firm of Peacock and Handley also made its contribution to county society. Anthony Peacock, son of one of its founders, married into the well-connected Fane family, built a country house at South Rauceby, and was for a short time M.P. for South Lincolnshire in the 1850s. Cracroft wrote of him: 'He always gives me the idea of being suspicious of detection, and yet I am sure no one would suspect that he never had a grandfather.'[39] Henry Handley, son of Benjamin Handley, the other principal founding partner, also cut something of a social figure, marrying the daughter of a whig peer and representing South Lincolnshire in parliament from 1832 to 1841. The Handleys did not, however, found a dynasty like the Peacocks. The Garfits, the Boston banking family, joined the landed aristocracy of the county as late as 1888, when they purchased the Kenwick estate near Louth.

Lawyers had much more trouble in unlocking social doors. George Tennyson of Tealby was not only a very successful businessman, and the confidant of several Lindsey gentry, but also a substantial landowner in his own right, even before he embarked on the partly speculative purchases that increased his holdings to about 6,000 acres by the time of his death in 1835. He was even made a justice of the peace, an exceptional distinction for a retired solicitor. But his pretensions were not much relished by those who could recall his origins in an attorney's office. His second son Charles, whom he chose to establish the family dynasty, took the additional

[39] Quoted in Hill, *Victorian Lincoln*, p. 72.

name of D'Eyncourt to emphasize his mediaeval origins, turned Tealby Cottage into the baronial pile of Bayons Manor, and had an interesting if not ultimately very successful career in parliament. On a smaller scale were the ambitions of John Fardell, who gave up his diocesan registrarship in 1821, acquired a small country estate at Holbeck near Horncastle, and educated his son for the life of a gentleman of independent means. He had much trouble, however, in persuading Lord Brownlow that he was eligible for the county bench.[40] Perhaps the last Lincolnshire legal family to rise into the gentry during the nineteenth century were the Smiths of Horbling. Benjamin Smith, whose business had included banking as well as legal work of many kinds, died in 1858 leaving £140,000. His nephew Henry had acquired an estate of over 3,000 acres by the 1870s.

In the late eighteenth and early nineteenth centuries it was possible for land agents to make large fortunes, especially from inclosure business, and in this way the Parkers of Hanthorpe, Bournes of Dalby, and Craggs of Threekingham rose into the minor gentry class. Their fortunes were eclipsed by that of John Burcham of Coningsby, who left £400,000 when he died in 1841; but he had not used his wealth to build up a great territorial interest, perhaps because he had only two daughters to succeed him.

Only those farmers who operated on a very extensive scale or became successful ram breeders could accumulate enough money to purchase large estates. Even then they frequently lacked the social ambition to make gentlemen of their heirs. There were, however, occasional exceptions among the well-established farmers of northern Lindsey and the wealthy graziers of Holland. Thomas John Dixon of Holton-le-Moor near Caistor inherited land from his father in 1824, married a Roadley heiress, carried on a successful farming business, and at his death left a much enlarged estate which he entailed in the approved aristocratic manner.

His neighbours and relatives the Skipworths did even better for themselves. In 1802 Philip Skipworth of Aylesby, a member of a wealthy family of wold farmers, joined with George Tennyson and others in the speculative purchase of the lordship of South Kelsey, an estate of some 4,500 acres.[41] But what began as a speculation became an attempt to found a new county family. Skipworth acquired a sole interest in the estate in 1808, and when he died he left it to his third son George, just as his friend Tennyson had also

---

[40] Mary E. Finch, 'Some Correspondence of John Fardell', *Lincoln Record Society*, vol. 66 (1973), p. 50; 4 BNL box 2.
[41] DIXON 1/F/1.

favoured a younger son. George Skipworth was sent to Oxford, a new house was built on the property, and he took up residence there on his marriage in 1824. He farmed some of the estate himself, however, as did his brother William, and his marriage to a Dixon did not markedly advance his gentrification. There was some hesitation, therefore, despite his ample landed property, when the question of his becoming a magistrate arose in 1837. The Revd William Cooper described both George Skipworth and his brother-in-law Thomas John Dixon to Lord Brownlow as 'highly respectable and very opulent yeomen'—the word yeoman being here used to imply owner-occupying farmers. 'Their education has not fitted them completely for magisterial duties;' Cooper went on condescendingly, 'but they would not disagreeably oppose their more experienced brethren.'[42]

In the last quarter of the century the fortunes on which to build dynasties were no longer being made in the Lincolnshire countryside. What new blood there was came from elsewhere—some of it surprisingly blue blood too. Viscount St Vincent at Norton Disney, the earl of Londesborough (a passionate amateur fireman) at Blankney, and the earl of Liverpool at Hartsholme, were all latter-day additions to Lincolnshire's native nobility. One industrialist to set up as a country gentleman late in the century was George Hodgson, the Bradford manufacturer and banker who bought the Nocton estate in 1889. At the level of the smaller gentry there were occasional recruits from outside the county, such as W. D. Gainsford, who 'agreeably surprised' the snobbish Rawnsleys when he came to live at Skendleby in 1873.[43]

New wealth within the county was now represented by the urban businessmen, the ironfounders, merchants, and shipowners. The pioneer was Joseph Shuttleworth of Lincoln, who resided at Hartsholme for a time before buying the Old Warden estate in Bedfordshire. His partner Nathaniel Clayton bought the Withcall estate, but continued to live in Lincoln, although his co-heir Nathaniel Clayton Cockburn later established himself at Harmston. Joseph Ruston did not invest extensively in land, but both the Hornsby brothers acquired country seats, William at Burwell and James at Laxton (Northamptonshire). Joseph Cliff, the Frodingham industrialist, built himself a country house at Scawby Grove in 1889, and died there in 1914 leaving £233,206.[44] He was high sheriff of Lincolnshire in 1901. The following year the high sheriff was J. D.

[42] 4 BNL box 1.
[43] Diary of Catherine Rawnsley 1873–6.
[44] SM 13 Sept. 1889; DIXON 15/1, Kirkby Pedigrees vol. 7, p. 95.

Sandars of Gainsborough, who was to acquire the Gate Burton estate from the Hutton family in 1907.

In the late nineteenth century more fortunes were being made at Grimsby than anywhere else in the county, but it is remarkable how few Grimsby capitalists set themselves up as country gentlemen. In the early twentieth century the Wintringhams settled at Little Grimsby, and branches of the Bennett family at Brackenborough and Oxcombe. But the Doughtys, Bannisters, Smethursts, and Sutcliffes appear to have contented themselves with more suburban grandeur.

CHAPTER III

THE MIDDLING SORT

ATTORNEYS, AGENTS, AND BANKERS

'I HAVE long been of the opinion,' wrote Sir Charles Anderson, 'that the county of Lincoln is ruled chiefly by agents and attorneys, and that in no other county have they such power.'[1] Together with the country bankers these were the professional groups most closely involved with the agricultural economy and most directly concerned with the relations between landlord and tenant. The attorney would draw up the farm agreement; the agent would see that the farmer observed its conditions; and the banker might lend money to both parties, to the tenant against the next harvest and to the landlord against the next rent day. In mid-nineteenth-century Lincolnshire the number of people occupied in banking, legal work, and land agency was very small. There was only a handful of country bankers, some of them almost indistinguishable from the gentry. In 1861 there were 200 qualified solicitors in the county, supported by 337 law clerks. Only 156 people were described in 1861 as land agents or surveyors. The influence of these groups was out of all proportion to their size. Resident landowners valued their expertise, and non-resident landlords, of whom there were many connected with Lincolnshire, relied absolutely on their men on the spot.

The attorneys seldom made large fortunes, but they had unique opportunities for acquiring local influence. They were generally of higher social standing than the agents, and they touched the life of the rural community at more points than did the bankers. Indeed, it was not uncommon for attorneys to act as agents to one or more landowners, supervising the financial as well as the more purely legal side of estate management. A really large estate might employ as head agent a man of legal training, with local agents to provide a knowledge of agriculture and to exercise day-to-day supervision. For some years the firm of Tallents and Co. of Newark acted in this capacity for the Yarborough estate as well as for a number of Kesteven gentry. At a later date J. F. Burton and Robert Toynbee of Lincoln acted for the Blankney and Burton estates respectively.

[1] Quoted in Hill, *Georgian Lincoln*, p. 182.

Attorneys with capital to deploy and with a detailed knowledge of the local economy were in a good position to become country bankers, and several did so in Lincolnshire, especially before the growth of joint-stock banking. Benjamin Smith of Horbling combined a legal practice with banking, and so, as late as the middle of the century, did Titus Bourne of Alford.

The most successful attorneys were often of good grammar or later even public school education, and locally well-connected. They came sometimes of clerical families, like John Hett of Brigg, son of a pluralist priest-vicar of Lincoln cathedral. Benjamin Cheales, head of the leading legal firm at Sleaford in the early nineteenth century and clerk of the peace for Kesteven, came from a family of landowners at Hagworthingham. A later member of the same firm and Cheales's eventual successor in the Kesteven clerkship was Maurice Peter Moore, whose father, the Revd William Moore, was for many years chairman of quarter sessions at Spalding. The need to serve one's articles with an established attorney and the expense of buying a practice helped to preserve the middle-class tone of the profession. Legal families tended to perpetuate themselves. Joseph Daubney, for instance, was articled with Messrs Tennyson and Main of Market Rasen, and later founded a practice in Grimsby, dying in 1837. In the next generation there were three solicitors in the Daubney family—William Heaford at Grimsby, Joseph at Caistor, and Robert at Market Rasen.[2]

For the high fliers the way to positions of trust and influence in the county was to attract the attention and patronage of the gentry and nobility. One means of achieving this was to appear on behalf of clients at quarter sessions, as did W. E. Tallents of Newark and J. H. Hollway of Spilsby. Another was to engage in political agency work. For Frederick Burton the patronage of the Chaplins led to the Conservative agency at the North Lincolnshire elections of 1835 and 1841, and this in turn led to the clerkship of gaol sessions for the county in 1842. His son, J. F. Burton, was educated at Rugby and eventually became clerk of the peace for Lindsey, the pinnacle of the legal profession of the county. When he died in 1891 Lord Oxenbridge described him as 'a perfect gentleman', and indeed his successor, Charles Scorer, was appointed at the undeniably gentlemanly salary of £2,500 a year. The Kesteven and Holland clerkships at this date produced less than £1,700 between them.[3]

The sphere of most country solicitors, however, was the market town. Firms such as Nicholson, Hett, and Freer of Brigg built up

[2] *Archivists' Report* 9 (1957–8), pp. 18–19.   [3] *SM* 24 April, 5 June 1891.

extensive practices among the farmers and landowners of their neighbourhoods. The leading firm of a flourishing market town could expect to accumulate a number of clerkships to bodies such as the magistrates in petty sessions, the board of guardians, the commissioners of sewers, and the turnpike trustees. Where the conditions were favourable, attachment to a political interest could bring further business. John Hett was retained by the Liberal party in North Lincolnshire, and transacted local legal work from time to time for the second earl of Yarborough. Attorneys in smaller towns, with a more restricted range of clients, might find it unprofitable to take sides so openly.[4]

Although many solicitors allied themselves to a local landed interest, some of them exerted independent and frequently powerful interests of their own. Attorneys flourished in parts of the county full of small freeholders, and they were particularly numerous in Boston, Barton, and Gainsborough. The sale and purchase of small farms created much legal work in the days before short titles and land registration, and some plots could almost have been covered by the square yards of parchment evidences relating to them. Not only that, the small farmers were usually in need of a mortgage loan, and the attorneys were in an ideal position to arrange for an accommodation. The favour of a loan created an obligation that could be brought into play particularly at election times. A political survey of the county made for Lord Yarborough in 1825 gave full weight to the pull of such firms as Jebb of Boston and Codd and Heaton of Gainsborough.[5]

The presence of a number of solicitors in a fairly small town such as Barton may well have encouraged the litigiousness of its inhabitants. When customers failed the attorneys could always go to law with each other. 'The Spilsby lawyers continues there warfare,' reported Lord Willoughby's agent in 1854: 'they have a case at Lincoln next week, William Walker v. Thomas Thimbleby, defamation of character.'[6]

The first half of the nineteenth century was a golden age for Lincolnshire solicitors. They were involved in most of the great improvements in agriculture and communications, from inclosure and turnpikes to the coming of the railways. Much of the money locally raised and locally invested passed through their hands, and often the legal work involved in obtaining an act of parliament led to a permanent position in the form of a clerkship to a trust. After

[4] R. J. Olney, *Lincolnshire Politics 1832–1885*, 1973, pp. 75–7.
[5] Lincoln City Library, D Coll/SMI.
[6] Janet E. Courtney, *Recollected in Tranquillity*, 1926, p. 59; 3 ANC 7/23/66/58.

1850 these opportunities lessened. Investment patterns changed, and conveyancing simplified itself a little. The wealthy Lincolnshire client might now invest in railway shares rather than in mortgages, and the railway line might take him not to his local solicitor but to a London firm with local connections, such as Frere, Cholmeley, and Co.

Whereas the value of the attorney to his employer resided in his knowledge of copyholds and covenants and entails, the agent made himself indispensable by his thorough knowledge of soils and farming practice. Some agents, indeed, were tenant farmers whom their landlords employed on estate business. James Martin of Wainfleet was a farmer who built up a successful agency practice in eastern Lindsey. At an earlier period the Bournes of Dalby established reputations as agents as well as graziers, and through being recommended from one landowner to another acquired an extensive practice.[7] An agent for one of Lincolnshire's large estates, of 10,000 acres or more, was in a position of considerable trust, recommending which tenants should pay more or less rent, which should be offered more land, and occasionally which should lose their holdings. He handled large sums of money and was responsible for large investment programmes. Not surprisingly a good many nests were feathered, and small tenants often went more in awe of the agent than of their landlord.

At the top of the profession were those who were called in over the heads of the lesser agents to conduct valuations of estates. John Cragg of Threekingham did much work of this kind in south Lincolnshire around 1800. In Lindsey, and beyond its borders, the leading valuer in the early nineteenth century was John Burcham of Coningsby. His knowledge of land management and the land market was second to none, and his importance may be gauged by the fact that the first earl of Yarborough retained him at a salary of £2,000 a year. A large part of his immense fortune was laid out in mortgages on the Brocklesby estates in the 1830s. Both Cragg and Burcham helped to mould the Lincolnshire landscape, as well as line their pockets, by their work as inclosure commissioners. In manners and appearance they were probably more like well-to-do farmers than gentlemen, and the gentry liked them none the less for their lack of airs and graces. Cragg was described in 1806 as having a rough exterior, but as strictly honourable and 'of first rate Talents in his way'.[8]

[7] TYR 4/1.
[8] CRAGG 1/7–9; DIXON 16/3 pp. 236–8 (for a sample of Burcham's conversation); YARB 3/2/7; STUBTON VII/E/11.

Long before the inclosure movement reached its peak the drainage problems of Lincolnshire had fostered the local growth of surveying as an independent profession. The Grundys of Spalding were its outstanding eighteenth-century representatives. The surveyor was called on to draw plans of estates, but he was frequently also an engineer, designing bridges, locks, and new cuts for the navigable drains of the county. James Sandby Padley (1792–1881) first came to Lincolnshire in connection with the Ordnance Survey. He met its leading subscribers, particularly Charles Chaplin, settled in Lincoln as a surveyor and engineer, and soon secured the post of surveyor of county bridges for Lindsey.[9] Another occupation fostered by local conditions was tenant-right valuing. With the development of the so-called Lincolnshire Custom, valuers were called in when farms changed hands to assess the sum due from the incoming to the outgoing tenant. Although this work became one of the mainstays of many firms of land agents it was often entrusted to farmers with local reputations for knowledge and wisdom. The Lincolnshire Association of Land Agents and Valuers was formed in 1873.

Banking in nineteenth-century Lincolnshire was closely connected with the farming economy. A small farmer might depend on a bank loan to enable him to stock his newly entered holding. In times of depression it was the withdrawal of credit that precipitated many a failure. Early in the century, however, it was the banks themselves that were prone to failure. The collapse of a small private bank like Marris and Nicholson of Barton in 1812 or Ingelow of Boston in 1825 caused great hardship in its locality. There were rumours of a run on Garfit's bank as late as 1873. By the middle of the century, however, Lincolnshire's once numerous private banks had been reduced to a handful of prosperous concerns. Smith Ellison and Co. had a widespread landed and farming clientèle in the north of the county. Messrs Garfit of Boston were strong in east Lincolnshire, whilst Kesteven supported Hardy's of Grantham and Peacock's of Sleaford. Alongside these family concerns there were two joint-stock banks. The Stamford, Spalding, and Boston flourished in the far south; and in 1833 the Lincoln and Lindsey Bank was founded, with Lincoln lawyers prominent among its supporters. Despite the intrusion of the National Provincial and the Capital and Counties Banks, these Lincolnshire banking establishments were still holding their own at the end of the century.

The bankers were a small and highly respectable social group.

[9] James Sandby Padley, *The Fens and Floods of Mid-Lincolnshire*, 1882, pp. vi–viii.

The rise of families like the Willsons and Garfits into the gentry has already been noted. There was also movement the other way, for banking (unlike trade) was still considered an acceptable occupation for gentlemen's sons. The Fanes of Fulbeck had especially strong banking connections, and one of them took over the management of the Sleaford Bank when Anthony Willson died in 1866. William Parker of Hanthorpe was for a time connected with the same concern as a trustee for its agency at Bourne. His second son, C. J. B. Parker, married the only daughter of John Hardy and eventually succeeded to the control of Hardy's Bank at Grantham.[10]

As providers of capital for public works the banks achieved a semi-official status in the county. The Sleaford Bank, for instance, advanced £20,000 to the Deeping Fen inclosure commissioners in 1802. Smith Ellison and Co. were made treasurers for the rebuilding of the county hall in the 1820s. When Henry Pye of Louth, the Lindsey treasurer, absconded in 1868 owing the county over £9,500, it was Smith's Lincoln Bank that made an advance to meet the deficit. Later that year A. S. Leslie Melville of the Lincoln Bank and William Garfit were appointed joint county treasurers.[11]

DOCTORS AND CLERGYMEN

Unlike the agents and attorneys, the doctors and clergymen of nineteenth-century Lincolnshire stood at one remove from the rural economy. Their primary object was not to make money but to minister to the needs of their neighbours. The squire and the labourer were alike prone to sickness and to sin, and doctors and parsons aimed to acquire the confidence of all classes. The parson might lunch with the squire and then visit the poorest of the squire's cottage tenants. G. M. Porter, a flourishing Caistor doctor around the middle of the century, numbered among his clients the earl of Yarborough (who is said to have paid him a retainer of £100 a year), some of the well-to-do Brocklesby farmers, and the paupers of the Caistor union.[12] Nevertheless neither clergy nor medical men could stand outside the class system of rural society. Their status was defined partly by their income and family background, and partly by their education and professional training.

The clergy, with their university degrees and distinctive dress, approached most nearly to a social caste, but there were wide

[10] *Archivists' Report* 17 (1965–6), pp. 24–5; KQS, Sleaford Bank papers 1841.
[11] L. S. Pressnell, *Country Banking in the Industrial Revolution*, 1956, pp. 354–5; LQS minutes Aug.–Oct. 1868.
[12] MCD 707.

variations within the clerical body. At the head of the country clergy were the relatives of the aristocracy, men like the Revd Edward Chaplin of Blankney or the Revd F. C. Massingberd of South Ormsby, holders of good family livings and active magistrates. Massingberd, indeed, achieved wider distinction. As a comparatively young man he wrote a highly regarded book on the Reformation, and later, in 1862, became chancellor of Lincoln cathedral. Some beneficed clergymen enjoyed the income of lesser squires. The Revd William Cooper, hereditary incumbent of West Rasen from 1802, acquired the even better living of Waddingham in 1808 and held both until his death in 1856, deriving from them a gross income of about £1,800 a year. He had considerable influence in the Market Rasen neighbourhood, and was a leading magistrate. On the other hand the county had 300 livings worth £150 a year or less in 1809,[13] and below these poor incumbents was a layer of unbeneficed curates struggling to maintain their clerical status on stipends of £80 a year or less. Clerical poverty lessened during the first half of the century, but the profession continued to contain members who were looked on as scarcely gentlemen in their neighbourhoods, and whose elevation to the bench was sometimes strenuously opposed by parsons who were already magistrates.

Differences within the medical profession were even more profound. In 1804 Dr Fawssett of Horncastle surveyed a region of Lindsey that included Horncastle, Tattershall, Alford, and Spilsby. He found that it contained only five physicians, all with Edinburgh training. There were eleven surgeons and apothecaries trained by apprenticeship, twenty-five druggists, sixty-three midwives, and forty quacks. During the century the medical profession of Lincolnshire continued to be led by a small group of physicians, men as distinguished as Edward Parker Charlesworth and Robert Gardiner Hill of Lincoln. The country doctor remained a surgeon and an apothecary, performing operations when necessary and dispensing his own drugs, but his status and professional qualifications rose markedly as the century progressed. The first major step, the examination and licensing of apothecaries under an act of 1815, owed its achievement in part to the activity of the Lincolnshire Medical Benevolent Society and the influence of Sir Joseph Banks.[14]

[13] 3 CC 3.
[14] Edward Harrison MD, *Remarks on the Ineffective State of the Practice of Physic in Great Britain, and the Resolutions of the members of the Benevolent Medical Society of Lincolnshire*, 1806, p. 38; Charles Newman, *The Evolution of Medical Education in the Nineteenth Century*, 1957, pp. 58 ff.

The social position of clergymen was often dictated by local factors beyond their control. Incumbents of the rich livings of Holland, where the gentry class hardly existed, had perforce to give a lead in parish and local society. Where a large landowner was non-resident, a parson sometimes stood in as his representative in the district. Thus the Revd Charles Barnard of Bigby acted in the Brigg neighbourhood on behalf of his relative Robert Cary Elwes, and the Revd Thomas Hardwick Rawnsley, perhaps the last great Lincolnshire pluralist, upheld the Willoughby de Eresby interest in the Spilsby area. In other parts of the county the clergy had stronger social links with the upper reaches of the farming class, and this was especially the case in parts of the Wolds. Successful farmers occasionally purchased advowsons as a provision for younger sons who had no farming vocation.

Doctors might also belong to local middle-class families. Dr Samuel Turner of Caistor (1764–1825) was the great-nephew of a Caistor solicitor, the son of a farmer, and the father of a clergyman (the rector of Nettleton). But the majority of doctors came as strangers to the county, many of them being of Scottish extraction. When Dr John Gay of Spilsby died in 1899 his practice, worth about £800 a year, was advertised for sale at £1200. Applicants wrote from Dublin and North Devon as well as from within the county, the ultimate purchaser coming from Berkshire. Parsons might also come from different parts of the country. The Revd John Morton was a Scot who after a short spell in a Devon living somewhat reluctantly accepted the offer of Holbeach from his patron Earl Grey in 1832. But once arrived in Holbeach Morton had a well-defined sphere of influence, and was soon (although a whig) put on the bench. Doctors operated in a less clear-cut locality, based on a market town or large village, and they were not considered suitable for the magistracy until quite late in the century.[15]

Both doctors and clergy were separated by impenetrable cultural barriers from the indigenous village population of Lincolnshire, the small craftsmen and tradesmen and 'the poor'. The parish clergy had to contend against the twin forces of dissent and superstition, and often made very little spiritual headway against them. Where a parson succeeded in partially civilizing his parish, as the Revd Ayscoghe Floyer did at Marshchapel, it was primarily through the provision of material comforts. Archdeacon Bayley complained in 1823 that his Messingham parishioners believed in 'witches, the evil

[15] *Archivists' Report* 20 (1968–9), pp. 31–2; MISC DEP 306.

eye, the casting out of devils, etc., etc., and look upon him when they go to church on Sunday to be a perfect noodle'.[16] In the same way herbs and spells were cheaper and possibly no less efficacious than a doctor's prescription.

At a county level, however, the presence of some five hundred educated and professionally vocal clergy had a considerable influence. Their prominence on the bench probably detracted from their usefulness in other ways, and their strongly Conservative outlook made them look askance at progressive movements, but they played an important part in educational and charitable work. The doctors were more independent-minded and more in sympathy with the march of science. They explained to their neighbours the importance of drains and pure water, and at the end of the century gave lectures in technical education. Their contribution to botanical studies in the county has been noted by Miss Joan Gibbons.[17] They were also the professional group most prone to Liberalism in politics. At different times doctors such as Benjamin Abbott of Brigg (a Catholic Irishman), Samuel Trought of Louth, and Edwin Morris of Spalding lent weight to the Liberal cause in their respective towns.

FARMING FAMILIES AND FORTUNES

The farmers of Lincolnshire varied so widely in wealth and style of living that it is almost meaningless to describe them as a middle class. But it may be helpful to start by imagining the 'average' farmer, as he lived about the middle of the nineteenth century. His farm is about 120 acres—one that can be worked by four horses—and it lies on rather poorly drained clay soil. The farm house, a brick and tile affair of three bays and no architectural pretension, stands a few hundred yards out of the village. Most of the fields lie together within easy reach of the farmstead, and the holding is rented from a landlord who lives many miles away. The buildings, partly tiled and partly thatched, stand around a small yard very close to the house, and the whole group has an unromantic and unsheltered appearance. The farmer is in his thirties, and has been set up in the farm with money lent him by his father, who is still farming a few miles away. His wife is somewhat younger than himself (the daughter of an innkeeper), and they already have three young children. He puts his hand to most of the jobs on the farm,

---

[16] DIXON 16/3, p. 258.
[17] *The Flora of Lincolnshire*, 1975, pp. 53 ff.

and the rest of the regular labour force is made up by a head waggoner, a second waggoner, a lad, and a boy. His wife has one domestic servant, a girl of about sixteen from one of the labouring families in the village. The head of the family attends the market once a week (in his chimney-pot hat), but holidays, excursions, and social calls are almost non-existent. He reads little except the county newspaper and keeps no accounts. His farming methods could be most kindly described as 'traditional'.

In certain parts of the county the medium-sized farm just described would have counted as a large one, whilst in other regions it would have seemed comparatively small. The Fens and the Marsh, together with the Isle of Axholme, teemed with those small farmers who, as we have just seen, could so easily fall into the clutches of the attorneys. A typical farmer of this class might rent or own a holding of around ten acres, small enough to be worked by family labour. He might own the field attached to his cottage, where he grazed a cow, and also rent another small field or two at a little distance where he could raise crops. These cottagers were often the descendants of the small yeoman class of former times, valuing their independence and managing to live in frugal comfort. But the life of a smallholder could be hard, and owners with mortgages to pay off suffered more in times of agricultural depression than those tenants who were able to obtain concessions from their landlords. A smallholder's family might work harder and live more roughly than some day labourers' families, and there was no great social difference between the two.

At the other end of the scale were the farming aristocrats of Lincolnshire, men of considerable capital established on very large, generally upland, holdings. Of these farmers the Marris family of Great Limber is a good example. Thomas Marris (d. 1834) farmed 831 acres under the second baron Yarborough, and lived in the large end house in Limber known as 'The Other End', or even more simply 'The Marrises'. He was succeeded by his eldest son Thomas in the Limber farm, but in 1848 the second earl of Yarborough took the very unusual step of terminating the tenancy, because Marris had wrongfully evicted a labourer. Thomas was succeeded, however, by his brother William, who had farmed previously at Ruckland. At the time of the 1851 census William had a wife and seven children, six domestic servants (including a governess and two nursemaids), and six indoor farm servants. Altogether he employed a labour force of forty on a holding of 1,050 acres. Another brother, George, became a solicitor at Caistor, and yet another brother, Charles, held a Yarborough farm at Croxton. Two sisters married members of the Skipworth family, whilst a niece, Mary Maunsell, married William Richardson of the Top House at Great Limber. It was John Maunsell Richardson, son of William, who married the dowager Lady Yarborough in 1881.[18]

Altogether fifteen of the leading tenants on the Brocklesby estate in the early 1830s held upwards of 675 acres each. Farms of this size were of course comparatively few even in Lincolnshire and were confined mainly to the Wolds. In the 1830s the county contained perhaps twenty-five farms (or rather single occupations) of over 1,000 acres. The largest farm of all was the parish of Withcall, held as one farm by the Dawsons under Lord Willoughby de Eresby, and comprising no less than 2,655 acres, including the glebe in Withcall and seventy-seven acres in the adjacent parish of Welton-le-Wold. The chalk hills of Withcall had once been largely warren, but had responded well to high farming. The Dawsons held the farm on lease at a rent of £2,000 a year, and made a fortune out of it. Withcall House was enlarged in 1825, to provide among other additional accommodation a housekeeper's room and an extra bedroom for the farm servants, who ate and slept at the back. In 1842 the house was described as 'very commodious, and fit for the occupation of a large genteel family'. Dawson, however, unlike Marris, did not occupy land at the heart of a great estate. Withcall was a long way from Willoughby's other Lindsey properties and in 1842 he decided to sell it. Dawson was aggrieved, but unable despite his personal and family means to buy the estate himself. It was knocked down to George Tomline, and some years later was re-sold to Nathaniel Clayton.[19]

These substantial wold farmers formed a tightly knit community, bound together by family connections despite the miles of poor roads that often separated one isolated household from another. A key family such as the Marrises were related to most of their social equals for some miles around. Fathers did their best to set up their sons in good farms, and landlords like Lord Yarborough were content to let farms pass from generation to generation of the same family, knowing that this was the chief way in which farming capital accumulated. To enter on an arable farm of some 400 acres might require an initial capital outlay of £1,000, and thereafter it was necessary to maintain a large expenditure in labour and manure. The upland farms were not naturally fertile, and in the days of 'high

[18] YARB 9 (letter books); 1851 census (enumerator's return for Great Limber); DIXON 15/1, vol. 20, p. 67; Mary E. Richardson, *The Life of a Great Sportsman, John Maunsell Richardson*, 1919.
[19] YARB 5 (surveys); 2 ANC 7/62/7; 3 ANC 7/23/43; *SM* 5 Oct. 1888.

farming' whole fortunes were laid out in the form of artificial manures such as bones.[20]

The wold farmers of the mid-nineteenth century were not gentry, although they sometimes received the appellation of squire from their neighbours. They were sometimes of good grammar school education, and some even sent their sons to university. They lived in large houses that had in some cases once been manor houses, with three or four indoor servants. They would keep a chaise or gig, riding horses, and probably hunters as well. Their wives, though they might attend to household duties in the morning, would pay and receive afternoon calls in a ladylike manner, their refinement no doubt contrasting in some cases with the market-place manners of their husbands.

Just as we can compare the smallest farmers with the labouring class, and the medium farmers with the more substantial type of tradesmen, so in reaching the topmost ranks of the agriculturists we find a group in which professional people of good education might feel at home. How far was it possible to rise by farming in Lincolnshire, in the same way that one could rise in other counties through trades and manufactures? How easy was it for a labourer to get started on a small farm; how quickly might a small farmer turn himself into a large one; and how many substantial farmers managed to elevate themselves into the gentry class during the nineteenth century?

All these are questions to which only tentative answers can be given. In the early nineteenth century Lincolnshire probably saw more movement between the labouring and farming classes than it did in later years. Inclosure, especially in the Fens, created many small freeholds of which enterprising labourers, with the aid of savings or a timely legacy, could take advantage. Even in the latter part of the century examples can be found of labourers managing to scrape up capital by keeping a village shop or by doing a little cattle dealing. An allotment—a rood or two of garden ground rented from a large landlord or from charity trustees—might be a useful start. The regions of very small holdings were obviously the area of greatest social mobility at this level.[21]

It was harder to progress from a small farm to a large one. Theoretically the successful farmer, having made money from a twenty-acre holding, would move to a fifty-acre one, and so on,

[20] See also J. A. Perkins, 'The Prosperity of Farming on the Lindsey Uplands 1813–37', *Ag. Hist. Rev.* 24 (part 2), 1976, p. 126.

[21] For a rising labourer (and his energetic wife) in Digby in the 1880s see Fred Gresswell, *Bright Boots*, 1956, pp. 20–22.

increasing his working capital in proportion. But farming was an unpredictable business, and one or two years' profits could easily be wiped out by an outbreak of sheep rot or a slump in wheat prices. In good times farms were often in short supply, particularly those under reputable landlords, whilst in bad times it was a brave man who took on new commitments. Some landlords made a point of promoting deserving small tenants to larger holdings, but in some parts of the county there was a discouraging gap between the very small farms and the very large ones. On the Wolds there were few small farms. Even a big open village such as Binbrook had only a handful of small farms of under twenty-five acres, and one or two medium-sized occupations: the rest of the parish was laid out in farms of 300 to 1,000 acres. The earliest income tax returns for Dunsby, a fen-side parish near Bourne, reveal a similar gap between rich and poor farmers.[22]

Yet even the large farmers had not been wealthy from time immemorial. The prosperity of the Brocklesby tenants did not go back many generations. The Revd John Parkinson noted in the 1820s after a conversation with Mr Nelson of Limber that Nelson's predecessor had given only £100 a year for his farm and had died insolvent. Mr Byron's father had given the same sum and had been hard set. 'They had but two pot-days in the week at that time, and seldom any bread in their houses but what was made from barley and oatmeal.'[23] Their fortunes were made in the war period, when corn rose to starvation prices and large tracts of the Wolds were inclosed and ploughed up. Some farmers remained proud to the end of their lives that they were self-made men. When John Booth of Kelstern Grange, an influential wold farmer, died in 1853, a Gothic wall tablet in Kelstern church proclaimed that, 'commencing life with humble means, he created by industry and skill in his calling an ample fortune.' After the middle of the century there were more opportunities for losing than for making fortunes, and by 1900 many of the wold farming dynasties were extinct.

Farmers were not averse to investing their fortunes in land. The wold farmers often bought marsh land for agricultural purposes. But particularly in Lindsey a few successful farmers, among the earliest of whom were the Grants of Oxcombe, went in for whole lordships, of 1,000 or 1,500 acres. In 1873 an estimated sixteen Lincolnshire farming families each owned over 1,000 acres in the

[22] R. J. Olney, ed., *Labouring Life on the Lincolnshire Wolds: A Study of Binbrook in the Mid-Nineteenth Century*, Occasional Papers in Lincolnshire History and Archaeology no. 2, 1975, p. 15; 2 TAX 2/10.

[23] DIXON 16/3, p. 265.

county. Of these families, twelve were in Lindsey, three in Holland, and only one (the Marfleets of Bassingham and Boothby Graffoe) in Kesteven. An estate of 1,000 acres was large enough to support a modest country gentleman, and some of these farmers could have retired from business and let their land. But generally they did not do so: they preferred to carry on farming. Sometimes they took their newly-acquired land in hand and exploited it as a single farm. More often they let their own estates but continued to rent somebody else's land. William Whitlam acquired Biscathorpe in 1834, but he let that property to the Kirkhams, and continued to live at Great Tows near Ludford, where he rented an excellent farm of nearly 1,000 acres. Later in the century William Hudson continued to farm under Lord Yarborough at Kirmington Vale, although by 1873 he had acquired land at Barnetby and elsewhere to the extent of nearly 2,000 acres. The Nelson family bought the Wyham and Cadeby estate around 1850, but George Nelson (1808–65) merely farmed Wyham in addition to the family farm on the Brocklesby estate at Great Limber.[24]

Farmers, unlike the gentry, did not believe in primogeniture. When they died they liked to leave their property equally between their sons. Sometimes one son would inherit the land, but be obliged to pay his brothers' shares out of it. When William Dixon of Holton-le-Moor died in 1824 he left his land equally between his two farming sons, Thomas John and James Green Dixon. Thomas John, the better businessman of the two, bought his brother out and went on to consolidate the estate by further purchases.[25] There were cases, however, where farmers' wills directed the sale of all their lands, either to avoid family quarrels or because there was no obvious heir. In 1822 Lady Banks sold the Toft Grange and Toft Hill estate near Revesby to Thomas Brailsford of East Barkwith. But after Brailsford's death in 1866 the property was auctioned and bought back by Sir J. H. Hawley, one of the co-heirs of the Banks estate.[26] In a similar fashion the Monson family sold off North Carlton to Samuel Slater, a well-to-do farmer and sheep breeder, in the 1830s. But forty years later, after Slater's death, they took the opportunity to buy it back. Those wealthy farmers who did not buy land might lend their spare capital to their neighbours. Mortgage securities were preferred, but in the earlier part of the century many farmers lent money in the form of bonds. The capital invested in mortgages, bonds, or local concerns such as canals brought a greater

[24] *Return of Owners of Land* (1873); county directories; DIXON 15/1.
[25] *Archivists' Report* 22 (1970–1), pp. 17–24.
[26] 2 HAW 1/C/1/24–34.

and more trouble-free return than the same amount of capital invested in land, and money lent locally helped to foster the rural economy.

OLD STYLE AND NEW STYLE FARMERS

So far we have considered social change within the farming class mainly in economic terms, concentrating on sizes of farms and the acquisition of land. But during the nineteenth century other changes caught the eye of contemporaries—changes in manners, habits, and social attitudes. In two of his dialect poems Alfred Tennyson, nephew of Charles and grandson of George, contrasted the old style Northern Farmer with the new. The old style farmer had no doubt made money by his efforts, but his success had not given him ideas above his station. He thought in terms of a local community in which he had a recognized place. He could look back over his life and die in the knowledge that he had done his duty both by the squire, to whom he owed his farm and his position of trust, and to the land, upon which the whole community was based. The new style farmer had equally rigid ideas, but they were based not on duty but on gain. When the new style farmer cantered his horse along the 'ramper' or highway he heard 'proputty, proputty, proputty'. His aim was to lay field to field, and if that put the squire's nose out of joint so much the worse for the squire. He had married for money, and wished his son to do the same. Extending this idea a little, we can imagine the old style farmer deferring to his landlord in political matters, and giving at least the appearance of religious conformity, whereas the new style farmer believed instead in the laws of economics, of supply and demand. He would regard his relations with both landlord and labourer in a purely business light, and consider himself bound to neither by any tie of obligation or duty. Toynbee wrote to Monson in 1883: 'I fear gratitude no longer enters into the relations between Landlord and Tenant, which are now resolved into mere matters of bargain.'[27]

Another view of changes in the attitudes and behaviour of farmers is expressed in the following lines, quoted by Jabez Good of Burgh-le-Marsh in his *Glossary*:

> *Agricultural Customs in 1800*
> Farmer at the plough,
> Wife milking cow,

[27] MON 25/13/18.

Daughter spinning yarn,
Son threshing in the barn,
All happy to a charm.

Agricultural Customs in 1900

Father gone to see the show,
Daughter at the pian-o,
Madame gaily dressed in satin,
All the boys learning Latin,
With a mortgage on the farm.

The idea that a new race of idle farmers with genteel families had
arisen was one that cropped up time and again during the nineteenth
century. At the Northampton show in 1879 Lord Burghley
declared that farmers' wives and daughters should give up the piano
and French lessons and 'put their shoulders to the wheel'. The
Saturday Review satirically suggested that the recently appointed
royal commission on agricultural depression should have a statisti-
cal appendix on pianos, comparing the yields on farms with and
without the instrument.[28]

These two models of the new style farmer are in some ways
contradictory. If his principal aim was to amass property, he would
be unlikely to pander to his womenfolks' extravagance or neglect
his own business to the extent of impairing his capital. Tennyson's
new style farmer in fact shows no tendency to social pretension. His
Lincolnshire accent could not be broader, and he opposes his son's
contemplated alliance with a clergyman's daughter because her
father, although undeniably a gentleman, is a poor, debt-ridden
curate. Another trouble with these myths is that neither the period
to which they referred nor the level of farming class was ever
specified. Musical or linguistic talents appropriate to a Miss Marris
or a Miss Skipworth, and acquired at a lady's school such as Mrs
Gardiner's at Elsham Hall, might be less fitting for the daughter of a
small working farmer. What contemporaries probably resented
was firstly the growing wealth of the large farmers, which *might*
make them less deferential to their landlords, and secondly the
tendency of the small farmers to ape their betters, and allow their
holdings to run down in the process.

There were two principal periods which encouraged the spread
of these myths. The first was the Napoleonic war period, when the
large farmers in particular had a chance to make fortunes. But at this
stage pianos had scarcely begun their descent through successive

[28] *SM* 3 Oct. 1879.

layers of the middle class, and in the comparatively lean years that followed, from the 1820s to the 1840s, tenants of quite large holdings remained essentially working farmers. In 1851 a wold farmer such as John Fieldsend of Orford near Binbrook, farming 380 acres, still had five farm workers living in his house, and only one maid, in addition to his wife and unmarried daughter, to look after them. Miss Fieldsend cannot have had much time to practise her scales. The next twenty-five years, however, were on average much more prosperous, and further social up-grading took place. Large farmers left more of the day-to-day supervision to foremen, and the foreman's wife in many cases took over the lodging of the confined men. The title of esquire, usurped by a few leading farmers earlier in the century, began to spread downwards. Farming families were tempted by the good times to adopt modes of life that could not always be maintained in bad times: and this is the background to Lord Burghley's remarks, made during the long depression that closed the century.

It is thus impossible to say that at a certain point the new style farmer ousted the old style farmer. It was rather a matter of the penetration of successive layers of farming society by social and economic ideas that were themselves changing and developing. Belief in the iron laws of economics, however, did not penetrate very far; or, if it did, it had surprisingly little impact on the older social values of the tenant farmer. Farmers may have shown less 'gratitude' to their landlords in times of depression, and it is in that context that Toynbee's remark in 1883 should be read; but at other times even those farmers who laid field to field still tended to defer to the gentry in political and other matters. As for farmers' wives, some worked harder than their husbands. They may not have done the dirtier jobs about the farm, and few liked their daughters to do field work. But, apart from household tasks, there was usually the cow to milk or the chickens to feed. And some women, often on the deaths of their husbands, took over the management and even the legal tenancy of farms. Of the 10,973 farmers in Lincolnshire in 1851, as many as 784 were women.

COMMERCE AND CRAFTS

The farmers and farm workers were far and away the largest occupational group in mid-nineteenth-century Lincolnshire. But next to them in numbers were the tradesmen and craftsmen. In 1861, when rural craftsmen and tradesmen were at or near their numerical peak, there was a total of about 26,000 persons in the county engaged in trades and crafts, compared with about 66,000 in agriculture.

The market towns were filled with shopkeepers large and small, dependent on rural as well as urban custom, and with craftsmen who ranged from solitary workers to owners of substantial businesses. In 1856 White's *Directory* listed no less than thirty-five shoemakers in Spalding, a town of little more than 7,000 inhabitants. These shoemakers were of course masters of their trade, employing journeymen and apprentices. Even a small town such as Caistor had nine shoemakers listed in the same directory. One of these, as we know from the 1851 census, had twelve men working for him. Two apprentices lived in his house, much as young farm servants were boarded and lodged with their masters.

The tradesman, that is, the retailer, was an urban phenomenon which spread to the countryside as items such as tea and sugar established themselves in the rural diet. By 1856 even the smallest villages normally had a 'shopkeeper', somebody who kept a small store of necessaries and who may often have had another job as well. At Rothwell Robert Waller, described as a herdsman in the 1851 census, combined labouring and shopkeeping. Most villages also had a blacksmith and a wheelwright, and larger settlements might also support a shoemaker and a tailor. A notable feature of Lincolnshire was the large open village which provided services for a tract of surrounding countryside. Keelby, a village on the eastern edge of the Wolds between Caistor and Grimsby, had 859 inhabitants in 1851. Among the master craftsmen and tradesmen listed in the 1856 directory were seven shopkeepers, six shoemakers, four tailors, and three blacksmiths. Binbrook had a working population of 532 (out of a total population of 1,269 resident inhabitants) in 1851, and of these as many as 140 were engaged in crafts and retail trade.[29]

Despite the large numbers and widespread incidence of these occupational groups, it is hard to assess their contribution to rural society and to the life of the county. They were lacking in homogeneity, and never spoke with one voice. The distinction between masters and men has already been mentioned, and it is interesting in that connection to note that a movement for a union among the journeymen shoemakers of Louth took place as early as 1853.[30] In 1872 similar, more widespread movements had an important influence on the formation of the labourers' unions. In the

[29] White's *Directory*, 1856; Olney ed., *Labouring Life on the Lincolnshire Wolds*, *passim*.
[30] *SM* 15 July 1853.

countryside there was another distinction, between craftsmen who travelled from village to village or farm to farm and those who put down roots in their native parishes. In the same way pedlars and travelling salesmen contrasted with village shopkeepers. But the most important distinction was between those who depended on the farmers for most of their custom and those who met the personal and domestic needs of all classes among their neighbours. Blacksmiths and wheelwrights were closest to agriculture: on the Wolds some of the large farms employed full-time blacksmiths. At the other extreme were grocers, who dealt with urban whole-salers, and whose interests lay with the consumers rather than the producers.

On the one hand, therefore, the small rural craftsman was vulner-able to the influence of his more powerful customers, the gentry, the clergy, and the farmers. On the other hand the possession of tools and working capital, the ownership in many cases of his house and perhaps a field or two besides, and the existence of a range of small customers, some of whom might owe him money, all tended to make him a potentially independent figure in the local com-munity. In a moderate-sized Lincolnshire village the leading craftsmen and tradesmen, together with the innkeepers and carriers, probably influenced local opinion more than the clergymen, who belonged to a different class, or the larger farmers, who often lived outside the main settlement.

The clearest illustration of this is in the religious history of the county, which in the nineteenth century was one of the great strongholds of both Wesleyan and Primitive Methodism. Wes-leyanism was particularly strong among the craftsmen and trades-men, some of whom found outlets for their energy and qualities of leadership by becoming local preachers. In 1859 the Willoughby agent at Spilsby wrote to the head agent in London about a possible tenant for a tailor's shop.

I believe he is steady and sober, a single man and a member of the Wesleyan connection, as most all tailors and shoemakers are here. Perhaps the parson may consider the Church in danger if we accept this man. It is difficult in matters of this kind to know what to do in a small town like this for it is sure to reflect the country do what we will. I believe purely as a matter of business there is trades that can be more favourably carried on in connection with the Methodists than in connection with the Church and vice versa.[31]

[31] 3 ANC 7/23/97/174; James Obelkevich, *Religion and Rural Society: South Lindsey 1825–1875*, 1976, pp. 195, 202.

Village and small town tradesmen might show their independence of squire and parson in religious matters, but it was more
difficult to hold out against political pressure from above, particularly at election times. Some were bold enough to speak out. In 1882
Isaac Nutsey, a Baptist and a leading Alford tradesman, addressed a
Liberal meeting at Wainfleet on that very subject. 'A great many
were afraid to declare their politics, he said, for fear of losing a
customer, but as a businessman for thirty years he had taken his
stand and said "I sell my goods and not myself".'[32] He may just
have remembered the prolonged tory campaign of 1850–2 in North
Lincolnshire, when farmers threatened to withdraw their custom
from those tradesmen who did not support the Conservative and
protectionist candidates. At the general election of 1852 many gave
one vote for the tory and the other for the Liberal, hoping to please
both sides. Nevertheless the Liberals were in a majority among the
shoemakers, tailors, and drapers. The blacksmiths and butchers
leaned towards the tories.[33]

In the later nineteenth century the rural crafts and village trades
were affected both by the depression in agriculture and by the
growth in urban commerce and manufacture. A classic case was
that of the millers, caught between poor harvests on the one hand
and the growth of powered roller milling in Lincoln and Grimsby
on the other. Farmers spent less on waggons, and labourers went
into the towns to buy cheap manufactured boots and shoes. The
number of shoemakers in the county fell dramatically, from 3,900
in 1861 to 1,905 in 1891. Some village craftsmen struggled on into
the twentieth century, but by 1900 the large service villages such as
Keelby and Binbrook had seriously declined.[34]

THE MIDDLE CLASS AND THE COMMUNITY

The occupational groups described in this chapter contained men of
widely differing incomes and status. Up to about 1860 there were
roughly four main layers. At the top were the bankers and the
superior clergy, men who but for the fact that they had definite
occupations were hard to distinguish from the leisured and landed
upper class. Below them came what was in Lincolnshire at least a
very important group in early nineteenth-century rural society.
This was the group comprising the upper crust of farmers, the less

[32] *SM* 7 April 1882.
[33] Olney, *Lincolnshire Politics*, p. 137.
[34] See also G. E. Mingay, *Rural Life in Victorian England*, 1977, pp. 181–3 *et
passim.*

well-connected clergy, the reputable doctors and lawyers, and a few merchants and manufacturers. Below these again subsisted a rougher and much larger group of working farmers and tradesmen. Millers and innkeepers belonged to this layer: they sometimes rented a farm of forty or fifty acres in addition to their main occupation. Then, finally, there were the village craftsmen and the smallholders, who were culturally little different from the labouring class. A recent study of a sample of south Lindsey craftsmen showed that their sons more frequently married daughters of labourers than daughters of other craftsmen.[35]

A good proportion of this chapter has been devoted to the second layer, the farming and professional people with incomes ranging between three and twelve hundred pounds a year, because these were the people who for two-thirds of the century dominated the middle class of rural Lincolnshire. But during the latter part of the century, assailed by the twin factors of urban expansion and rural decay, the clergy, agents, attorneys, and superior farmers lost ground to newer middle-class elements. The lesser farmers and the tradesmen became more vocal in county and local affairs, and they were joined by a growing army of managers, accountants, civil servants, and elementary school teachers.

This development can be illustrated from the progress of middle class education during the century, and in particular from the decline and revival of the grammar schools. In 1800 most Lincolnshire market towns could boast a grammar school, probably endowed with income from land by its Elizabethan founder and occupying venerable if uncomfortable buildings. These schools were mostly small, with under fifty scholars, and they were presided over by masters who had to be clergymen of the Church of England. They offered a strictly classical education, generally free to local boys, but by 1800 the demand for Latin and Greek was strictly limited. The inhabitants of the Wainfleets, it was noted in 1818, were 'almost without exception of the middle and lower orders of society', and their children, 'not likely to be profited by a classical education', were drilled instead in reading, writing, and arithmetic. In 1829 no scholar was studying Greek at Wainfleet grammar school, and the Latin grammar in use was 'Ruddiman's Rudiments'. Heighington grammar school sank to the level of a local elementary school, and when visited by a Commissioner from London in the 1860s was found to be 'not full, as many of the boys were employed in the fields'.

Some schools survived by offering a more practical curriculum to

[35] Obelkevich, *Religion and Rural Society*, p. 61n.

those parents willing to pay fees of a few shillings a quarter. The better schools attracted boarders, paying fifty or sixty pounds a year, from a much larger catchment area. If a master acquired a good reputation, gentlemen and clergymen would be prepared to send their sons to him as a preparation for the university. The leading school in Lincolnshire in 1800 was Louth grammar school, where scions of county families rubbed shoulders with the sons of well-to-do lawyers and farmers, and where the Revd John Waite instilled a severely classical curriculum with frequent recourse to the birch. Gainsborough grammar school, revived shortly before the turn of the century, was another popular school under the Revd James Cox.[36]

During the first half of the century these schools declined, the victims of growing class divisions and widening horizons. The gentry began to look farther afield, to the great public schools of England: Louth was especially hard hit by the 'facilities for sending boys further from home'—in other words by improved communications. At the same time the upper class became less willing to support those endowed schools that offered places to the sons of the poor. By the mid-1860s Brigg grammar school was favoured by 'only a part of the more respectable inhabitants of the town'. 'Their principal objection,' it was reported to the Endowed Schools Commission, 'seems to be the mixed character of the school, to which boys of all classes are admitted.'[37]

It was not only the upper middle classes that became discontented with the grammar schools. Dissenting tradesmen saw less and less advantage in sending their sons to a clergyman to learn dead languages. At Lincoln, where the control of the grammar school was divided between the dean and chapter and the city, the question of educational reform arose in the wake of municipal reform in the late 1830s. A series of disputes resulted forty years later in the physical separation of the upper and lower schools: the upper school learned the classics under dean and chapter auspices above hill, while the lower school was turned into a modern or commercial school below hill. Elsewhere efforts were made to modernize the curriculum. French and German were introduced at Gainsborough in 1839, and mensuration and land surveying at Brigg in 1847. In 1863 a new middle school was opened at Market Rasen, putting to good

[36] Edmund Oldfield, *A Topographical and Historical Account of Wainfleet and the Wapentake of Candleshoe*, 1829, pp. 52–3; Adam Stark, *The History and Antiquities of Gainsburgh*, 1843, pp. 317–26; Richard W. Goulding, *Some Louth Grammar School Boys*, 8 parts, 1925–32.

[37] *Parliamentary Papers*, 1867–8 XXVIII, part xiii.

use at last part of the Spital charity endowment. But in the mid-1860s the 'want of a commercial education' was still a frequent subject of complaint in towns like Alford and Sleaford.

Following the Endowed Schools Act of 1869 efforts were increasingly made to modernize the buildings of the old grammar schools, as well as to extend the range of subjects taught. At Brigg new buildings were designed by James Fowler of Louth, and Greek gave way to book-keeping. But schools partly dependent on agricultural income were hit by the depression towards the end of the century, and it was not until after 1900 that they blossomed forth with gymnasia and science laboratories. It was at these reformed grammar schools that Lincolnshire's middle class was prepared for the new industrial and commercial age.[38]

The fact that the grammar schools were sited in the market towns was not without its social significance. The rural middle class of clergy and farmers was thinly scattered over the county, but the market towns provided centres where they could transact business, meet friends, and discuss current affairs. The clergy assembled officially at archdiaconal visitations, but the farmers came regularly to the weekly corn markets. When T. M. Richardson of Hibaldstow decided to attend the newly revived market at Kirton-in-Lindsey, the change of allegiance from Brigg was not undertaken lightly. 'He left kindred spirits ..., friends of his childhood and his youth, and it therefore could not be surprising that he should be found clinging to home with its endearing recollections and associations.'[39]

The flourishing or declining state of local markets was therefore an important factor in Lincolnshire society throughout the nineteenth century. Swineshead, for instance, caught between the rapidly expanding markets of Sleaford and Boston, was already in decline by 1800, and thirty or forty years later the only vestige of its market was an evening gathering of the farmers at one of the inns for recreation and a little business. Saltfleet's market was killed by the Louth Navigation, and Crowle, Burgh-le-Marsh, Wainfleet, and Corby all declined in the early nineteenth century. Folkingham followed them into obscurity, and Wragby and Caistor were doing very little business by the 1880s. But as they went down others came up. A market started at New Bolingbroke in 1821 did not flourish, but Long Sutton (1823) and Winterton (1826) were more successful. The revival of the Kirton-in-Lindsey market in 1849

[38] Hill, *Victorian Lincoln*, pp. 57, 282–3; Frank Henthorn, *The History of Brigg Grammar School*, 1959, pp. 143 ff; J. N. Clarke, *Education in a Market Town: Horncastle 1329–1970*, 1976, pp. 37–44.
[39] *Lincolnshire Chronicle*, 4 Oct. 1850.

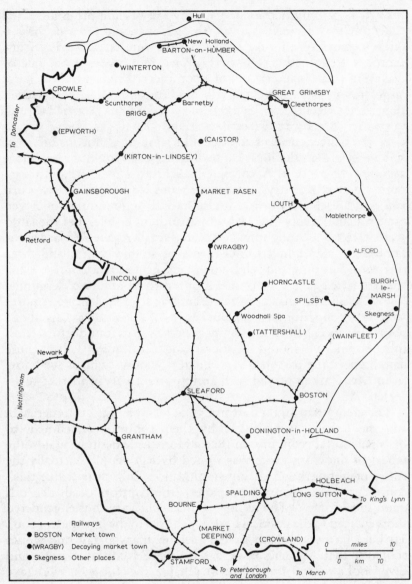

Figure 5   *Lincolnshire in 1885, showing market towns and railways*

proved to be only temporary, but the railway did bring increased trade to Crowle, albeit at Epworth's expense, and towards the end of the century fortnightly cattle markets were established at Scunthorpe and Barnetby. The overall picture, however, was one of declining small markets, and of a commercial concentration in the larger towns with good rail communications. The twenty-seven flourishing weekly corn markets of the county in 1800 had shrunk to twenty-two by 1885 (see Figs. 1 and 5).

A good-sized market town could support a not insignificant middle class—in the local context upper class might be the more accurate description. According to White's *Directory* Louth supported eleven attorneys, eleven surgeons, and a dozen or so corn and coal merchants in 1856. It also had the high number of eleven esquires and twenty-five clergymen, although several of the latter were in fact dissenting ministers. On a smaller scale Sleaford at the same date had eight attorneys, five or so merchants, and three surgeons, but only four clergymen and no resident esquire. On a smaller scale again, Caistor had four attorneys and two clergymen (the vicar and the master of the grammar school). Its two esquires were really superior farmers, but the town's position as capital of a poor law union helped it to support no less than four doctors. In all three towns we should of course add the leading ladies, those daughters of the parsonage and genteel widows who as we know from Mrs Gaskell played such an important part in market-town society.[40]

The clergyman and the attorney, no less than the corn merchant and the farmer, were linked by their common attachment to the agricultural economy. In 1826 a Horncastle petition against the repeal of the Corn Laws was signed by 847 people, virtually the entire neighbourhood of any significance. 'In a district like this', commented the county newspaper, 'the comfort of all depends upon the farmer.'[41] The feeling of local solidarity thus engendered showed itself in the political hostility shown to the free trade school. To hear farmers discuss the subject on market day one would conclude that Manchester was full of cruel cotton masters and Liverpool a nest of fraudulent merchants. Yet the men who gave tongue to these sentiments were by the 1860s running their farms in quite an industrial way. They thrashed by machinery. A few tried ploughing by steam power. Horrible accidents were frequent in the early days of thrashing machines, and women and children suffered

[40] For a local novel see Edward Peacock's *Mabel Heron*. It should be noted that White's *Directory* used esquire sparingly, to 'avoid invidious distinctions'.

[41] *SM* 29 April 1826.

working conditions in the fields that could be as bad as in any mill.

Locally the very solidarity of the middle class was enhanced by the fact that farmers, merchants, and manufacturers were interdependent and sometimes inter-related. Lindsey farmers sold their corn to the Lincoln miller Charles Seely and bought machines from Nathaniel Clayton despite the Liberal and free-trading politics of both those gentlemen. When the foundry of Robey and Co was established at Lincoln in 1875 several well-known Lindsey farmers were ready to put their capital into it; and at a later date the Riggalls and Sharpleys became connected with Rustons of Lincoln. It was not only the great ironmasters, moreover, whose fortunes found their way back to the land. William Foster (*c.* 1816–76) was not such an outstanding capitalist as Joseph Ruston or Nathaniel Clayton, but his career is equally instructive. He came from Manchester to set up as a merchant, miller, and thrashing machine maker in Lincoln in the 1840s. But he married into a farming family, the Cartwrights of Kirmington. In 1888 his son Henry Munk Foster married the niece and heiress of William Hudson of Kirmington Vale, and the family soon afterwards acquired the Abraham property at Barnetby-le-Wold.[42]

Whether or not the respectable leaders of market-town society were connected with commerce, they shared a respect for the ways and traditions of landed society. To keep two or three servants, to possess some family silver and a portrait of a grandfather, to meet the gentry on business and even to enjoy the occasional social visit to the big house—these were the things that marked off the merchant and the professional man from the clerk and the shopkeeper. The emphasis on solidity and respectability, moreover, helped to conceal the unpleasant fact that it was all too easy to slip from the path of virtue into the slough of disgrace and poverty. In nineteenth-century Lincolnshire business failures were common. Farmers drank themselves to death, and suicides were frequent in bad times. Attorneys absconded, leaving their affairs in disorder, and even clerical households were liable like Framley Parsonage to invasion by the bailiffs. Perhaps towards the end of the century life became more secure for the rural middle class, but then its opportunities for making 'ample fortunes' had certainly diminished.

[42] *Archivists' Report* 21 (1969–70), p. 10; DIXON 15/1; SB (Sills and Betteridge deposit), Foster deeds.

CHAPTER IV

FARM LABOUR AND VILLAGE LIFE

OPEN AND CLOSED PARISHES

BETWEEN 1801 and 1851 the population of the county nearly doubled, from 208,625 to 407,222. By 1851 the number of agricultural labourers, farm servants, and shepherds (males and females of all ages) had reached 52,046. Detailed figures are not available before 1831, but the number of farm workers probably grew fastest in the period 1801 to 1831. This was not only a time of general population expansion but also a time when in Lincolnshire the spread of intensive arable cultivation was most rapid.

The population of rural Lincolnshire grew principally by its own natural rate of increase. Those who swelled the numbers in the most rapidly expanding settlements came mainly from only a few miles away. The county was haunted by Scottish vagrants early in the nineteenth century, and during the 1820s the seasonal influx of Irish labourers reached considerable proportions; but few of these visitors settled in the villages. By 1850, in fact, Lincolnshire was on balance an emigration rather than an immigration county. As early as the 1820s Lincolnshire natives began to look for employment and a new life outside the county. Some went to the Yorkshire woollen towns, some to the colonies. Only after 1850 did emigration begin to have an appreciable effect on the county's agricultural labour market.[1]

The consequences of these demographic changes on the lives of Lincolnshire farm workers were far-reaching. They became less of a peasantry, more of a proletariat. They lost their cows and their common rights. By 1850 the typical farm worker lived not in an insanitary but pretty cottage in a small village but in an insanitary and ugly row of tenements in a new and featureless rural settlement, or in the back streets of an overcrowded market town.

[1] Arthur Redford, *Labour Migration in England, 1800–50*. 2nd edn., ed. W. H. Chaloner, 1964, pp. 142–7, 197.

Twenty-one Lincolnshire market towns doubled in size between 1801 and 1851. Labourers walked out from towns such as Louth to the surrounding farms. In the 1860s Spalding was said to be composed chiefly of semi-employed and demoralized farm workers.[2] As many as 158 rural parishes or townships also doubled their population in the same period. The greatest increases were in the Lindsey and Holland Fens, and such Kesteven fen-side parishes as North Kyme, Billinghay and Metheringham. Spectacular growth also took place in some wold parishes in Lindsey such as Belchford, Tetford, Ludford and Donington-on-Bain.

On the other hand twenty-six rural places had actually fewer people in 1851 than they had had fifty years before. Binbrook (excluding Orford) grew from 484 people to 1,285, but the neighbouring parish of Kirmond-le-Mire shrank from sixty-nine inhabitants to sixty-two. Contemporaries and later writers have explained these differences in terms of open and closed parishes. Binbrook was, if not exactly an open parish, certainly an open village. No single landed proprietor dominated it, and its land and houses were owned by a number of different people. Kirmond was a closed parish, owned entirely by the Turnor family. Over the county as a whole the majority of the expanding parishes were open ones, and the contracting ones closed parishes.

It seemed obvious to many contemporaries that the owners of the closed parishes were to blame for this imbalance of population and its consequent social evils. Not content with failing to build new cottages on their estates, it was said that they let existing cottages fall into decay or even pulled them down. They did these things partly to exclude undesirable people from their estates, but mainly to keep down the poor rates and thus preserve the letting value of their farms. The result was that the local labour supply was crowded into neighbouring open parishes, which became notorious for poor housing and lawlessness.

For Lincolnshire at least it can be suggested that this is much too simple an explanation. Some landlords did fail to pursue an enlightened cottage-building policy. Some even cleared old dwellings away and failed to replace them. But how far this was due to a desire to discourage the settlement of paupers or potential paupers is very hard to establish. The 1851 census explains a decrease in the population of South Owersby by referring to the removal of some cottages by the proprietor (Angerstein), but this appears to have been part of a policy of farm consolidation. Shortage of capital to invest in cottage building probably held back many landlords.

[2] *Parliamentary Papers*, 1867 XVI, p. 98.

Where great landowners pursued policies of estate improvement they built cottages as well as cattle sheds. Whilst Kirmond shrank, the nearby closed parish of Wold Newton on the Brocklesby estate showed a modest increase of population. Of the 158 expanding places mentioned above as many as thirty-seven were parishes or townships where one proprietor owned all or most of the soil.

On some estates the decisive factor may have been the attitude of the farming tenants. Farmers may have urged on their landlords the need to build or rebuild cottages for their shepherds or foremen. With a tied cottage there was not much risk of a growth in the pauper population of the parish. For day and casual labour, however, the farmer might well prefer to draw his supply from a neighbouring open village, in this way avoiding responsibility for workers when they became sick or infirm.

It was the pattern of demand for agricultural labour, particularly in the Fens and on the Wolds, that in the early nineteenth century exacerbated the problem of the open village. The demand for day and casual labour greatly increased, and only the open villages could supply it. In the 1860s Edward Stanhope wrote of the Wolds: 'The bad distribution of cottages in this district, as in most other parts of Lincolnshire, arises not from the destruction of cottages by the large owners to save the rates, but from its being in many respects a new country.'[3]

It must be said that in other parts of the county the problem was not as acute as it was on the northern Wolds or in Deeping Fen. Many parishes were in mixed ownership, with one or two large but several small estates. Some parishes, formerly closed, were broken up by sale during the nineteenth century. A few, such as Corringham, Tealby, and South Rauceby, were transformed from near-open to near-closed parishes by the purchasing policies of their chief landlords.[4] A parish owned entirely by an absentee corporation might well give the appearance of a run-down, open settlement. Also to be considered are the vagaries of the parochial system. It was possible to have two townships in one parish, one of them closed and the other open (South and North Kyme). It was also possible to have an open village in an otherwise virtually closed parish (Binbrook).

<hr>

[3] *Parliamentary Papers*, 1867–8 XVII.

[4] For Rauceby see A. Rogers ed., *Stability and Change: Some Aspects of North and South Rauceby*, University of Nottingham Department of Adult Education, 1969.

VILLAGE SOCIETY

The classic examples of open parishes were to be found surrounded by closed parishes, and contemporaries always had in mind the contrast between the two. That is why more was written about the large wold parishes than about the equally open parishes of the Marsh or the Fens. Landowners liked tidy estates and well-behaved cottagers, but the necessary corollary was the large, untidy, lawless village two or three miles off, with its collection of drunks, ruffians, and poachers.

Is this a fair description of the manners of an open village? Were they places of deservedly ill repute? And if so, what was it in their social structure that inclined them to be so? For the Revd Samuel Hopkinson, incumbent of Morton with Hanthorpe and Hacconby with Stainfield in the early nineteenth century, there was no doubt about the contrast in behaviour between his two sets of parishioners.

> The inhabitants of these places, tho' adjoining parishes, are as different as in two clans or counties. The former [the Morton people] have, always, time immemorial, been proverbially bad: the latter far better than the common run in any of the surrounding towns. Of the one not less than 7 or 8 have been sent abroad besides many more subjected to minor punishments within the last 30 years; of the latter not above one or two. Ninety sheep, within 20 months, were either, in part, slaughtered on the ground *sub noctem*, or driven away in flocks from 7 to 13 together. Nearly two years together, foot-pad robberies real and sometimes fictitious for the purpose of exciting compassion and obtaining money, frequent housebreaking attended with open and outrageous violence by a gang of masqued thieves, who came armed, burglaries and petty thefts, mischievous acts cruel to both man and beast, kept the public and private mind in continual alarm: assassinations were in two cases particularly plan'd, pistols were fired and other injuries used.[5]

After great efforts two gangs were eventually tracked down and their members brought to justice.

Sheep stealing and burglary were especially common in times of unemployment or high prices, but they were crimes that were often traced to outsiders rather than to village people. Hopkinson blamed two groups of people in particular, the convicts who were released in England instead of being transported and the 'horde of itinerant

[5] DIOC MISC 1/10.

and gigantic bankers' who were employed on drainage and other projects. More truly indigenous crime, however, could be violent enough. The curate of Whaplode, the Revd Samuel Oliver, recorded the vagaries of his flock on the fly leaves of the parish registers.

> Memorandum. Jany. 27th. 1820. At the last Lammas Assizes, John Bimrose, of this Parish, was capitally convicted of wilfully firing a gun about midnight, into the Chamber window of William Wilders of the Star public house (pretending to suppose that his wife, whom he had turned out, was there) ...
>
> It ought not, by any means, to be omitted recording, that, among the principal people of this Parish, Shooting into Houses; breaking open doors; demolishing windows; and such like transactions, in the Night, has been, for some years, a common drunken frolic, which was always made up, in a day or two, by paying for the damage done; and spending a few shillings by way of a treat!!!![6]

These frolics were indulged in, then, by the 'principal people' of the place, and they were not regarded as crimes. The parish went to great lengths to secure a reprieve for Bimrose, sending a messenger after the judge to Derby and raising a subscription to pay the expenses of £21 thus incurred.

At Ruskington in the 1830s street fights were common. Hephzibah Scott, a coarse female who died in 1845 aged twenty-two, once fought another woman stripped to the waist in a public house yard. 'This was before the Rural Police force were established,' recorded the schoolmaster of the parish, 'when parties like those could fight to their hearts' content without fear of molestation.'[7] In contrast the villagers of Scopwick on the Chaplin estate were well behaved. 'The sobriety of the Scopwickians is proverbial,' wrote the Revd George Oliver (Samuel's better-known son) in 1838, 'and consequently no Temperance Societies are wanted here.' There was only one habit that constituted 'a dark shade in the religion of this otherwise quiet parish': the farmers' servants spent their Sundays gambling for halfpence in the public street.[8]

Hopkinson was sure that the division of land in Morton had much to do with its social character.

[6] WHAPLODE PARISH, register of baptisms 1813–42.

[7] 'A few of the Persons I have Known', by Thomas Ogden. Copy of MS (in private possession) at Grimsby Public Library. I owe this reference to Mr R. W. Ambler.

[8] Revd George Oliver, *Scopwickiana*, 1838.

Let magistrates be ever so active, let the resident clergy be ever so attentive, while the property of this large parish continues divided and in so many hands, each individual proprietor will consider himself at liberty to act independently. His example is insensibly imitated by his inferiors, who gradually growing up in progressively lawless habits, have no notion of that decent deportment and necessary subordination visible in market towns, and villages belonging solely either to some virtuous nobleman, or to a resident gentleman. Hacconby is almost the Property of Sir Gilbert Heathcote. To what other cause, then, is the moral state of the people, so very different in these two contiguous villages, to be attributed more than to that above assigned?

In Morton, as in Whaplode, the tone was set by the more substantial residents, and these were generally owner-occupying farmers. Men of little or no education, they guarded their properties against outside interference, and had few recreations beyond family quarrels and feuds with neighbours. Some of the farming families in Ruskington went back several generations, during which period hard liquor and inbreeding had in some cases led to a deterioration in morale. Perhaps the unmarried sons of these families were the most inclined to violence, adding juvenile delinquency to the village problems of drink and drugs. Opium was extensively taken in the early nineteenth century, and not only in the Fens. The example to the labouring population thus provided was reinforced by the way in which open villages were haunted by vagrants, escaped convicts, and local 'characters'.

The personal influence of the squire in a close parish can easily be exaggerated. Hopkinson omitted to state that Heathcote lived some miles from Hacconby across the Rutland border. But the fact that farmers and cottagers shared the same landlord gave some cohesion to the parish community. The structure was more of a hierarchy—squire, parson, tenant of the largest farm, and so on downwards. In open villages the social structure was much looser, and there was a lack of focus around established institutions. The Church was generally weak, the incumbent being either non-resident or even if resident looked on as an outsider. When Oliver first came to Whaplode as resident curate in 1802 the forces ranged against him were led by the vicar's churchwarden, the schoolmaster (an infidel), and the parish clerk. At Ruskington the parish clerk used to withdraw to the Black Bull during the sermon, and once announced an auction sale during the service. The presence of a number of tradesmen and craftsmen helped to diversify the society of the open village, and the population distribution within the parish also had its effect. A subsidiary settlement, especially down in the fen part of a large parish, might be even more lawless than the parent village, and little love was generally lost between the two.

The open village, however, was not entirely lacking in a sense of community. It benefited from a greater stability than the closed parish. The old families in an open village might decline and new ones might rise, but family traditions were preserved, and even black sheep would after years of wandering come back to die in their old homes. Such villages probably had a higher than average percentage of native-born inhabitants.[9] A village could also show its solidarity when confronted with an outsider. Samuel Oliver had to contend with hostility from his parishioners for several years, culminating in an attempt to blow him up: only later was he adopted as a feature of the parish. At Morton the inhabitants dropped their plans to assassinate one another in order to drive out the Methodists who came to preach to them. The 'invaders were defeated', recorded their incumbent (and resident magistrate), 'and the church people came off with as much credit as usual in [such cases]'.

FARM WORK AND WAGES

Much of the history of the English farm worker in the nineteenth century remains obscure. This applies even to the basic facts of wages and conditions of work, and it is particularly true of the period 1800–50. Statements are common enough that in a particular county, at a certain date, the labourer earned so many shillings a week. But earnings and wages were different things. Wages could vary from district to district, from farm to farm, from season to season, and from occupation to occupation. This last is particularly important, for not all farm workers did the same unspecialized job. There was, especially on the larger farms, a well-defined division of labour and a corresponding range of terms of employment. The principal division was between farm servants or confined men, and ordinary or day labourers.

On a large Lincolnshire farm the foreman, shepherd, yardman, and waggoners (or horsemen) were all confined men. The foreman and shepherd might live in tied cottages. The waggoners, who were usually young and unmarried, might live either with the farmer himself or with the foreman. But however accommodated they were all on yearly hirings, generally from old May Day (14 May). In

[9] Olney, ed., *Labouring Life*, p. 18.

contrast to the great seasonal farming operations such as hay time and harvest the tending of livestock needed a regular labour force, living conveniently close to its work and available all the year round. Farm servants could bargain with their masters at the statute or hiring fairs, but once on the farm they were bound to work their full year and could be prosecuted if they absconded.

Payment of farm servants was partly in kind. When Richard Hill went to serve Thomas Skipworth of South Kelsey as foreman in 1808, he was to have £20 a year, a house, nearly a rood of garden ground, and the keeping of a cow and two pigs. Four years later his wage and allowances were doubled when he agreed to board and lodge two of his master's servants. At the end of the century farm servants in the Caistor rural district were receiving allowances in the form of rent-free cottages and gardens, potatoes, beer, and bacon. The custom of cow-keeping, however, declined during the early nineteenth century, and by 1850 survived in only a few areas of Lindsey. Farmers did not object to pig raising and potato growing, but cow keeping was thought to take up too much of the men's time and make them too independent. When John Cragg valued the parish of Metheringham in 1802 he advised its owners to turn the cow common into a few fair-sized closes: the cottagers could easily obtain wood from elsewhere on the estate, and too much land interfered with their usefulness as labourers. Wage rates for farm servants also declined during the period 1800 to 1850, in the case of a first waggoner from about £16 to £12. In 1894 the rate was £19, but fifth waggoners were still getting about £6 10s., only 25s. more than in 1851. No wonder the young farm lads of the 1890s were attracted to the shorter hours and higher wages of the towns.[10]

Ordinary labourers were paid by the week but they were in reality hired by the day, and the practice of laying off hands unpaid on rainy days did not die with the nineteenth century. In 1794 Thomas Stone wrote that wages rates fluctuated very much with supply and demand, thus bringing out the near-casual nature of day labour. Wages varied from season to season, and even in 1900 the winter wage averaged 13s. 6d., compared with a summer wage (for longer hours) of 15s. From season to season wages fluctuated with the price of corn, a phenomenon observable in Lincolnshire until the early 1890s. During the mid-century depression wages dipped down to 10s., less than the level of fifty years before. The rise of the early 1870s, when 18s. was briefly reached, was followed by a fall to

[10] LNPS 1/10; MISC DEP 270; Arthur Young, *General View of the Agriculture of the County of Lincoln*, 1799, pp. 397 ff; *Parliamentary Papers*, 1893–4 XXXV, p. 740.

around 13s. 6d. or less, with rates beginning to rise again slowly after 1895.[11]

Allowances for day labourers were few, apart from beer at harvest or straw for the pig. But piece-work could help to swell the farm worker's meagre wages, and during the nineteenth century operations such as hoeing, turnip pulling, and potato lifting were increasingly done on that system. The great opportunity for extra earnings was the harvest, which in a good season might bring the labourer as much as £10. A bad harvest, however, such as that of 1860, meant a shortage of new shoes and winter clothing for many a family.[12]

Lincolnshire was a comparatively high-wage county. In 1902 the average estimated total weekly *earnings* of the farm worker in cash terms were 18s. 8d., not far below his fellow-workers in Nottinghamshire (19s. 9d.) or Northumberland (21s. 7d.). Lower rates prevailed in the arable counties to the south and south-east of Lincolnshire. The comparable figures were 16s. 1d. in Cambridgeshire, 15s. 6d. in Suffolk and 15s. 3d. in Norfolk. In fact earnings in south Lincolnshire, especially around Spalding, were close to those of Norfolk, whilst earnings in northern Lindsey approached those of north Nottinghamshire and Yorkshire. In January 1903 actual wages varied from 13s. 6d. on some farms in the Sleaford and Spalding districts to 16s. 6d. in north-west Lindsey.[13]

In its proportion of farm servants to day labourers Lincolnshire again bore more resemblance to the pastoral northern counties than to its southern corn-growing neighbours. The proportion in 1851 was one farm servant to every four labourers in Lincolnshire, compared with one to two in the North Riding of Yorkshire but as low as one to eleven in Norfolk. In mid-nineteenth century Lincolnshire a surprising number of small farmers employing no outdoor labourer still had a farm servant living with them.[14]

For most of the century the day labourer had to contend with chronic insecurity as well as low wages. Women and children were increasingly employed as potato growing developed in the Fens and as elaborate turnip cultivation became part of the routine of high farming on the less fertile uplands. The shilling a day earned by the wife or the sixpence by the child could add appreciably to the

[11] Thomas Stone, *General View of the Agriculture of the County of Lincoln*, 1794, p. 24; *Report by Mr Wilson Fox on the wages and earnings of agricultural labourers in the U.K.* (Cmd 346 of 1900).

[12] *Parl. Papers*, 1861 L, p. 592.   [13] *Parl. Papers*, 1905 XCVII.

[14] The 1851 census distinguished between 'indoor' and 'outdoor' labourers, and probably included some farm servants among the latter. See also the article by J. P. D. Dunbabin in *Ag. Hist. Rev.* (1968).

income of a labouring family, but they adversely affected the bargaining power of the labourer himself. Women and children were
not his only competitors. His crucial harvest earnings were frequently depressed when the labour market was flooded by immigrants. Thomas Stone wrote in 1800:

> I have on a fine morning been obliged to arise at the Inn, at Long
> Sutton, and march long before my avocations required it, on
> account of the assemblies of harvestmen under my windows,
> talking as many different dialects as the builders of Babel, Irish,
> Scotch, and Welch, upwards of fifty in a body, bargaining with
> the farmers for the work of that day.[15]

But winter unemployment rather than summer underemployment
was the final disaster that drove many labouring families on to
parish relief.

By the early 1830s, when the Poor Law commissioners investi-
gated conditions in Lincolnshire, the parochial system was in many
places breaking down. At Coningsby in 1833–4 there were thirty
families on out-relief and fifteen in the parish workhouse. Assistance with emigration and the provision of allotments had failed to
improve matters, and the rates stood at eight shillings in the pound
gross estimated rental. The payment of cottage rents by the overseers and the erection of cottages by the parish were other remedies
extensively tried in Lincolnshire, to the disgust of the poor law
reformers.[16] But the reformers' answers, the grouping of parishes
into poor law unions and the replacement of out-relief by the
workhouse test, caused as much misery as it alleviated.

The efforts of enlightened landowners concentrated on the provision of better housing and allotments. At Saxby near Barton-
on-Humber the ordinary labourers in the early 1840s had the chance
to rent good cottages for only thirty shillings a year and an acre of
garden ground for a further twenty-eight shillings.[17] But such
places were the exception. Allotments became more common after
1870, but housing was still deplorable in many villages at the end of
the century.

During the nineteenth century two direct attacks were made on
aspects of the Lincolnshire agricultural labour market. One was on
the hiring fairs. Farm servants stood in the open market place to be
inspected by prospective employers, and the business of hiring was

[15] Thomas Stone, *A Review of the Corrected Agricultural Survey of Lincolnshire by
Arthur Young Esq.*, 1800, p. 307.
[16] *Parl. Papers*, 1834 XXIX, esp. pp. 142–3.
[17] *Journal of the Royal Agricultural Society* V (1844–5), p. 282.

followed by the drunken and roisterous pleasures that marked the one holiday of the year for their participants. The Lincolnshire General Servants' Amelioration Society was formed in January 1858 with the object of getting the hirings off the streets and into registration offices.[18] But custom proved too strong, and statutes were still a feature of Lincolnshire labouring life in 1900.

The other and more successful attack, conducted more at a national than a local level, was against the gang system. The system had developed in the 1820s in areas of intensive arable farming but unevenly distributed population. In Lincolnshire 'public' gangs, groups of workers controlled by a gangmaster and travelling from farm to farm, were particularly in evidence on the high Wolds between Caistor and Louth and in Deeping Fen. Objections to the gangs might have been expected to centre on the hardness of the work, especially for the often very young children employed, and on the fact that it kept them out of school. The landowners and farmers of Lincolnshire tended on the contrary to consider healthy outdoor work a better education than book-learning for the future farm labourer, although by the 1860s a growing minority disagreed with that view. There was unanimity, however, on the immorality of the gangs. There is no doubt that some of the casual female workers were rough types, and that bawdiness would sometimes seize even respectable farm workers out in the fields. But over-crowding in cottages probably deserved far more attention than the gangs as a source of social evil in the countryside. Public gangs were outlawed in 1867, but at the end of the century private gangs, hired directly by the farmers, were not unknown in the south of the county.[19]

REPRESSION AND RESISTANCE

The instincts of paternalism, though present in some farmers as well as in many landlords, could not have much beneficial effect upon a large class of workers depressed to near subsistence level. Nor could the ancient responsibilities of the parish community survive into an era dominated by the iron laws of supply and demand and the forbidding brick bastilles of the New Poor Law. Nor again could a concern for the morals of the poor bridge the cultural gap that separated Hodge from his masters.

An acute shortage of alternative work, lack of opportunities for self-advancement, and above all lack of education all combined to

[18] *SM* 22 Jan. 1858.   [19] *Parl. Papers*, 1867–8 XVII.

I County Hall, Lincoln Castle. Built 1823–6. The Grand Jury Room is in the centre, above the entrance, with the assize courts on either side. Lincoln Central Library, Local Collection.

II County Gaol, Lincoln Castle. Built 1787–8 and in use as a gaol until 1878. Lincoln Central Library, Local Collection.

III Judges' Lodgings, Castle Hill, Lincoln. Built 1810–12. Lincoln Central Library, Local Collection.

*IV Spilsby Sessions House and House of Correction. An engraving dated
1866. Built in 1824–5. The prison was closed in 1876 and afterwards
demolished, but the Sessions House survives. Lincolnshire Archives
Office, Foster Library.*

*V Folkingham House of Correction. Built 1824–5, and in use until 1878.
Only the gatehouse, incorporating the governor's house, survives. Lincolnshire Archives Office, LLHS 16/2/6.*

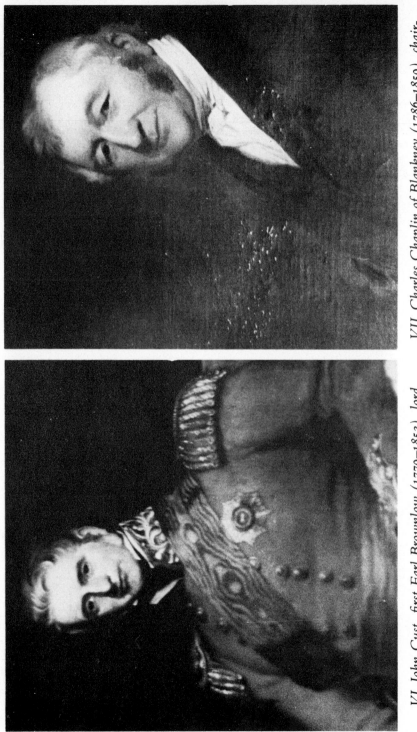

VII *Charles Chaplin of Blankney (1786–1859), chairman of Kesteven Quarter Sessions at Sleaford 1817–59. Detail of portrait.* Grand Jury Room, County Hall, Lincoln Castle.

VI *John Cust, first Earl Brownlow (1779–1853), lord lieutenant of Lincolnshire 1809–52. Detail of portrait.* Grand Jury Room, County Hall, Lincoln Castle.

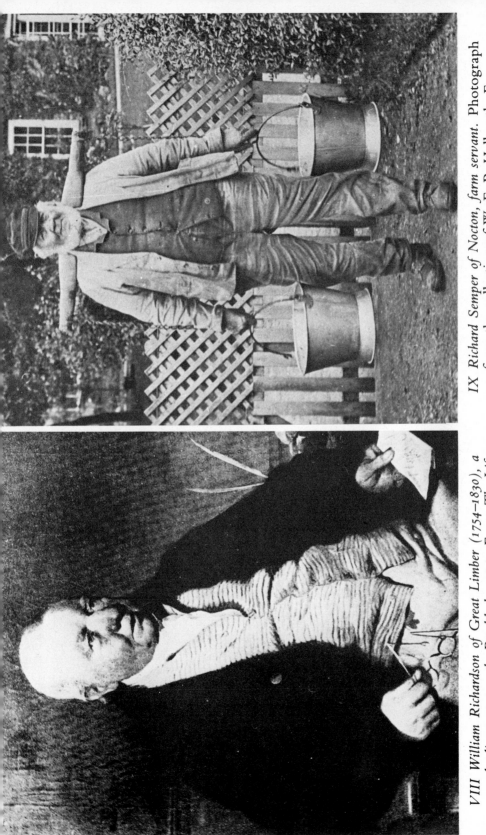

VIII *William Richardson of Great Limber (1754–1830), a leading tenant on the Brocklesby estate. From* The Life of a Great Sportsman, *John Maunsell Richardson, by Mary E. Richardson, 1919.*

IX *Richard Semper of Nocton, farm servant. Photograph from the collection of W. E. R. Hallgarth, Esq.*

X An Evening Party at Redbourne. Watercolour by Charles Uppleby of Barrow (1780–1853), 1812. The flautist is Lord William Beauclerk, later eighth duke of St Albans, and members of the Uppleby and Nelthorpe families are also present. Lt-Col R. Sutton–Nelthorpe. Photograph: George Tokarski

XI *A Hunting Scene. Watercolour by Charles Uppleby, 1814. The farmer maintains the traditional good relations with the Brocklesby hunt, but his labourers appear none too pleased. Professor and Mrs John Barron.*

XII Harlaxton House. Drawing by C. Nattes, 1803. Lincoln Central Library, Banks Collection.

XIII Harlaxton Manor. Built as the successor to Harlaxton House, mainly between 1831 and 1844, and the most striking country house of its day in Lincolnshire. National Monuments Record. Photograph: M. W. Barley.

keep the labourer literally in his place. 'If I were a scholar I shouldn't be here,' said one, 'and that's the reason why the farmers hold against this 'ere scholarship.'[20] Despite the growth of elementary education in the first half of the century, about 30 per cent of men and 50 per cent of women in Lincolnshire were still illiterate in the 1840s. In some of the expanding villages illiteracy had actually increased in the 1830s. In the 1840s the illiteracy rate among men in Tetford was 43 per cent, in Binbrook 40 per cent, and in Wintering-ham 38 per cent. Among labourers the percentage must have been greater still.[21]

Why should the poor need to write? The labourers were not expected to play any part in parish affairs, and except for a few who owned their cottages they lacked the political franchise. Reading was well enough, if confined to religious literature and not extended to radical tracts and inflammatory journals. For attempts at combination the law had its remedies, and for non-political crimes punishment was fierce enough. In the early 1820s persons found armed at night with intent to kill game were liable to seven years' transportation.[22]

The social attitudes that supported this system of repression are hard now to understand. John Cragg, a Lincolnshire land agent of long and wide experience, gave it as his opinion in the early 1830s that 'the deterioration of the morals and industry of the labouring class had been constantly augmenting'. According to Miss Boucherett, a lady known for her good works, labourers were not just lazy but also stupid. 'No sink or other communication with drains', she considered, 'ought to exist in labourers' houses. The inhabitants have not intelligence enough to keep such things in order.'[23]

Three things followed from this state of affairs. The labourers deeply resented their plight; they blamed it upon the unfeeling behaviour of their superiors; and when their resentment erupted into action, as it did in periods of extreme hardship, it took a violent form. The characteristic expression of discontent, in Lincolnshire as in the eastern counties, was the incendiary fire. The motives for arson were very varied, from a personal grudge against an employer to an attempt to intimidate a whole farming community. The miserable winter months were the usual season and the stack yard

[20] *Ibid.*, p. 144.
[21] Rex C. Russell, *A History of Schools and Education in Lindsey, 1800–1902*, Lindsey County Council 1965–7, i. 49–56. Lincolnshire was slightly more literate than most southern English counties (E. J. Hobsbawm and George Rudé, *Captain Swing*, 1969, p. 64).
[22] 57 Geo. 3, cap. 9 (repealed 1828).
[23] *Parl. Papers*, 1834 XXVIII, p. 600; 1867–8 XVII, p. 524.

the common target. Here the farmers' harvest produce was assembled in the form of unthrashed corn. Thrashing was one of the few occupations available for the day or casual labourer at certain times during the winter, and the anger aroused at such times by machines or imported labour was correspondingly intense. Fires were sometimes preceded or accompanied by threatening letters such as the following:

> Mossop you are damd baden and you may look out for we are geten game on you without you destroy your misheen and get out of your farmen men and shepherdes and take them home to their one parish with in ten dayes we will burn you up in all parts.
>
> We are not speeking on you alone but all that imployes them that dont belong hear so you may all out to your corn and hay blast and buger your eyes if you do not imploy your hone poor we will burn you in your bed.[24]

Lincolnshire was relatively quiet during the troubled year of 1816, and in 1830–1, the time of Captain Swing, unrest was slow to reach the county. When it did so it took the form of arson rather than of rioting and machine breaking. Incendiary fires spread from Norfolk and Cambridgeshire in November 1830, and by the end of November the county was seriously alarmed. Cavalry troops were formed to quell possible riots, and the home secretary was asked to provide arms and equipment for them. Special constables were enrolled and protection associations formed among the farmers. The actual disturbances were not in proportion to these alarmist preparations. According to a recent authority there were twenty-eight fires in Lincolnshire between mid-November 1830 and mid-March 1831, although this must be an underestimate. Only twelve court cases resulted, compared with over one hundred in each of several southern counties.[25]

The slightly higher level of wages in Lincolnshire may be one reason for its relative quietness. Sir Robert Sheffield wrote to Lord Brownlow on 17 December:

> The Wages in this Part are 2s. a day, and if any refractory spirit should shew itself here among the Labourers it will be for an increase of Wages. Two shillings a day is sufficient at present and if Corn should rise much more I dare say it would be met by the farmers by an advance of 3d. or 6d. but a stand will be made at present at two shillings.[26]

[24] 4 BNL box 2.
[25] Hobsbawm and Rudé, *Captain Swing*, pp. 308–9.
[26] 4 BNL box 2.

This refers to the north-west of the county. In the south-east wages were probably lower, and it was in that region, the Holland and Kesteven Fens and Lindsey Marsh, that the fires were most frequent. When it comes to the incidence of crime it must also be remembered that some of the fen places were at the best of times the most lawless areas in the county. The Revd T. H. Rawnsley, writing to the Home Office in March 1831 about fires in Leake, Friskney, and Butterwick Fens, stressed the local lack of settled paupers and the dependence on foreigners from Norfolk, Cambridgeshire, Yorkshire, and other places. Some of these people came to work, others to escape the law.[27]

Why were there not a number of attacks on thrashing machines in Lincolnshire, as there were in parts of Huntingdonshire and Norfolk and some southern counties? It was not because the machine was little used in Lincolnshire. Production in the county had begun around 1810, and by 1830 its use was widespread.[28] Perhaps by November, when the fires began, much of the harvest had already been thrashed out. Perhaps also the Lincolnshire farmers were able to appease their labourers by a prompt abandonment of machine-work when resentment was shown. On the Grimsthorpe estate the tenants gave up using the machine early in December, 'until some time after tranquillity is completely re-established (if they use it at all in future)'.[29]

In Lincolnshire it was not the thrashing machine that caused rioting but the Irish harvesters. The presence of the military was considered necessary in Holland for several seasons in succession, but the worst disturbances were in 1831, especially at Boston, and 1832, especially in south Holland. In the former case the problem was aggravated by political excitement, and in the latter by the presence of bankers (or navigators). On 5 August 1831 Francis Thirkill reported to Brownlow that the Irish had been driven out of Boston with bludgeons and pitchforks. 'In this Town the persons are generally loose Characters, and not Agricultural Labourers; tho' otherwise in the Country. . . . I am afraid the farmers are somewhat to blame in rather restricting the Wages of our own Men.'[30]

Fires raged again in the closing weeks of 1834, and frightening events they must have been. A blaze at Thoresthorpe lit up the sky and drew spectators from nearly twenty miles around. They demanded refreshment, and the scene became one of saturnalian

[27] Public Record Office, HO 52/14.
[28] Sir William Tritton, 'The Origin of the Thrashing Machine', *Lincolnshire Magazine* 2 (1934–6), pp. 7 ff.
[29] 3 ANC 7/23/23/103.
[30] 4 BNL box 2.

wildness.[31] Wage reductions were a major factor, but a new element of bitterness was added by the introduction of the New Poor Law. George Booth, agent for the Lindsey Coast estates of Lord Willoughby de Eresby, wrote to the chief agent in November: 'I am afraid the new Poor Law Bill has caused a great sensation in the Country and is partly the cause of these diabolical acts, another cause is the low price of corn as the farmers are compelled to lower the wages.' At Laceby the overseer reduced the wages of labourers employed by the parish from 1s. a day to 10d., and received the following note: 'Firing is no warning to you at Laceby, you must not try the Poor any longer, for they will not submit to work for 1s. per day, young men are fools to stand it any longer. ...' A protection association for Grantham and district had subscriptions of over £2,000 by early December. It urged farmers to insure themselves adequately, and set itself to combat the 'notion entertained by many persons that the Farmers and Parish Officers are to be intimidated, by the conflagration of their property, into giving higher wages or greater parochial relief'.[32]

THE UNION MOVEMENT

The winters of 1843–4 and 1850–1 in particular saw further outbreaks of incendiarism, and isolated cases were reported down to the end of the century. The 1850s and 1860s were more peaceful, however, and when the farm workers of the county next launched a widespread movement, it was an agitation of a different kind. Lincolnshire played a prominent part in the 'Revolt of the Field', the trade union movement which developed with astonishing rapidity among the farm workers of England in the early months of 1872. Instead of isolated acts of despair there was a new optimism and a new ability to organize.[33]

The earliest known meeting in Lincolnshire was at Leverton near Boston on 5 January 1872: the labourers there invited William Banks of Boston, a stationer by trade and a republican in politics, to address them. During the next few weeks there was increasing activity around Boston, and meetings were held in several Lindsey towns and villages. Early in March the labourers on some of the

[31] SM 27 Nov. 1834.
[32] 3 ANC 7/23/29/9; SM 13 March 1835, 6 Dec. 1834.
[33] The following paragraphs are based mainly on Rex C. Russell, *The Revolt of the Field in Lincolnshire*, 1956, and files of the *Stamford Mercury*.

larger farms in Deeping Fen struck for a wage of three shillings for a nine-hour day. In April the Long Sutton Nine Hours' Labour League made similar demands, and embarked on a long struggle with the employers. Elsewhere in the county more moderate objectives were achieved by peaceful negotiation, and some of the newly formed local unions laid their emphasis on mutual aid and emigration rather than militant industrial action.

These local unions rapidly came together in larger organizations. At the end of April a conference was held at Grantham, when it was decided to form a union for the whole county, and at a meeting in Lincoln on 13 July the constitution of the Lincolnshire Labourers' League was settled. Banks became its secretary, and under his leadership it expanded until by the beginning of 1873 it had branches in Lincolnshire, Norfolk, Nottinghamshire, and Yorkshire. Branches were also set up in places like Sheffield and Sunderland to ensure that members who migrated to jobs in foundries were not lost to the union. Nearer home, the first union at Frodingham appears to have been a branch of the League.

Joseph Arch's National Agricultural Labourers' Union had been formed in Leamington in 1872. He first visited Lincolnshire in April 1873, and his visit was followed by the adherence of the Market Rasen Labourers' Protection and Emigration Society to the National Union. In August the union at Spalding also joined Arch. By the middle of 1874 the North Lincolnshire district of the National Union (centred on Market Rasen and Caistor) had about 1,800 members and the South Lincolnshire district (Spalding and Bourne) about 1,300 members. The Lincolnshire membership of the League, however, was by this time probably well over 12,000.

In 1872 the principal scene of activity had been the south of the county, but the great battle of 1874 was fought in Lindsey, mainly on the Wolds. The usual seasonal reduction of wages was resisted late in 1873, and in the spring of 1874 the labourers prepared to make a push for 21s. The large farmers got together and countered the League's policy of selective strikes by a lock-out of union members. The struggle lasted from March to May, when the unionists were obliged to accept a compromise. After this there was no further large-scale confrontation with the farmers over wages. In the latter half of the 1870s the unions turned to other issues—emigration, friendly society benefits, and the franchise question. Both the National Union and the 'Federal Union' (which the League had joined) were rocked by internal disputes, and in the depression years 1879–81 their organizations collapsed.

Several questions arise which are of interest to local historians and labour historians alike. Why did the movement suddenly emerge when it did? Why was it stronger in some parts of the county than in others? Why did some local unions join Arch's union and some Banks's?

The events of 1872 would have been inconceivable without some important though not easily charted changes that occurred during the middle years of the century. Illiteracy declined, newspapers became cheaper and more easily available, and railway travel increased mobility and broadened horizons. Labourers were acquiring experience of organization and public speaking in chapels and friendly societies. The chronic under-employment of rural labour was becoming, in some districts and at some seasons, a thing of the past. Farm labour became noticeably scarcer—and dearer—in 1866, and scattered reports of industrial action soon started to appear. A large Lindsey farmer reported in 1867 that 'there is a growing independence about the labouring population, they don't like standing like beasts to be sold. They begin to enquire about their master's character. They are beginning to combine a little for some purpose. I notice it at the threshing machines, and they combine for extra holidays. I had to give one the other day.'[34]

Undoubtedly Lincolnshire farm workers were less quiescent in the few years before 1872 than has sometimes been supposed, although evidence is very hard to come by. But there were certain precipitating factors which brought matters to a head early in 1872. Prices began to rise in 1870–1, threatening labourers with a fall in living standards, but at the same time their hands were strengthened by changes in the labour market. The townsmen were in full employment, and the Irish failed to turn up for the fen harvest of 1871, enabling local labour to command higher prices. All the farm workers needed now was an example to encourage them, and that came from the urban unions. In 1871 a movement for shorter hours swept the country; by the autumn it had reached Lincolnshire. In October foundry workers at Lincoln, Gainsborough, and Boston obtained a reduction in hours. In December the movement spread to the building trade, and early in the new year it reached the journeymen builders and shoemakers in the market towns. At Alford, for instance, the journeymen boot and shoemakers combined early in February 1872 to secure an increase in wages as well as a reduction in hours.[35]

Urban influence, therefore, was important in the early stages of unionism in Lincolnshire. The leadership of a townsman like Banks

[34] *Parl. Papers*, 1867–8 XVII, p. 519.   [35] *SM* 9 Feb. 1872.

is significant, as is the way in which farm workers at Long Sutton and elsewhere took up the nine hours' demand. But not all the towns of Lincolnshire gave a helping hand. Gainsborough saw little activity, and even Lincoln and Grantham were disappointing centres. Areas of rural militancy were defined mainly by local labour conditions. In the Fens the day labourers were concentrated in towns and large villages, where movements could rapidly spread, and where there was a tradition of militancy going back to the Swing period. The failure of the Irish harvestmen to arrive in 1871 was a tremendous encouragement to the local workforce, but conditions were different at the following harvest, and the period of militancy was soon over. The remote areas of the Wolds took longer to organize, but there too there were the ingredients of conflict. There were similar concentrations of day labourers, and more class feeling between employers and men than in other parts of the county.

Even on the Wolds and in the Fens support for the unions was patchy. Some villages had active branches, others none at all. Much research could be done on the distribution of village unions, but it can be suggested that the large open villages were the most likely to have active branches. Such places had concentrations of labourers and often a degree of social independence. They were also likely to have friendly societies, temperance organizations, and flourishing Primitive or Free Methodist congregations. A significant proportion of Lincolnshire labourers' leaders in the 1870s were Primitive Methodists.[36] The unions were not preached or publicized in the chapels—that indeed was frowned on by connectional leaders.[37] The important thing was that individual laymen received valuable experience in public speaking, just as the treasurer of a sick club was the obvious choice for a union branch officer.

These were important conditions for the formation of a strong branch, but it needed a more direct stimulus to bring a village movement to life. In some cases—Leverton was one—it was the existence of a dispute over a parochial charity which provided an excellent introduction to parish politics and a chance to fan class feelings against the parson and leading farmers (who were often the charity trustees). At Long Sutton the charity question was involved with the allotments question and led to prolonged parochial battles

[36] Information kindly communicated by Mr Nigel Scotland, of the University of Aberdeen.

[37] The Wesleyan local preachers of the Spalding circuit condemned the agitation work of Brother Harrison as an 'error of judgment' in 1876. (Reference kindly supplied by Mr N. Leveritt.)

in the early 1880s. The existence of vigorous leadership at parish level was essential: if one bold man spoke up many would follow. And that leader would have most success where he could appeal to a local tradition of militancy. Such a tradition existed, for instance, at Normanby-by-Spital, where the labourers' memories went back to a meeting about wages in 1834.[38]

Once village unions became branches of larger organizations their individual characters were to some extent lost. This was particularly the case with the National Union, which exercised a tight financial control over its branches. With the emergence of the big unions the history of the labourers' movement becomes more institutional than local. Yet there is something to be learned from the way in which part of Lincolnshire joined Arch and part stayed faithful to the county's own union body, the League. The programme of the League, with its demand for 18s. a week, was more ambitious than that of the National Union. Yet the Long Sutton labourers, who had less hope of achieving a wage of 18s., joined the League, whereas the better-paid workers of the Caistor district gravitated towards the National Union. It was partly a question of local leadership, partly one of ideology. Banks's League was the heir of the nine hours' movement. Most of the village unions which demanded shorter hours as well as higher wages ended up in the League. Banks established relations with trade unionists in London, whereas the important links of the National Union were with Liberal politicians, especially those of Birmingham. Banks's League can also be seen as appealing more to the friendly society side of village culture, whereas Arch captured the imagination of the non-conformists with his revivalist style.

Despite the rapid success of the unions in Lincolnshire and their strong impact on the public mind they could claim at their peak a membership amounting to probably less than half the county's agricultural labour force. Despite various successful strikes, they may not have done much more—as far as wage levels were concerned—than accelerate the rise of the early 1870s and delay the fall that inevitably followed. The day labourers, the main supporters of the movement, were caught between the farm servants on the one hand and the casual workers on the other. The day labourers came into demand on the farms in spring, when the rhythm of work changed and the days lengthened; and this was the obvious time to negotiate for an advance of wages. But the gains of the spring could still be wiped out at harvest by the appearance of 'foreign' labourers,

[38] R. J. Olney, 'The Class Struggle in Normanby-by-Spital, c. 1830–1900', *Lincs. Hist. and Arch.* 11 (1976), p. 39.

and the early onset of a hard winter could dash any hopes that remained. It made sense, therefore, for the unions to turn to migration and emigration as a more permanent solution to the rural labour problem. By sending its own members abroad, however, the union was not only weakening itself numerically but also depriving itself of the leaders that it so badly needed.

CONFLICTING CULTURES

The 'Revolt of the Field' registered the entry of the farm workers into the modern world of economic values, class interests, national institutions, and widespread publicity. It was an important step in the process described by some historians as the decline or defeat of the old rural culture. The trade union district, like the Methodist circuit, the Temperance league, and the friendly society order, was an institution removed from the spontaneity of village feasts and seasonal celebrations. But how far was there an antithesis between the two cultures, and how complete was the triumph of the new over the old?

The decline of parish feasts had already begun in Lincolnshire by 1800, although many survived into the 1840s and a few until the end of the century. Dancing around a pole on May Day was already obsolete at the beginning of the century, although Henry Winn of Fulletby, writing in 1877, remembered children dressed as the May king or queen and sent round to collect halfpence. Plough plays, which seem to have had deep roots in the arable county of Lincolnshire, survived in a few places into the twentieth century, although their decline was being noted in newspaper reports of the 1870s and 1880s. Winn also recalled that Shrove Tuesday used to be the great day for cock fighting 'before the cruel sport was put down by law'. The 1840s seem in Lincolnshire to have been the decade when the most dramatic progress was made against cruel sports and noisy popular demonstrations. The last bull running at Stamford took place in 1839. The jollities of statute hiring fairs, as we have seen, took longer to subdue. They must have owed their resilience to the fact that they were an integral part of the farm workers' year.[39]

The old culture rested on custom and was reinforced by community tradition. It did not understand public order as the nineteenth-century magistrate saw it, and it had a generally low opinion of the law. The extra-legal but in some eyes binding transaction of selling one's wife was prevalent in Lincolnshire in the early

[39] WINN 3/1; *SM* 10 Jan. 1879, 13 Jan. 1888; Robert W. Malcolmson, *Popular Recreations in English Society, 1700–1850*, 1973, pp. 126–33.

part of the century. As late as 1847 the *Stamford Mercury* printed the following characteristic report from Barton.

> On Wednesday . . . it was announced by the cryer that the wife of Geo. Wray of Barrow . . . would be offered for sale by auction in the Barton market-place at 11 o' clock: . . . punctually . . . the salesman made his appearance with the lady . . . having a new halter tied round her waist. Amidst the shouts of the lookers-on, the lot was put up, and . . . knocked down to Wm. Harwood, waterman, for . . . one shilling, three-halfpence to be returned 'for luck'. Harwood walked off arm in arm with his smiling bargain, with as much coolness as if he had purchased a new coat or hat.

On occasion a community took the law into its own hands, showing its disapproval of a wife-beater or other moral offender by ran-tanning him, or 'riding the stang'. This custom, the less picturesque Lincolnshire equivalent of the Wessex skimmington ride, was revived at Horncastle in July 1862, 'in consequence of Thomas Dutton, a well-known "renovator" of seedy hats, having thrashed his wife in a most brutal manner'. 'All the worn-out tin ware and horns, as well as the stentorian lungs of a large body of the lads of the town, were called into operation to give Dutton a concert of rough music.' If the performance was repeated for three nights the participants were believed to be immune from legal consequences.[40]

Just as custom was more real than law, so the devil was better known to many villagers than the parson. It was extraordinary how superstitions were attached even to the churches themselves, where devils might be invoked with greater ease than anywhere else. Institutional religion cannot have had much hold on the minds of the villagers of Willoughton, where for many years the parish clerk was a noted witch. Towards the end of the century Lincolnshire labourers were still noted for their obsession with tales of witchcraft, and their folklore continued to involve much torture of frogs and toads.

Among the enemies of the old culture much the most potent, it may be thought, was education. By 1900 illiteracy, so widespread in the 1840s, had been reduced to negligible proportions. Statistics compiled from marriage registers indicate a significant fall in the 1850s, and another marked drop after 1880. In 1851 the Church, by

[40] *SM* 12 March 1847, 1 Aug. 1862. (References kindly supplied by Mr Rex C. Russell.) See also Ethel H. Rudkin, *Lincolnshire Folklore*, repr. 1973, p. 54. Ran-tanning survived well into the twentieth century.

far the largest provider of elementary education in the county, controlled only 250 schools, but by 1895 the total had risen to 449. The Education Act of 1870 enjoined the creation of school boards where voluntary provision was inadequate, and by 1895 there were 119 board schools in the county. Elementary education became free in 1891, but irregular attendance, the bane of rural schools earlier in the century, was not wholly eradicated in the 1890s. The schoolmaster at Waddingham recorded in his log book in 1896 that four members of his board were setting a bad example by employing boys who should have been at school.[41]

The Church had taken the lead in establishing day schools in the county, and it had clung to that lead with great tenacity throughout the nineteenth century, despite the strength of nonconformity in Lincolnshire. From the start, when Brownlow chaired a meeting in support of the National Society in January 1812, the aims of the Church party were clear—to 'make useful members of the community, and to render inviolate the Constitution, in Church as well as in State, by enforcing a system adapted to our Establishment'. In 1839 a diocesan Board of Education was formed, well supported by the leading tory landowners of the county, and after 1870 the diocese struggled, by maintaining and extending voluntary effort, to prevent the spread of the non-denominational board schools. As Bishop Wordsworth said with characteristic aggressiveness, 'The battle of Christianity is to be fought in our schools.' Despite the agricultural depression, which affected the subscriptions of landowners and farmers, most of the county's elementary schools at the end of the century were still in connection with the established Church. The Methodists, though supporting hundreds of Sunday schools, had only twenty-six day schools in the county in 1895.[42]

The education provided by the National schools in the smaller villages of Lincolnshire was certainly not favourable to the old culture. It was supervised by parsons, whose own cultural background was an alien one. The teachers themselves were often strangers to the agricultural community: of fifteen teachers recorded by the census enumerators at Market Rasen in 1851, only one had been born in the parish.[43] The curriculum was narrow and tedious, and subjects were seldom related to the immediate experience of the pupils. For the brighter boys the chance to acquire a neat

[41] Russell, *A History of Schools and Education in Lindsey, passim.*
[42] See especially Russell, *Schools and Education in Lindsey*, part 3, *The Church of England and the Provision of Elementary Education* (1966).
[43] Market Rasen W.E.A. Branch, *An Early Victorian Town: Market Rasen in the 1850s*, 1971.

hand and some proficiency with figures may well have spoiled them for farm work. On the rest the days spent in chanting the names of the kings and queens of England or learning the Catechism probably left little permanent impression.

The early Methodists set their faces determinedly against many aspects of the old culture, and were opposed to 'theatrical exhibitions, cricket-matches, steeple-chases, etc.'. Sabbatarianism was strong, and Henry Winn recalled the 'old Methodists' who might wipe their shoes on Sunday but regarded it as sinful to grease them.[44] By 1850 most Lincolnshire parishes had at least one Methodist chapel, around which a whole new way of life developed. The village calendar filled up with red-letter days that had nothing to do with the public house or the village green. There were love feasts, prayer meetings, chapel anniversaries, and Sunday school outings. Visiting preachers provided Sunday evening entertainment, and the perils of routine were avoided, at least during the early days, by periodic schisms and revivals. Though not energetic providers of day schools the Methodists gave a great stimulus to adult education through their bible readings and class meetings. Methodism grew best where the forces of the Establishment were weakest, and the open villages became its rural strongholds. A rough village like Navenby might shut its ears to the first appeals of visiting preachers, only to become in a few years one of the leading societies in its circuit.

Methodism struck at two centres of the old parish community, the church and the public house. In place of parish loyalties it demanded loyalties at once narrower and broader, to the chapel and to the circuit. The centre of the circuit was a market town, from which the ministers of the connexion would visit the country societies. In the wake of the Methodists, with their new standards of respectability, came the Temperance reformers. Where the movement was strongest Temperance halls were built as rivals to the public houses. Eight of them were built in Lindsey between 1839 and 1851—Alford (1839), Grimsby (1840), Binbrook (1840), Barton (1843), Barrow (1843), Waltham (1849), Winterton (1850), and Tetney (1851).[45]

The money saved by abstinence from liquor could be invested in one of the friendly societies that offered insurance against sickness, unemployment, or (occasionally) old age. Some societies were in existence in the late eighteenth century, but the decline of the parish

[44] Revd Joseph Dixon, *The Earnest Methodist, a Memoir of the late Thomas Dixon of Grantham*, 1871, p. 53; WINN 3/1.
[45] Particulars kindly supplied by Mr Rex C. Russell.

as a source of social security in the early nineteenth century was a great spur to independent effort. By 1857 there were over 300 registered societies in the county. Lincoln had thirty, other large towns between ten and twenty, and large villages two or three. Even remote settlements such as Hawthorn Hill and Littleworth Drove, composed mainly of labourers, boasted a club. The Fens appear to have been particularly well covered.[46]

Like the chapels, the friendly societies, with their annual services, dinners, and processions, became important village institutions. Like the Methodists, too, the members of the village societies acquired wider loyalties. Many Lincolnshire benefit clubs were affiliated to the Ancient Order of Foresters or the Manchester Unity of Oddfellows. On the other hand the village friendly societies mostly accepted a closer relationship with the Establishment than did the Methodists. The annual services were generally held in the parish church, not a nonconformist chapel, and meetings were usually at inns, although a handful met in school rooms, Temperance hotels, or chapel vestries. In 1857 one, the Grantham Independent Labourers' Self-aiding Medical Club, met in the board room of the union workhouse.

The old culture was slow to die, for it was not lacking in the strength and suppleness to adapt itself to changing conditions. It was defeated in the end, but as much by the depression in agriculture and the exodus from the countryside as by the assaults of urban culture. Even in 1900 it was by no means extinct. It might take only one policeman to suppress a village football game, but it took many years of lessons, sermons, and propaganda to eradicate deeply held superstitions. Many of those who went to chapel must have continued to believe in witchcraft. And while there remained horsemen on the farms, preserving the primitive mysteries of their craft, there remained a residue of ancient magic in the countryside.

[46] KQS, register of friendly societies under the Act of 1793; *A List of the Friendly Societies in the County of Lincoln*, 1857.

CHAPTER V

THE LIEUTENANCY AND MAGISTRACY

THE LIEUTENANCY

LORD Brownlow became lord lieutenant of the county in 1809, in time to implement the Local Militia Act of the previous year. He took an active interest in his military duties, taking on the colonelcy of the Lincoln and Kesteven Local Militia which assembled at Stamford. In 1811 he gave himself a more important job, becoming colonel of the Royal South Lincoln Militia.

Just as the regular army reflected the social dominance of the landed classes of the country, so militia appointments were a mirror of county society. The colonels, lieutenant-colonels, and majors were chosen from the ranks of the 'county', the families of Sibthorp, Ellison, and Cracroft taking a prominent part. When Sir John Thorold offered Brownlow his services in whatever capacity they might be useful, Brownlow told him that somebody of his rank, property, and time of life could not possibly be less than a major.[1] Lieutenants and captains had to be gentlemen, but not necessarily of county status.

In 1835 the death of Lord Portmore, the late duke of Ancaster's son-in-law, created a vacancy in the command of the North Lincoln battalion. Brownlow promoted Lt-Col. George Tomline of Riby to the full colonelcy, but instead of promoting Major Richard Ellison of Boultham to be lieutenant-colonel he put in his own son Viscount Alford. Brownlow may have looked askance at Ellison's bar sinister, but the gentlemen of the county certainly disapproved of Brownlow's failure to promote according to seniority. Ellison had to wait until 1853 to receive his due.[2]

After the end of the Napoleonic Wars there were nearly forty years of decay in the militia system. The battalions were not called up between 1831 and 1853, and the machinery of lieutenancy sub-

---

[1] 4 BNL box 11.   [2] KQS, militia papers 1852–4.

96

divisions became moribund. The office of deputy-lieutenant lost its usefulness, and was prized mainly because it enabled its holder to wear a striking uniform on social occasions or when visiting foreign courts. In 1853 fears of a war with France led to a revival of the militia, but not (in Lincolnshire) the old balloting system, which the deputy-lieutenants had had to administer. The battalions of newly enrolled volunteers assembled in June 1853, after various initial difficulties had been surmounted. One of them was a quarrel between the marquis of Granby, the new lord lieutenant, and Colonel Tomline, a former tory who took an independent line in political as well as military matters.[3]

In the mid-1850s the county provided new headquarters for the militia, building storehouses for the North Lincolns at Lincoln (now the Museum of Lincolnshire Life) and the South Lincolns at Grantham. The latter site was the choice of Granby, whose interests were much connected with the Grantham neighbourhood, and some resentment was manifested from Holland as a result. Under the army reforms of the early 1870s the responsibility for the militia passed from the lord lieutenant to the War Office, which first rented the storehouses from the county and then built new headquarters, still in use today, at Lincoln. The North and South Lincoln militia became the third and fourth battalions of the Lincolnshire Regiment, the first two battalions being formed from an infantry regiment of the line, the Tenth Foot.[4]

The local yeomanry corps formed early in the century were disbanded in 1827, to the regret of those gentlemen and farmers who found themselves defenceless against the outbreaks of 1831. No regular army detachment was at that time permanently stationed in the county. One response to unrest among the labourers was the formation in 1831 of the North Lincolnshire Yeomanry Cavalry, headed by Lord Yarborough, but it does not seem to have survived beyond the mid-1840s. Then came the invasion scare of 1859, when in a few months rifle corps were formed in most of Lincolnshire's market towns. This seems to have been the last occasion on which the deputy-lieutenants met together to give a lead to the local movements. The old yeomanry tradition of the county, however, was not revived until 1902, when the Lincolnshire Imperial Yeomanry was formed as a result of the Boer War. The fourth earl of Yarborough took the lead, after the failure of an earlier effort promoted by the lord lieutenant, and contingents were

[3] KQS, militia papers; Hill, *Victorian Lincoln*, pp. 75–6.
[4] R. Donald Stokes, 'A History of the Lincolnshire Regiment (the 10th Foot)', *Lincs. Mag.* 1 (1932–4), pp. 66–71.

provided by the Brocklesby, South Wold, Burton, and Blankney hunts.[5]

The rifle volunteers had been organized into territorial battalions in the 1870s, and there was a further re-organization under the Territorial and Reserve Forces Act of 1907. The old militia units, the third and fourth battalions of the Lincolnshire Regiment, were merged into a third special reserve battalion, and the volunteers became the fourth battalion, based at Lincoln, and the fifth battalion, based at Grimsby.

THE MAGISTRACY

After the end of the French wars in 1815 Brownlow's military duties as His Majesty's Lieutenant for the county became less important, and his principal attention was devoted to his civil duties as custos rotulorum. In this capacity he recommended magistrates to the lord chancellor for appointment under the Great Seal. In putting names into the commission of the peace the lord chancellor was not bound to accept all those forwarded to him by the lord lieutenants of the counties; nor was he obliged to refuse applications from any other quarter. In 1838 Lord Cottenham, the whig lord chancellor, told Brownlow that beneficed clergy should not be put on the bench unless there were 'circumstances making it absolutely necessary'. In 1836 Yarborough and Pelham recommended to Lord John Russell (the home secretary) the name of Jonathan Dent of Appleby. Russell wrote to Brownlow asking if he had any objection. The latter did object. He had hitherto considered himself solely responsible to the lord chancellor, he told Russell stiffly; but he made enquiries, found that the 'gentlemen of the county' were prepared to overlook Dent's 'defective education', and accordingly acquiesced in the proposal and put the necessary machinery in motion.[6]

Despite these occasional difficulties Brownlow for the most part succeeded in bringing the appointment of magistrates for the county under his control. Under his predecessor the magistrates had drawn up their own lists, which the lord lieutenant had passed on to the lord chancellor with little or no amendment. Brownlow put a stop to this system when the commission was opened in 1820, on the accession of George IV. He did not attempt to foist on the different benches colleagues with whom they were not prepared to act, but he did censor the lists sent to him in 1820 by removing

[5] SM, 2 Feb. 1900; Collins, *Brocklesby Hounds*, p. 230.
[6] This and the following paragraphs are based on 4 BNL boxes 1–3.

names he considered unsuitable. Thereafter the only lists drawn up were private ones for Brownlow's eyes alone.

Because Lincolnshire was such a large county he could not have personal knowledge of all the names submitted to him. He relied, therefore, on chairmen of quarter sessions, particularly in later years on Sir Robert Sheffield for Lindsey and the Revd William Moore for Holland. These men shared his own views (Sheffield, however, being the least narrow-minded of the three), and they had the local knowledge, or means of obtaining it, that Brownlow lacked. When names came up, perhaps by a private application, that meant little either to Brownlow or his magisterial advisers, the clerks of the peace, with their middle-class connections, could be set to work. They generally came up with the simple fact that so-and-so was not a gentleman, which was why nobody had heard of him.

In November 1837, in response to a circular from Cottenham, Brownlow set out the criteria which guided his choice of magistrates. The class he preferred to recommend was the landed gentry.

> With the exception of heirs apparent to the gentlemen of old family or their immediate collaterals, I have usually thought it necessary that persons should be in possession of a clear landed property worth perhaps £2,000 per annum within the county, not being at the same time occupiers thereof as farmers, in which case I consider them as yeomen, and not of a class to be placed on the Bench, except in cases of necessity.

In the case of clergymen he expected them to have benefices worth at least £400 a year, unless they also had other property in the county. He had no strong objection to other professional people or merchants, or so he told Cottenham, provided that they also had 'claims from property'. But he did steadfastly refuse applications on behalf of attorneys in practice, and had only in three exceptional cases accepted the services of retired legal men.

This summary did not do full justice to the working of Brownlow's mind. The fundamental importance of landed property as opposed to other forms of wealth is clear enough, but a property qualification of £2,000 a year was not by itself sufficient as a social determinant. Brownlow's ideal was in fact to restrict the magistracy to the ranks of county society. Only the old county families had an adequate stake in the local society; only they had sufficient standing to appear as the natural upholders of law and order. They also had the right educational background: they might know nothing of the law, they might scarcely be able to write a legible letter, but they had been brought up to be gentlemen. Thus Brownlow put on to the Bench people of old family such as G. W. Maddison of Partney, whose income from land was well under £2,000 a year, whereas able and well-educated business and professional people were seldom even considered, although they were not always devoid of landed wealth. The case of George Skipworth, who did just scrape in, has already been quoted.

When Brownlow had to widen the social range, the class he preferred to go to was the clergy. Again the property qualification was not all-important, but the holders of the better livings were usually well-connected and quite frequently had additional means of their own. In the case of relatives of the gentry it is indeed hardly correct to speak of widening the social range. Other clergymen, however, were definitely beyond the pale. Of one Brownlow was informed in 1817 that neither his appearance nor his manners bespoke the gentleman; of another that his promotion to the Spalding bench would cause the immediate retirement of its two principal members.

It is still interesting, however, that Brownlow could raise to the magistracy clergymen who by county standards had neither large means nor distinguished local connections. He favoured them for three reasons: they were resident in areas where the gentry were thin on the ground; they understood public business; and they were in the broadest sense politically sound. They stood for authority, as representatives of the Established Church, and they were frequently staunch tories. Brownlow could see little difference between dissent, radicalism, and treason, and neither could they. 'I own I wish for more Laymen among the Magistrates,' wrote C. B. Massingberd to the lord lieutenant in 1820, 'but I know your Lordship will pay due regard to Men's Principles in these times.' In 1838 Sheffield recommended the rector of West Halton, one of the best livings in Lindsey, as 'an active sensible man and of good conservative Principles'.

Brownlow's policy had far-reaching effects on the life of the county. It helped to harden the divisions between the classes, and to foster an upper crust with a clear-cut social and political philosophy. It also created administrative problems, by keeping Lincolnshire short of justices. In 1831 it had only 111 qualified magistrates, compared with over 170 in Norfolk, Devon, Kent, and Sussex. Of those 111 no less than fifty-two were clergy, one of the highest proportions in the country. (The lords lieutenant of Derbyshire and Sussex refused to have any clergy at all.)[7] When faced with complaints of local shortages Brownlow would point to the dearth of

[7] *Parl. Papers*, 1831–2 XXXV, pp. 231 ff.

suitable gentlemen in certain parts of the county, and lament that
even where there were gentry they could not always be persuaded
to act. In 1842 there were fifty-seven large landowners, of over
3,000 acres in the county, who could have made at least an
occasional appearance at quarter or petty sessions, but only
twenty-nine (excluding eldest sons) had taken the trouble to qual-
ify. In such circumstances, thought Hollway, the Lindsey clerk,
Brownlow would have to descend to 'a class of persons not hereto-
fore thought of sufficient weight and influence in the county to
sustain the dignity of the judicial bench'. But only a very few
concessions were made; reports continued to reach Brownlow
from time to time of petty sessions having failed to take place for
want of two magistrates, or of the inhabitants of disturbed open
parishes having to go several miles to obtain a warrant.

The social composition of the bench differed in the three
divisions of the county. Holland was always the least exclusive, as
the following table shows. The column loosely labelled 'gentry'
refers to landowners of over 1,000 acres in the division for which
they sat, together with their eldest sons, a qualification a little lower
than Brownlow's £2,000 a year. The clergy include unbeneficed
clerks.

HOLLAND MAGISTRATES[8]

	gentry	clergy	others	total
1807	2	6	4	12
1842	0	9	3	12
1872	5	10	7	22
1900	4	6	24	34

The acute shortage of gentry eased a little in the middle of the
century, but the five magistrates who represented this class in 1872
were a mixed bag—Lord Kesteven (not a Holland resident),
Colonel Moore of Frampton Hall (not a very large landowner
though undeniably gentry), and three others who might be called
semi-gentry, that is, substantial local figures but not quite *county*
(Richard Gleed, Robert Everard, and Adderley Howard). The
clergy had to make up for this shortage, their numbers increasing
during Brownlow's reign. After the middle of the century Holland
led the way in the introduction of middle-class elements, and by
1872 its bench included a Spalding physician, a Sutton merchant,
and two Holbeach farmers.

[8] For this and the two following tables lists of acting magistrates in 1807 have
been constructed from quarter sessions minutes. For 1842, 1872, and 1900 the lists
provided for the county directories of those dates have been used.

The Kesteven bench, in contrast, was able to keep its gentrified character for much of the century.

KESTEVEN MAGISTRATES

	gentry	clergy	others	total
1807	11(39%)	14	3	28
1842	25(54%)	17	4	46
1872	35(54%)	17	13	65
1900	41(45%)	5	46	92

The gentry, in fact, increased their representation during the first half of the century, a testimony to the effectiveness of Brownlow's policy in the division where admittedly the circumstances were most favourable. But after 1870 the number was kept up only by putting on relatives of leading landowners. By 1900 several representatives of the old families, although still counted as acting magistrates, had left the county: their houses were let to tenants, who themselves quickly found their way on to the bench. Bankers, doctors, and retired Lincoln industrialists were already starting to infiltrate the Kesteven magistracy by 1872, but these were people whom gentry were accustomed to meet on fairly easy social terms. In the last quarter of the century there were far fewer farmers and tradesmen on the Kesteven than on the Holland bench.

Lindsey, with its large area, sparse population, and absentee landowners, presented more judicial problems even than Holland. But until the 1860s the demand for more magistrates was met chiefly from the ranks of the gentry and clergy. In 1900 there was still a good number of clerical justices, but as in Holland they had been swamped by new men.

LINDSEY MAGISTRATES

	gentry	clergy	others	total
1807	21(40%)	21	10	52
1842	25(38%)	29	11	65
1872	44(40%)	43	22	109
1900	45(28%)	23	94	162

By 1872 the Lindsey bench included a Gainsborough maltster, a retired Louth grocer, and probably the first working farmer to be a Lincolnshire J. P., Edward Carr of Beltoft in the Isle of Axholme. Farmers were increasingly called on, and by 1900 there were sixteen in the Lindsey commission. But they were outweighed by urban elements. The growing wealth of Grimsby was represented in 1900 by nine county magistrates (not all, however, still living in Grimsby or actively engaged in business), whilst Gainsborough interests accounted for a further seven. Louth was represented by seven justices, and Lincoln by six. The magistrates of the Isle of Axholme were almost entirely farmers and tradesmen.

By 1900, therefore, the Lincolnshire magistrates were much more socially representative of the county than they had been in the first earl Brownlow's day. The change took place mainly after 1860. Landed wealth was relinquished as the essential requirement, allowing the entry of a few bankers, industrialists, and retired professional people. The next step, and perhaps a bigger one, was the inclusion of people actively involved in business—land agents, merchants, farmers, and even the occasional shopkeeper. In Lindsey this development can be dated to the early 1880s, whereas in Kesteven and Holland it seems to have come towards the end of that decade.

The change was not simply a matter of lowering social standards. It was also a change from government by a rural ruling class to government by a partly urban élite. The magistrates of 1900 were all highly respectable and well-to-do people, more representative of the wealth than the populace of the county, but they had been chosen, at least in some cases, because of their proven experience as public leaders, mainly as county or district councillors. They stood for a tradition of administrative service that went back some decades—to the institution of the boards of Poor Law guardians.

No lord lieutenant after the first earl Brownlow exerted such a strong personal influence on the composition of the bench. Under Granby, a stranger to the business of the county, the initiative reverted to the chairmen and clerks of the quarter sessions.[9] The appointment of the second earl of Yarborough was an opportunity to make a break with tory traditions, but his reign was short and ineffective. Lord Aveland, his successor, was no political bigot, but his ideas on suitable magistrates were socially conservative. An acute shortage in the Isle made him swallow Carr of Beltoft, but in 1867 Hollway was able to advise firmly against Samuel Cropper of Minting, a respectable man farming his own land but not socially acceptable to the magistrates acting at Horncastle.[10] The commission was still most inadequately filled in the Axholme, Barton, Wragby, and Alford districts. During the outbreak of cattle plague in 1866 some farmers in the Isle had to travel twelve miles merely to obtain a licence to take a cow to the bull.

Ironically it was under the Conservative third earl Brownlow,

[9] KQS, clerk's correspondence on the commission of the peace 1855–6.
[10] LQS bundle 535 (letters from Aveland to Hollway 1862–7).

lord lieutenant from 1867, that the major change took place. His own views are not known, but it is probable that they became increasingly unimportant towards the end of the century as pressures from the towns and the middle classes became more insistent. Particularly in Lindsey, the pressures were reinforced by political developments and by the emergence of more Liberally minded chairmen of quarter sessions. In Kesteven and Holland it was the introduction of the county councils in 1888–9 that was the decisive factor.

QUARTER SESSIONS: LINDSEY

In the early nineteenth century county magistrates had no schools to maintain, no regular police force to supervise, no main roads to keep in repair, no allotments or smallholdings. The most conspicuous and costly obligation was one that in fact they lost later in the century, the upkeep of houses of correction. The policy of a court of quarter sessions with regard to its prisons can tell the historian much about the quality of the magistrates' bench, and about the local pressures that moulded administrative policy within each division. The building of prisons involved a heavy charge on the ratepayers of the county, and the choice of a site, in a period when roads were poor and travel expensive, could lead to acrimony.

The provision of prisons was a matter closely related to the holding of sessions. As described in Chapter I, Caistor and Gainsborough lost both their houses of correction and their status as sessions places in 1791, when the new prison and court house at Kirton came into use. It was an uneasy compromise. Kirton lay not far off the turnpike road between Lincoln and Brigg, as well as roughly mid-way between Caistor and Gainsborough. But the magistrates were stretching a point when they recommended Kirton for its ability to provide adequate markets, medical supplies, and other 'assistances' necessary for a large public establishment.[11] It was not an important market town, and even its railway connection with Brigg and Gainsborough in 1849 did not do much for it.

Nevertheless Richard Ellison and his fellow justices designed a substantial prison, capable of holding long-term convicts for the whole division. Built of local limestone, it provided thirty-two separate cells as well as other accommodation for a further eighty-four persons. The male and female wings flanked a central court house and grand jury room with governor's house attached. By 1866, when the prison was showing signs of age, a government

[11] LQS, minutes, 14 July 1789.

surveyor found the female cells particularly objectionable. They were 'very small, badly lighted, and without ventilation, except by opening the cell window'. The only means of heating them was by 'an unprotected gas burner, also used as a light at night', and the installation of water closets had only made such confined quarters more unwholesome.[12] Gas lighting, ventilation, and sanitation were all, of course, nineteenth-century features undreamt of by the magistrates of the 1790s. At that date Kirton was an improvement on the damp and squalid rooms into which prisoners had been indiscriminately herded at Caistor and Gainsborough.

Dissatisfaction with the centralization at Kirton came from those eastern parts of the subdivision which now found themselves even further from Kirton than they had been from Caistor. The Market Rasen magistrates, led by Ayscough Boucherett, favoured the re-division of Lindsey into three parts, based respectively on Kirton, Louth, and Spilsby. Magistrates and parish officers from the wapen-takes of Walshcroft (including Market Rasen) and Bradley Havers-toe could then attend sessions at Louth instead of Kirton every quarter. But the prospect of three subdivisions all disagreeing with one another was too dreadful for most of the magistrates to con-template. When the question came up for the second or third time in 1831 Brownlow settled it by transferring Bradley Haverstoe and East Walshcroft to the Louth and Spilsby subdivision, making it the larger of the two. The Rasen magistrates were thus relieved of the obligation to attend Kirton, but they were not much better off, since Louth continued to hold sessions only twice a year rather than quarterly as had been hoped.[13]

In 1806 the house of correction at Louth was condemned as beyond repair, and the opportunity arose of building a prison at a place nearer the centre of the Louth and Spilsby subdivision. The proposal of Horncastle received strong support from Spilsby, which was nearer to Horncastle than to Louth. Louth, however, was not keen to lose its prison, and the magistrates at Kirton were firmly opposed to the expense of building a second large prison for the division less than twenty years after the first. This argument appears to have been decisive, but it is interesting to speculate what the result would have been if Sir Joseph Banks had put his full weight behind the Horncastle scheme.[14]

The Louth house of correction was improved, therefore, in 1808.

[12] LQS, prisons, papers 1866–8, printed minutes of prison committee (Oct.–Dec. 1866), p. 10.
[13] 4 BNL box 3.
[14] Spalding Gentlemen's Society, Banks and Stanhope Papers 22.

But when the Prisons Act of 1823 came into force the accommodation there was found to be insufficient for the required segregation of different classes of prisoner. The magistrates of the subdivision, meeting at Louth in November 1823, decided to adapt the Louth prison as far as possible to the requirements of the act, but it was also clear that a new building was required, and it was resolved to erect it at Spilsby. The Spilsby magistrates had made a determined effort to secure this result, and in the end only Dymoke urged the cause of Horncastle.[15] A London architect, H. E. Kendall, drew up plans for a prison whose central feature was a court house fronted by an impressive Doric portico. A site was acquired from Lord Willoughby de Eresby, and the building was finished in 1826 at a cost of £26,400. The clerk of the peace and his records were installed, and Spilsby could now stand on its dignity as the administrative capital of Lindsey. It was a town of only about 1,300 people in the mid-1820s, but its new importance was partly justified by the great increase in population and judicial business that had recently occurred in south-east Lindsey following the drainage and inclosure of the Fens.

The prison system thus established in Lindsey lasted for the next forty years. It survived the pressure on accommodation caused by the growth of vagrancy in the 1840s; it even survived the increasing insistence of government inspectors on the 'separate system', which condemned prisoners to isolation at night and silence during the day. But it could not survive the Prisons Act of 1865, which abolished the old distinction between gaols and houses of correction and brought all prisons under a uniform code of discipline based on separate confinement and hard labour. The new regulations governing the size of cells and construction of buildings rendered Kirton obsolete, and extensive alterations were also required at Louth and to a lesser extent at Spilsby. Faced with an inevitably large bill, the magistrates turned their thoughts to the possibility of a new central prison for the whole division.[16]

The choice of site was between the two largest centres of population, Lincoln and Grimsby. A number of influential magistrates, led by Weston Cracroft Amcotts and the seventh baron Monson, argued that it was inefficient and extravagant for the division to maintain more than one prison. They also wished to seize the opportunity to do away with the system of two separate benches, with all the delays and disagreements it engendered. The Lindsey of

[15] 3 ANC 7/23/10/30.
[16] For the Lincoln and Spilsby prison question 1866–8 see the LQS minutes, and the extensive clerk's correspondence and papers under LQS PRISONS.

the railway age was not too large to have a single seat of quarter
sessions, and that seat, they reasoned, should be Lincoln. It had the
advantage of good railway communication and adequate hotel
accommodation; it also had historic claims to be the capital of
Lindsey. The county hall was a suitable place to hold sessions, and
the Lindsey quarter sessions were already adjourned there occasionally to allow the magistrates of both subdivisions to confer
together. On 21 June 1867, at a joint sessions at Lincoln, the Lindsey
magistrates agreed by a majority of one to build a new prison at
Lincoln and to unite the division for quarter sessions purposes.

The result was an outcry from the ratepayers of eastern Lindsey.
The ancient dignity and modern conveniences of Lincoln were
nothing to them compared with the ease of railway travel between
Boston, Spilsby, Alford, Louth, and Grimsby. For the inhabitants
of Spilsby a day trip to Lincoln was a tedious business, and to avoid
being benighted they had to leave the city by the 3.15 train. The
ratepayers were already in a disgruntled mood. Farmers had been
irritated by the restrictions imposed on them by the magistrates
during the cattle plague outbreak a few months earlier. There was
much grumbling over the rising county rate, and talk was spreading
of elected boards to replace the magistrates as controllers of county
expenditure. By agreeing to the erection of a costly new prison at
Lincoln the magistrates were now defying the ratepayers' wishes as
expressed in over three hundred parochial memorials.

Faced with this strength of feeling the magistrates of the Louth
and Spilsby subdivision reconsidered their position, and decided to
withhold their co-operation from the Kirton magistrates in implementing the scheme. The ensuing stalemate was broken only when
both sides agreed to hold a joint 'peace-making' sessions at Grimsby
in January 1868. The new Lincoln prison, replacing the moribund
houses of correction at Kirton and Louth, was to be proceeded with,
but the Spilsby prison was to survive. County business was to be
transacted in a general quarter sessions for the whole division, to
be held alternately at Lincoln and Grimsby. There were to be
adjournments to Spilsby for trials and appeals, however, and for
these purposes Spilsby was assigned a district consisting of the petty
sessional divisions of Spilsby, Louth (including the borough), and
Alford, together with the hundred of Hill. To mark the change
from Spilsby to Lincoln as an administrative centre J. H. Hollway
retired as clerk of the peace. His successor, John Francis Burton, was
a Lincoln man.[17]

[17] Technically Burton acted as Hollway's deputy until the latter died in 1877.

The arrangement was less a reprieve for Spilsby than a stay of execution. By 1872 the Lincoln prison, accommodating 160 male and 40 female prisoners, was finished. The Kirton prisoners were transferred to it, and the Louth prisoners were sent to Spilsby, where alterations had been carried out. But the Lincoln prison was only half-full; and it became apparent first to the Home Office inspector and then to the Lindsey magistrates that it was wasteful to continue two separate establishments. The Spilsby prison was finally closed in 1876, and sessions ceased to be held there in 1878. The question of Lincoln versus Grimsby, however, continued unresolved for another twenty years. The adjourned sessions at Grimsby, abandoned in 1872, were resumed in 1879 for the convenience of the northern and eastern half of the division. They continued despite the unsatisfactory accommodation at Grimsby Town Hall, and despite the fact that Grimsby acquired county status and its own court of quarter sessions in 1891. From 1891 to 1898, in fact, the Lindsey sessions were held alternately at Lincoln and Grimsby, and meetings at Grimsby were abandoned only in the latter year, when the question of payment for the use of the town hall was raised.

QUARTER SESSIONS: KESTEVEN

The economy of one prison for the whole division, achieved in Lindsey in 1876, was already enjoyed in Kesteven in 1800. The old house of correction at Folkingham, however, was a very primitive affair. In 1808 it was abandoned and a new prison built in the yard of the castle, on a site acquired by the county from the Heathcote family. The building was greatly altered and enlarged in 1824–6 to meet the new requirements for the classification of prisoners and the provision of hard labour. Complete with chapel, treadmill, and accommodation for seventy prisoners, the improvements were designed by Bryan Browning and executed at a total cost to the Kesteven ratepayers of nearly £8,300.[18] It was thus a small and cheap affair compared with the new prison at Spilsby, which cost three times as much, but it was dignified with a rusticated stone entrance building, not part of the original design, which caused some grumbling on the Sleaford side of the division. The work was energetically supervised by Colonel W. A. Johnson of Witham-on-the-Hill, chairman of the Bourne bench since 1818 and perhaps the

---

[18] KQS, papers and plans relating to Folkingham house of correction. For Browning, a native of Thurlby, near Bourne, see Royal Commission on Historical Monuments, *The Town of Stamford*, 1977, p. lxxxiv.

ablest and most progressive magistrate of his day in Lincolnshire. He had the support of Brownlow, who in the 1820s was active as a Kesteven magistrate as well as lord lieutenant.

Before 1820 the magistrates held their quarter sessions in buildings which they did not own themselves, but which were traditionally provided for them by the manorial lords of those towns in which they met. At Bourne the town hall was the property of the marquis of Exeter. At Sleaford Lord Bristol provided accommodation which was mixed up with a public house next door. At Folkingham the place of meeting was the public house itself. The Heathcotes had pulled down the old town hall in about 1789 and had provided instead a room attached to the Greyhound inn. The position was regularized first at Bourne, where the magistrates built a new court house on a site conveyed to them by Lord Exeter in 1821. Apart from the main court room it provided retiring rooms for the magistrates and the juries, and was at first-floor level to accommodate market stalls underneath. The architect, as at Folkingham house of correction later, was Browning. At Folkingham matters did not proceed so smoothly. The magistrates regarded the Greyhound as a place of meeting consistent neither with the dignity of the law nor with 'the present Habits and State of Society'. But they could not convince Heathcote of his obligation to provide them with a new court house, and they therefore decided in 1828 to discontinue the holding of regular sessions at Folkingham. For gaol business there was a justices' room in the new prison which met the needs of the visiting magistrates.[19]

At Sleaford the question was precipitated by Bristol's decision late in 1826 to sell the Mitre public house. The magistrates offered to buy the whole site, that is, the Mitre plus the town hall, but Bristol said he would accept nothing less than £2,500 for the lot. A negotiation followed in which Charles Chaplin (chairman of the Sleaford bench since 1817) represented the magistrates. It was pointed out to Bristol that under a recent Act[20] he was liable to provide accommodation for the sessions. The building, dating from about 1755, was in bad condition, the court furnishings were in any case the property of the county, and the increasing pressure of business was bound soon to render the question of rebuilding an urgent one. In the end Bristol agreed to grant the site to the county in exchange for his release from further liability. In April 1828 the magistrates resolved to rebuild, and chose a Gothic design by H. E. Kendall. Bristol

[19] KQS, papers relating to removal of sessions from Folkingham, 1827.
[20] 7 Geo. 4 cap. 63.

approved, considering that Gothic would 'harmonise much better with the Town of Sleaford than Grecian Architecture'. The builder was Charles Kirk, of the Leicester firm who had been the chief contractors at Folkingham. He later became county surveyor for Kesteven. It is interesting that Chaplin did not have things all his own way, his fellow-magistrates acting as a brake on unnecessary spending. They wanted a 'plain, substantial and useful building, nothing fine or decorated, and it is intended that the expense should not be large'. Forbes, the clerk of the peace, secured the support of Chaplin and Sir Robert Heron for the erection of a county muniment room for his admirably kept records, and Brownlow as custos contributed £100 to the cost of setting it up.[21]

The work at Sleaford was finished in 1830, and marked the rise of the town in the first three decades of the century into an important if not populous commercial and administrative centre. But from the middle of the century Grantham, expanding rapidly as a railway and engineering town, began to exercise more influence on the division. Following the extinction of the soke, the boundaries of the northern and southern subdivisions were re-drawn along the Grantham to Bridge End road. The town itself remained a semi-independent jurisdiction, under the borough justices, but the suburb of Spittlegate was increasingly used for county business. It was the meeting place for a large petty sessional division, and in 1843–4 a good-sized police station was erected, where the county magistrates could hold occasional meetings. In 1868 regular adjournments from Sleaford to Spittlegate for financial business were begun; and in the following year, on the motion of William Parker of Hanthorpe, a formal finance committee was set up to audit the accounts. Henceforward, until the inauguration of the county council in 1889, the important administrative questions relating to police and prisons were debated at Spittlegate rather than at Bourne or Sleaford. From 1871 sessions were originated alternately at Sleaford or Bourne before being adjourned to Spittlegate, with the result that the ancient judicial centres of the division now had full sessions twice instead of four times a year.[22]

After the death of Charles Chaplin in 1859 and the retirement of Moore as clerk of the peace in 1866, personal as well as economic influence gravitated towards Grantham and Stamford. Moore's successor, Joseph Phillips, lived at Stamford. Sir John Trollope, who had succeeded Johnson as chairman at Bourne in 1850, lived at Casewick, not far from Stamford, and the Great Northern Railway

[21] KQS, Sleaford Sessions House papers.
[22] KQS, minutes, 2 July 1868, 19 Jan. 1869, 17 Jan. 1871.

enabled him to get to Grantham more easily than to Sleaford. Chaplin's successors as chairmen of the Sleaford bench—Allix, Packe, Welby-Gregory—all belonged to the Grantham rather than the Sleaford side of Kesteven. Sleaford and Bourne did eventually acquire railway communication, but Folkingham, once on a busy turnpike road, was left to dwindle into obscurity. Nevertheless the house of correction was enlarged in 1852, and it survived the Prisons Act of 1865. A warming and ventilating apparatus was installed and the number of separate cells increased to forty-six. The next upheaval in the country's prison system, however, made it an obvious candidate for redundancy, and it was closed by the Home Office in 1878.

QUARTER SESSIONS: HOLLAND

Holland began the century with one house of correction, but shortly acquired another. In 1808 it was decided not only to enlarge the Spalding prison, but also to build one for vagrants and short-stay prisoners at Skirbeck, a suburban parish of Boston lying outside the borough. The 1820s, however, saw the beginning of a shift to Spalding as the administrative capital of Holland. The southern subdivision was rapidly increasing in population following the drainage of the Fens. Also, being a non-corporate town, it lacked a rival bench of borough magistrates, a circumstance which caused a succession of disputes and difficulties at Boston. In the 1820s Spalding house of correction was much enlarged, at a cost of £15,000. The Skirbeck prison was not suitable for conversion, and from 1826 it held prisoners for trial only, the long-stay prisoners from the Boston quarter sessions being sent to Spalding. In 1837 the Boston borough justices, having had their own gaol closed as inadequate, offered the use of it to the county magistrates. The Skirbeck prison was thereupon closed, and the Boston gaol was refurbished as a short-stay prison for quarter sessions prisoners. Finally, in 1851, the Spalding prison was further enlarged; henceforth no quarter sessions prisoners at all were kept at Boston. The old Skirbeck building, having lain empty for some years, was turned into a lock-up in the late 1840s.

All these changes did not take place without hard feelings between the borough and the division. The borough tried three times, in 1836, in 1843, and again in 1848, to get its own court of quarter sessions. Had this move been successful it would have forced the divisional magistrates to surrender the borough gaol and build a new prison for the Boston subdivision. It would also have meant the loss of the county rate product from the borough and difficulties over the sessions house, built within the borough in the early 1840s. The last attempt, in 1848, was precipitated by a case in which the county magistrates, contrary to their usual practice, had interfered in a borough matter. Meaburn Staniland, who often defended prisoners at the Boston sessions, and who, it was said, wanted to become clerk of the peace for Boston, encouraged the borough council to base their petition for quarter sessions on the alleged incompetence of the county magistrates. The latter called in Trollope as county member to defend them to the home secretary, Sir George Grey, and Brownlow also wrote on their behalf. The Bostonians, unsuccessful in their attempt to achieve judicial independence, then agitated the question of the borough gaol; and it was their notice to the divisional magistrates to quit the gaol in 1850 that led to the concentration on improvements at Spalding.[23]

Spalding's ascendancy was also marked in other ways. William Moore succeeded his father-in-law Maurice Johnson as vicar of Spalding in 1824, and thenceforward, until his retirement in 1861, can be considered the most influential magistrate not just in south Holland but in the division as a whole. From 1829 the quarter sessions minutes accord him the title of chairman of the bench at Spalding. He got on well with Brownlow, and also with Trollope, who had estates and influence in the Spalding neighbourhood. In 1837 Brownlow, on Moore's recommendation, appointed J. R. Carter, clerk to the Elloe petty sessions, clerk of the peace for Holland in succession to the Bostonian Thirkill. At the midsummer sessions of 1843 Moore proudly declared open the new court house at Spalding, which he hoped was 'on a scale adapted to the business of the division, and such as became its inhabitants'.[24]

Later in the century it was Spalding's turn to decline, when it fought and lost the battle to retain its gaol. Although modernized during the 1870s at a cost of £2,300, it was threatened with closure by the home secretary in 1877 and reprieved only after a memorial from the Holland magistrates. They stressed in particular the slowness of railway communication with Lincoln: constables taking vagrants there from the Fens and Marshes would be obliged to spend part of two days away from home unless committals were made in the morning. Spalding was a good railway centre for south and east Lincolnshire, and the court house and prison were only a short distance from the station. The success of this pleading meant

[23] HQS, minutes, *passim*; papers relating to Boston borough quarter sessions 1843–8.
[24] *SM*, 7 July 1843.

that Spalding was the only prison in the county apart from Lincoln itself to survive into the period of direct Home Office control. But the threat of closure was renewed in 1884. The magistrates drew up another memorial pointing out that even after the railway journey to Lincoln, prisoners had still to be marched across the town 'through streets teaming [sic] with operatives, who in case of excitement might easily effect a rescue'. The Revd Edward Moore, chairman of the Spalding bench, wrote to the home secretary (Sir William Harcourt) a letter that expressed some of the frustration felt by the magistrates of a small local authority in a somewhat remote and neglected part of the country:

> Our Fen Country is almost reduced to the sad condition of Ireland and mainly from similar causes: the absence of Proprietors and consequent alienation of the wealth of the district to enhance other localities; [and] a want of sympathy from the authorities at a distance who are necessarily ignorant in great measure of our requirements.

But this time Whitehall was unmoved. All Moore achieved was the removal of the prison clock, donated by his father, to the sessions house next door.[25]

The three divisions of the county and the way the administration of justice in them developed during the nineteenth century had certain features in common. All three embarked on building programmes in the 1820s, although Holland did not acquire new court houses until the early 1840s. The stimulus came partly from prison legislation, partly from the pressure of increased business at quarter sessions, but partly also from a desire to embody the authority of the magistrates and the increasing prosperity of the county in dignified public buildings. The new or up-graded county centres—Spilsby, Sleaford, and Spalding—were all thriving towns near areas of rapidly expanding population. They were also independent of any borough jurisdiction that might try to cramp the style of the county magistrates. By the 1860s, however, when the next major changes took place, the debates over prisons and sessions towns were dominated by the all-important question of railway communication. Expanding industrial towns such as Grimsby, Lincoln, and Grantham were beginning to have more weight than the older centres of county government. Folkingham prison survived until 1878 only because it would have been

[25] HQS, minutes, 15 Oct. 1877, 13 Feb. 1884.

expensive to build an entirely new gaol elsewhere in the division. Spalding, in contrast with Folkingham, had good railway communication for its side of the county, but the pull of centralization towards Lincoln finally proved too strong for Holland, as it had already proved for eastern Lindsey.

CHAPTER VI

THE COUNTY AT LARGE

GAOL SESSIONS

THE year 1824 is an important one in the history of Lincoln-shire. Before that date there had been no regular machinery by which the magistrates of the three divisions could make orders affecting the county as a whole. The maintenance of the county gaol in Lincoln Castle, the main burden falling on the county at large, depended on the mutual agreement of the Lindsey, Kesteven, and Holland benches. In 1823 a Prisons Act was passed, affecting gaols and houses of correction, and requiring among other things the appointment of visiting magistrates and the submission of quarterly reports to the home secretary. It was to meet the requirements of this act that the Spilsby prison was built and the establishments at Folkingham and Spalding improved. But the parliamentary draughtsmen forgot as usual to cater for divided counties, and the following year a Gaol Sessions Act had to be added to the statute book. Under this act the Castle of Lincoln was declared to belong to all three divisions of the county, and gaol sessions were to be held there four times a year. The main sessions were in the autumn, as had been the pattern with the previous less formal magistrates' meetings. The autumn sessions were usually chaired by Brownlow, a frequent attender up till about 1840, and matters of general county interest were raised as well as routine gaol business. Reports on the state of the gaol and its inmates were received, accounts passed, and orders made for the levying of county rates by the divisions in the usual proportions. All county magistrates could attend gaol sessions; and there was quite a good attendance at the autumn meetings, held to coincide with the stuff ball, or when a new surgeon or chaplain was to be elected. The routine quarterly meetings, however, were attended mainly by magistrates from the neighbourhood of Lincoln, the most active in the 1820s being Sir Edward Bromhead of Thurlby. The improved financial control of the gaol after 1824 and the increased authority of the visiting magistrates enabled some advances to be made in efficiency and discipline. By 1827 Bromhead and his colleagues were ready to open the gaol to the inspection of 'respectable strangers interested in this new branch of social economy'.[1]

Brownlow appointed William Forbes, the Kesteven clerk and the county clerk of lieutenancy, to be clerk of gaol sessions, and made use of him for a growing range of county business. Forbes became the channel of communication with the Lindsey and Holland clerks, asking them for instance to supply lists of magistrates for the assize judges. The Lindsey clerk, who had once been frequently called in to advise on gaol matters, was left only with the business relating to insolvent debtors. As Forbes put it on one occasion to the Holland clerk, who was as liable as the Lindsey clerk to take umbrage, 'Situated as I am in the immediate vicinity of the Lord Lieutenant it constantly falls to my lot under his lordship's direction to carry into effect many arrangements affecting the county at large. . . .'[2] When Forbes died in 1842 Brownlow and Chaplin decided to separate the clerkship of gaol sessions from the office of clerk of the peace for Kesteven. They proposed a Lincoln man, Frederick Burton, and he was duly elected despite Chaplin's fears that the appointment would be attacked as a 'job'. Apart from being Chaplin's legal agent, Burton was a very competent petty sessions clerk for the Lincoln division of Kesteven, and there were obvious advantages in having a man on the spot. The clerks of the peace remained jealous, one of them addressing Burton in a moment of pique as 'the clerk to the county gaol'.[3]

Despite administrative difficulties the county had not lagged behind the divisions in improving its public buildings. In 1809–12 new judges' lodgings were erected on Castle Hill, on a site purchased by the county just outside the castle walls. To achieve this a special act of parliament was obtained, under which named magistrates from each division were made commissioners with powers to supervise the work, levy rates, and hold the property in trust for the county. The same procedure had to be followed in 1822, when an act was obtained for rebuilding the county hall in the castle grounds. The design, a slightly anaemic Gothic one by Robert Smirke, provided two courts and a grand jury room. It was in the grand jury room, with its semi-circular tables and portraits of leading magistrates, that much of the business of the county was to be transacted in the next few decades. Despite major problems with the foundations the new county hall was ready for use in 1826. It cost over

---

[1] County Committee records, CoC 4/1/2/135.
[2] CoC 4/1/5/154.
[3] CoC 4/1/16/142; 4/2/2, p. 354.

£24,000, at a time when other aspects of county expenditure were rising rapidly.[4]

Brownlow and Forbes did not yet regard their work as done. The castle was still the property of the duchy of Lancaster and only leased to the county. In 1831, therefore, at a further cost of £2,000, an act was obtained enabling the county to purchase the castle. The opportunity was also taken to vest the judges' lodgings in the county. This was not achieved without opposition from Boston and Spilsby, where the magistrates joined their clerks in resenting expenditure at Lincoln that would give little advantage to their side of the county. But the revolt was quelled, to the satisfaction of those whom Forbes described to Brownlow as 'the influential and sensible part of the County'. Bromhead was delighted to think that for once Lincolnshire was in advance of 'the boors of Yorkshire'.[5]

The county magistrates were immediately involved in the vexed question of the castle dykings, the moat and mound outside the walls. The duchy of Lancaster had long since lost control of this area, and some of its less desirable inhabitants were constantly perpetrating encroachments that threatened the stability of the walls and the security of the gaol. The magistrates had a battle lasting twelve years with the most persistent offender, Philip Ball. Having failed to establish any legal claim to the dykings they were reduced to buying them up piecemeal.

The other continuing problem of this period was the refusal of the local jurisdictions to contribute to the cost of lodging assize prisoners and transporting felons. Once the obligation of the county divisions to contribute to the county gaol was defined by the act of 1824, the grievance of the boroughs was felt even more strongly. It was no good expecting them to contribute to a county rate for general gaol purposes, but the county magistrates thought they should at least pay the expenses attending individual cases sent from the borough courts to the assizes at Lincoln. Grantham, with its large soke and considerable rateable value, was singled out for the first attack, but little progress was made. Later, in 1832, Boston was called on to make a contribution, but with equal lack of success. Eventually the problem was solved by the Municipal Corporations Act of 1835 and the boundaries act of the following year. The effect of these two measures was to deprive the boroughs both of their exclusive jurisdictions and their outlying liberties.[6] Only those boroughs which petitioned successfully for a separate court of

[4] J. M. Crook, 'The Building of Lincoln County Hall', Lincs. Arch. and Arch. Soc., vol. 9 part 2 (1962), pp. 151–7.
[5] CoC 4/1/5/170, 311. [6] 2 BNL 29.

quarter sessions, presided over by a recorder, could henceforth claim partial exemption from county rates. Grantham and Stamford were granted quarter sessions but not Boston or Grimsby, though Grimsby had its quarter sessions restored in 1891.

The next major project undertaken by the county magistrates in gaol sessions was the partial rebuilding of the gaol in Lincoln Castle. It was planned in a very different spirit from the erection of the judges' lodgings or the rebuilding of the county hall. This time it was insistence from Whitehall, and not county spirit, that was the motive force. Under the Prisons Act of 1835 a system of Home Office inspection was established, and the view of the Inspectors was that Lincoln Castle gaol ranked 'among the inferior establishments of the kind'. Their seventh *Report* in 1842 detailed its faults: the lack of an airing yard for female prisoners, the absence of an adequate infirmary, overcrowding in the male sleeping cells, and the impossibility of supervising the day rooms and exercise yard. The home secretary, Sir James Graham, brought this report to the attention of the magistrates and made it clear that 'immediate measures' to remedy the defects were required. After this *'peremptory desire* signified by the Higher Powers', as Brownlow described it to Burton, there was no alternative to obedience. In Brownlow's view 'Prisons are already too much like palaces, and when all the comforts are provided, which are now to be carried out, delinquency will be almost at a premium'. The magistrates reluctantly prepared a scheme of alterations costing about £2,600, but it was rejected by the Home Office, and in the autumn of 1843 the magistrates were persuaded by Colonel (later Sir Joshua) Jebb to rebuild the entire crown wing of the gaol.[7] Plans were prepared by W. A. Nicholson, the Lincoln architect who had recently built the city gaol, and they were approved by the magistrates and accepted by the Home Office towards the end of 1844. The old crown wing had stood at right angles to the front of the gaol: the new wing that replaced it was built parallel to the front range, with a new chapel between the two. The design provided 34 sleeping cells for men and 13 for women, in place of the previous total of 13 cells. Under normal circumstances, therefore, prisoners could now spend their nights under the approved system of separate confinement. The building also had a new-fangled ventilation and sanitation system designed by Messrs Hadens of Trowbridge.

After various delays the work was all but finished by the end of 1847, at a total cost of £11,000. Unfortunately the building was

[7] 4 BNL box 3; CoC 4/1/17/111; Sidney and Beatrice Webb, *English Prisons under Local Government*, 1922 (repr. 1963).

occupied by prisoners before it had dried out, the drainage and ventilation proved to be defective, and the result was an outbreak of fever lasting several months. The fever put an end to a short-lived experiment in total solitary confinement (by day as well as by night), and the fledgling bureaucracy of the Home Office was forced to admit the inadequacies of the building whose plans it had itself virtually dictated.[8]

A further responsibility was added in 1855, when the gaol sessions was appointed by an act of parliament to provide militia storehouses for Lincolnshire. From this point, however, the importance of the gaol sessions declined. After the retirement of Brownlow and the death in 1859 of Chaplin it lacked strong leadership, although the void was to some extent filled in the 1860s by Lindsey gentlemen—Anderson, Amcotts, and Monson. No further important building project was undertaken by the county. Its control of the castle gaol, its main responsibility, was progressively eroded by the Home Office, to whom it was finally surrendered in 1877. Emptied of their prisoners, the buildings were sold back to the county, but no satisfactory use was found for them until they became an archives repository after the second world war. The militia storehouses were rented by the War Office from 1872.

In 1889 the gaol sessions were replaced by a new County Committee composed of representatives of the three Lincolnshire county councils. Even in Brownlow's day the Lindsey magistrates had been able to vote in their candidate for the post of surgeon or chaplain to the gaol, through sheer force of numbers. Lindsey's numerical preponderance was now institutionalized on the County Committee, but Kesteven, the most 'county' of the three councils, reasserted its influence on the committee in the years after 1900.

THE PAUPER LUNATIC ASYLUM

The gaol sessions were the only regular and permanent means of unified action by the three divisions. But there are other examples of bodies set up for particular purposes which help to shed light on the way the county functioned in the mid-nineteenth century. One instance, from the declining days of Brownlow's lord lieutenancy, was the creation of a committee to build a county lunatic asylum. Under an act of 1845, as amended the following year, the justices of every county and borough were obliged to make special provision for those pauper lunatics who had previously been looked after privately or in workhouses. It was up to the various benches of

[8] CoC 6, building papers and plans.

magistrates in Lincolnshire, borough as well as county, to agree upon whether one or more asylums should be provided, and where. After much discussion a contract of union was entered into between the three divisions, plus Lincoln and Grantham, in 1847; Stamford originally planned to build its own asylum, but joined the county scheme in 1848.[9] Brownlow initiated the movement by getting the three divisions to send representatives to a joint meeting at Lincoln. Later he even circularized all the boards of guardians in the county in an attempt to discover the number of lunatics likely to be supplied from each poor law union. But he was now in poor health and losing his grip on county affairs; for much of the time he had to content himself with exercising remote control through the Kesteven clerk, M. P. Moore, who was formally elected clerk to the committee.

Brownlow's original view of the question was that there should be two establishments, one for Lindsey and the other for Kesteven and Holland. This was supported by places such as Stamford and Spalding, for whose lunatics commitment to an asylum near Lincoln would mean exile as well as incarceration. But Sir Robert Sheffield and other Lindsey magistrates did not see why their side of the county should be put to great additional expense for the sake of south Lincolnshire. Chaplin, who had interests north as well as south of the Witham, came down firmly for a single asylum, telling his fellow-magistrates that Brownlow had 'a wrong bias on the subject'. Economy prevailed, helped by the discovery that it was not necessary to cater for idiots as well as lunatics. A building designed to hold 250 lunatics would suffice for the whole county.

Plans were invited, and the committee met at Lincoln to consider them in May 1848. Brownlow was unable to attend but sent a letter expressing his views. Chaplin voted Sheffield to the chair, but from then on the meeting went from bad to worse. Instead of reading Brownlow's letter Sheffield summarized it in 'a very unintelligible way'. As to the cost, he announced, '"Lord Brownlow thinks it will come to £45,000, but, however, gentlemen" (and he then laid the letter down and winked to the meeting) "I think we shall be able to get off for a very different sum."' Chaplin, having failed to get the letter read in full, carried on a rearguard action by attacking all the lower estimates as Sheffield rambled through them. Magistrates with trains to catch started drifting away; and old General Johnson, sitting in indignant silence, 'had never witnessed any thing like it in the whole course of his life'.[10]

[9] KQS, Bracebridge Asylum papers.
[10] KQS, Bracebridge Asylum papers, draft by M. P. Moore, 25 May 1848.

Eventually, having received professional advice and the sanction of the Lunacy Commissioners, the committee accepted the designs of a Mr Hamilton of Gloucester. But Hamilton proved to be on the verge of a nervous breakdown. Thomas Parry, the Kesteven county surveyor, was associated with him to supervise the building work, and finally took over altogether when the unhappy architect resigned. 'I hope that poor man has not destroyed himself', wrote Sheffield to M. P. Moore. 'I have long been of opinion that he was not always right in his mind.'

The difficulties with the architect were discussed at country houses as well as in the grand jury room. Johnson visited Casewick, where Sheffield was staying with his son-in-law Trollope. Although uneasy about Trollope's influence over Sheffield ('I always look about me to see *what end* Sir John has in what he says and does'), Johnson was at least pleased to find Sheffield more in command of the subject. Later, in August 1849, Moore went over to Revesby, where James Banks Stanhope was host to a party that included R. A. Christopher, the tory M.P. for North Lincolnshire. It was there that it was decided to call in Parry. The building work, on a healthy site at Bracebridge, near Lincoln, now proceeded more rapidly. Described by Professor Pevsner as grimly severe, the asylum was completed at a total cost of over £54,000, by August 1852. Delays had been caused by the need to secure official approval for the plans and estimates and then by Hamilton's failure to provide adequate working drawings, but the chief difficulty throughout had been the working of the committee itself. Although dates were chosen in the usual way to coincide with the assizes, the gaol sessions, or the stuff ball, it was never easy to find a day that suited all the leading participants. When they did assemble they lacked a firm lead from the lord lieutenant. The result was friction between local interests, and arrangements made between rather than at meetings.

Nevertheless the unity of the county as regarded the asylum lasted until the 1890s. It was then broken by a series of bitter disputes. From 1889 the asylum Visitors were no longer magistrates but aldermen and councillors, made up, like the County Committee, of representatives from the relevant local authorities in fixed proportions. Resentment of Lindsey soon emerged, and as early as 1890 Alderman Winfrey was proposing a separate asylum for Holland. 'The more he saw of public bodies, the less he liked centralisation.' A new contract of union was entered into in 1892, on a population basis, but this only increased the bad feeling in Kesteven. In 1894 Kesteven and the borough of Grantham withdrew from the county union. Grantham then antagonized Kesteven by trying to get the new asylum built within the borough, but after further wranglings a site was purchased at Rauceby, between Grantham and Sleaford.[11]

THE COUNTY POLICE AND RURAL CRIME

In the early nineteenth century Lincolnshire had a rapidly rising population. It had incursions of migrant workers, mostly of an uncouth type—Irish harvesters, navvies for the drainage works, and railway builders. It also had a vagrancy problem that became acute at times of depression and unemployment. To keep all these people in order the county had to rely on an antiquated system of high constables and parish constables. The high constables were chosen from the substantial farmers of each wapentake, and (at least in Lindsey) they held office for life. The parish constables were unpaid, generally small farmers or tradesmen, and acted for one year only. Both high and parish constables were responsible to the magistrates in quarter sessions.

Holland, with its large open parishes, felt the need for an improvement in its policing most acutely, and in 1836 declared in favour of appointing salaried parish constables alongside the unpaid ones. Three years later the Lindsey magistrates at a joint meeting at Market Rasen also came out for the remuneration of parish constables, and they did in fact institute payments in vagrancy cases the following year. But when an act was passed in 1839 permitting the establishment of professional county police forces only south Holland showed an inclination to adopt it. The magistrates of the three divisions met at Lincoln in March 1840 and decided not to implement the act. They feared both the increased burden on the county rate and the erosion of their own control of police matters; and it was also claimed, in a petition from the southern division of Kesteven, that the introduction of paid strangers would destroy 'that chain of good neighbourhood upon which our glorious Constitution was founded'.[12]

Under an act of 1842 it became possible to build up a police force piecemeal. Petty sessional divisions could apply to quarter sessions for permission to build lock-ups and appoint salaried superintendent constables. The act was utilized most consistently in Lindsey, where the first lock-up, at Gainsborough, was built in 1843. The effect of establishing lock-ups in towns like Gainsborough and

[11] *SM*, 16 May 1890, 22 May 1896; KCC, Rauceby Asylum papers.
[12] 4 BNL box 3.

Brigg was to make the vagrants alter their routes and infest less well-protected parts of the division. These areas then demanded their own lock-ups, and by the early 1850s a number of police stations, with cells and magistrates' rooms attached, had been erected.[13]

In 1856 the county was obliged by act of parliament to establish a regular rural police. At first there was talk of independent forces for each division. Holland was reluctant to unite with Kesteven, but as Hollway remarked to M. P. Moore, 'How can that *ridiculus mus* Holland expect to have a police of its own?' Dr Moore of Spalding was more accommodating than some of the Boston magistrates, and wrote to his son that he did not think the Holland division as a whole regarded Kesteven as 'overbearing'. In the end the matter was settled at a meeting of county magistrates at Lincoln, convened by Lord Granby but chaired by Lord Yarborough, who was shortly to succeed him as lord lieutenant. Lincolnshire was to have one chief constable, and this meant a joint committee of magistrates from all three divisions to appoint him. The successful candidate was Captain Philip Bicknell (1818–1904), who according to Hollway was elected 'almost wholly by Holland and Lindsey men'. He held the office until 1902.[14]

The general establishment charges, including the expense of providing a county police headquarters in 1860, had to be met by the county at large and audited by a joint committee of the three divisions. The boroughs policed themselves. Each division decided on the strength and disposition of its own force, and the provision of lock-ups and other similar expenses remained charges on the division concerned. In 1865 the three Lincolnshire forces were consolidated, when pension rights were made transferable from one division to another, the superannuation fund being administered by a joint committee. It was only in 1937, however, that a regular county police committee, appointed by the standing joint committees of the three divisions, was set up.[15]

The new police forces were established on the basis of the old *ad hoc* arrangements. In Lindsey superintendents of various grades were put in charge of the police divisions (based on petty-sessional divisions), sergeants allotted to the more troublesome open villages, and less than a hundred constables spread round the division, with beats of about 9,000 acres each. These constables Bicknell liked

[13] LQS, minutes 1843–56 *passim*; F. C. Mather, *Public Order in the Age of the Chartists*, 1959, pp. 53–4.
[14] KQS, county police papers 1856–9.
[15] *Lincolnshire Constabulary 1857–1957*. Lincoln, 1957.

to recruit from the farm labourer class, provided that they were 'clean, active and intelligent, of a good height and well made'. They were paid little more than those on whom they had to impress the dignity of the law. But wages rose gradually later in the century, and the forces expanded to cover new areas of growing population. Scunthorpe received a lock-up in 1865, for instance, and Cleethorpes one in 1870. The magistrates came to rely on their uniformed police for administrative tasks such as inspecting weights and measures, and the police also took over duties at the assizes from the special constables. The chief constables of wapentakes were abolished in 1869, but at least one petty-sessional division was still appointing parish constables in 1900.

By the mid-1850s rural crime was diminishing, but its pattern was slow to change. The new police engaged in open warfare with poachers, and vagrancy remained a considerable problem. In the year ending 29 September 1868 766 vagrants were arrested in the county, 654 of them being committed to prison. In 1860 there were twenty-four presumed arson cases, ten of them in Kesteven. Throughout the century felonies affecting property heavily outnumbered offences against the person, the commonest crime being the theft of pigs and poultry from farm yards, the sale of corn or cake by farm servants, and thefts by domestic servants from their employers.[16]

CENTRAL AND LOCAL GOVERNMENT

It remains to consider the county in its relations with the state. On one level the relationship was of course a very simple one. Parliament passed laws: in appropriate cases the magistrates in quarter sessions, or later the county councils, were responsible for carrying them out. The magistrates were the upholders of the law: they could not decide to enforce some acts but ignore others. Where they disliked legislation they could have recourse only to delaying tactics. They could claim that the act in question was unworkable, that it could not be paid for, or that no machinery existed to implement it.

A case in point was the Weights and Measures Act of 1824, which provided no machinery by which the magistrates could ensure that every shopkeeper learned of the new requirements. 'Advertisements are necessary,' wrote Forbes to Brownlow, 'but my experience teaches me to discover, that a very great proportion of those

[16] *Lincolnshire Constabulary: Criminal, financial and miscellaneous Returns*, years ending 29 Sept. 1860 and Dec. 1900.

affected by this measure reside in remote villages, many not reading the newspapers, and if they do read, they do not or are unwilling to understand anything that makes a change in habit or discipline.'[17] The magistrates did not gird up their loins until 1826, but then on Forbes's suggestion they adopted a scheme whereby a trustworthy person was appointed to attend at a central town in each hundred, armed with the correct measures. Constables were to notify the shopkeepers of their obligation to take their weights and measures to be checked. Brownlow corresponded with the home secretary, Sir Robert Peel, about the cost involved. Later in the century the professional police were employed in similar circumstances. Sir Charles Anderson got the police to post bills explaining the Agricultural Children Act of 1873, under which no child under eight was to be employed in farm work, and no child under ten in a gang. The act, which came into force in 1875, was frequently violated, but this was attributed not so much to ignorance of its provisions as to a reluctance by individuals to prosecute.[18]

Where action by the magistrates was required the central government had various means of exhortation. Before about 1840 the Home Office, at that time the government department most frequently in touch with local authorities, had a very small establishment, and spent much of its time answering enquiries and collecting statistics. The circulars sent out to the counties were still a mere trickle compared with the later deluge, but they could be firm in tone. In 1824 Peel asked the custos rotulorum to 'impress upon the magistrates in the strongest terms' the necessity of a strict compliance with the prison legislation, 'as they must be aware that it is only by the adoption of one general and uniform system that the effects contemplated by the Legislature can be attained'.[19] A few years later the Home Office could do better: it could send a prison inspector to find out exactly what the magistrates had done or left undone. In the 1840s Captain Williams caused some ill feeling among the gaol sessions justices by his strictures on the county gaol. Brownlow was surprised that he met with so much countenance from the home secretary (Sir James Graham), since he had owed his appointment to the whigs. 'He seems to be an officious sort of fellow,' he wrote to Burton, 'and I suppose he thinks that unless he can find fault, he would not be *worth his salt*.'[20] A few years later Chaplin became equally irate with the Lunacy Commissioners over the new asylum.

[17] KQS, clerk's papers 1826.   [18] LQS, minutes, 16 Oct. 1873; 1 July 1875.
[19] KQS, clerk's papers, 28 June 1824.   [20] CoC 4/1/17/111.

The Home Office required returns to be made of the cost of prosecutions and the conveyance of prisoners from 1835 onwards, and the cost of maintaining prisoners from 1846. In the 1850s and 1860s the desks of the clerks of the peace began to groan under the weight of circulars on such subjects as prison diet. In the end, as we have seen, the Home Office took over the prisons altogether; but this did not ensure peace for the magistrates, for other government departments were also becoming more demanding. The Treasury, as it increased its grants in aid of county rates, also increased its vigilance over how the money was spent. In 1870, for instance, it insisted that police pay sheet vouchers should be stamped. The Lindsey magistrates asked their county members to try to get the order waived.[21] The Privy Council was drawn into the re-arrangement of polling districts and into the machinery to combat the cattle plague. From 1871 the local authorities had their own department, the Local Government Board, which continued the bureaucratic tradition of the Poor Law Board. County authorities, however, seem to have been treated with more latitude than the unions: witness the scope for local initiative in the establishment of county councils.

Earlier in the century the assize judges helped to make the short arm of government stretch a little further, by using their charge to the grand jury as a means of impressing aspects of ministerial policy on the county magistrates. The judges also had to approve prison rules, acting in this case as executive as much as judicial agents of the Crown. The leaders of the county became fond of Lord Denman, and the grand jury presented him with an address on his retirement as Lord Chief Justice. Mr Justice Maule was not so popular, how-ever, at least with Brownlow, who thought his way of dealing with the rape cases at the Lent Assizes of 1848 'must have proceeded in a great degree from his own filthiness of mind!'[22]

Brownlow was himself an important link between central and local government. Unlike the lord chancellor or the home secretary, he was conversant with local conditions, and, as already described, he was sometimes the only means of getting all three divisions of the county to act together to implement legislation. Unlike most local people, moreover, he was often personally acquainted with lord chancellors and home secretaries, at least the tory ones. As far as home secretaries went he was in closest sympathy with Peel and later with Graham, although disappointed by the latter's firmness over the county gaol. With Melbourne, and more particularly with

[21] LQS, minutes, 30 June 1870.
[22] CoC 4/1/21/97.

Russell, he got on less well, finding himself on some occasions informed rather than consulted.

But Brownlow was not simply an agent of government, and the influence was not all one way. The magistrates had various means of making their views known at Westminster and Whitehall. Petitions to parliament from quarter sessions were not uncommon in the early part of the century, expressing dissatisfaction with such disturbers of rural peace as the beer shops permitted under the act of 1830. The magistrates could also memorialize the home secretary, either direct or through the lord lieutenant. In August 1831, for instance, the Spalding magistrates sought military help in keeping the labourers in order. They sent their clerk, J. R. Carter, to find Brownlow in London and ask him to press their case on the home secretary. Carter did not find Brownlow, but called at the Home Office, where an application by the magistrates to the army commanders at Peterborough or Boston was sanctioned.[23]

County members could be as helpful as the lord lieutenant, especially when bills affecting county interests were being prepared and passed through parliament. The Lindsey magistrates got the lord lieutenant and their county members to join them in waiting on the home secretary on the subject of proposed vagrancy legislation in 1848. In 1876 Lindsey Quarter Sessions appointed a committee of magistrates to watch the progress of the Prisons Bill and to confer with the county members. It consisted of Anderson, Amcotts, and Heneage, none of whom was himself a county M.P. In 1878 these three were reinforced by Lord Monson, Edmund Turnor, Sir John Astley, Henry Chaplin, and Edward Stanhope, all the last four being in the House of Commons. Over the financial adjustments Anderson, Amcotts, and Monson negotiated directly with the Home Office.[24]

Chairmen of quarter sessions carried some weight when dealing with the government, and it was of great local benefit if they were also members of parliament. In practice, however, it was difficult to combine the two callings. Gentlemen like Sheffield, Charles Chaplin, or Amcotts did for a time represent their county in parliament, but they preferred local administration. The major exceptions were Sir John Trollope in the south of the county, and later Edward Stanhope, who between 1885 and his death in 1893 combined the vice-chairmanship of Lindsey Quarter Sessions with a distinguished political career.

[23] 4 BNL box 3.
[24] LQS, minutes, 1876–8 *passim*.

The county occasionally secured amendments in government bills to adapt them to local conditions. More rarely still it procured a local act, thus employing the central machinery for purely local purposes. Perhaps the best example was the act of 1831 to purchase Lincoln Castle. After Brownlow had discovered from Peel that there was no hope of the government's adopting a bill the county magistrates decided to proceed with their own measure. The petition for leave to introduce it into the Commons was to be presented by Chaplin, still at that date one of the two members for the county. The other member, the eccentric Sir William Ingilby, expected to take part in piloting the bill through parliament, but M. P. Moore wrote to Forbes that 'this would damn the concern of itself'. Forbes was put in charge of the legal work as solicitor for the bill, with R. Jones as the parliamentary agent. A committee of magistrates meeting at Brownlow's London house was appointed to watch over the progress of the bill. All was going well when in the spring of 1831 parliament was dissolved, Chaplin retired from his county seat, and the new member Charles Pelham had to be approached to introduce the bill all over again. It finally achieved the royal assent on 2 August 1831.[25]

A few years later the county again showed its vigour, this time in direct opposition to a governmental proposal. For once Holland showed zeal for Lincolnshire interests. The scheme was to create an assize district centred on Wisbech, which involved rating part of Holland. Thus those who had already contributed to the improvements at Lincoln would have to contribute again to the cost of the new buildings at Wisbech, whilst Lincolnshire would lose part of its rateable value for county gaol purposes. The indignation of the leading Lincolnshire protagonists was fuelled by party rancour. The duke of Bedford supported the scheme, and was supposed to have influenced his son Lord John Russell. Brownlow prepared for action, 'as far as the expression of county feeling may have weight with such a deceitful and tricky ministry as now rule the country'. At the request of the grand jury at the Lent assizes of 1837 Brownlow convened a county meeting of magistrates (technically a meeting of gaol sessions), at which decided opposition to the scheme was expressed. Lincolnshire's peculiar constitution was held to work very satisfactorily; it was feared that a precedent for dismemberment would be established; and it was declared, no doubt with the French example in mind, that 'anything like an approach to a departmental division of the country ought to be deprecated and

[25] CoC 4/1/5.

resisted'.[26] The subsequent withdrawal of the measure was not entirely due to the strength of the Lincolnshire opposition. Nevertheless the affair may be seen as a victory for local over central government and a high point in Lincolnshire's county consciousness.

[26] CoC 2/1, p. 360; 3/4/5.

CHAPTER VII

LOCAL AUTHORITIES AND REPRESENTATIVE GOVERNMENT

THE wapentakes or hundreds, the second-tier authorities of Anglo-Saxon and medieval local government, still had some life left in them in nineteenth-century Lincolnshire. The hundred courts, which in the Middle Ages had dealt with a variety of judicial and administrative business, had disappeared by 1800, but the hundred bailiffs continued to act as subordinate officers of the high sheriff. The high constables, not yet superseded by the professional county police force, were responsible for collecting the county rate in their hundreds and for implementing the orders of the magistrates.

In common with other Danelaw counties the name wapentake was preferred in Lincolnshire, but Hill, situated in the southern Wolds around Tetford, was usually known as a hundred. The sokes of Horncastle and Bolingbroke (the latter once a private jurisdiction of the earls of Lincoln) functioned as ordinary wapentakes, but the soke of Grantham, as already described, retained its privileged status into the early nineteenth century. Some wapentakes had two divisions, each with its high constable. Thus Boothby Graffoe had a high division, composed of certain parishes on the Cliff south of Lincoln, and a low division stretching westwards to the Nottinghamshire border.

The inhabitants of the wapentake remained responsible for the maintenance of certain roads and bridges, and down to 1886 it was possible to claim compensation from the hundred for damage caused by riot. The Revd John Mossop of Langtoft invoked the latter provision when his parsonage was burnt down, he suspected deliberately, in 1828.[1] The high constables continued to police fairs: Richard Healy of Laughton, one of the high constables for Aveland

---

[1] KQS, clerk's papers 1828.

wapentake, was given considerable trouble by the Stow Green fair
in the 1820s. Statute hiring fairs also came under the high constables' control. For Elloe wapentake a register of statute hiring
survives for the years 1767 to 1867, two years before the powers of
high constables were abolished by act of parliament.[2]

In the early 1830s local people were still familiar with the wapentake and its boundaries, and voluntary bodies such as yeomanry
corps or associations for the prosecution of felons sometimes
adopted it as the area of their operations. Wapentakes could even
have an identifiable political character. Loveden was distinguished
for its independence, Boothby Graffoe for its moderation. In July
1837 the Revd William Brocklebank of Carlton-le-Moorland told
G. J. Heathcote that 'a high Tory candidate would meet with little
support in the hundred of Boothby Graffoe—we are moderate
reformers, *not destructives*....'[3] Those who used White's *County
Directories* must presumably have known their wapentakes, since
the publication was arranged on that plan until redesigned for the
1882 edition.

Even the institutions that superseded the wapentakes were based
on the old boundaries, although some modifications were necessary. The courts of petty session were in part the successors of the
hundred courts. But most of them were held in market towns, and
took place on market days. Some wapentakes had no market town
within their boundaries, and were therefore grouped together or
split for the convenience of witnesses and parish officers. Thus the
Lindsey petty sessional division based on Lincoln embraced Lawress, Aslacoe, and part of Well.[4] The hundred of Hill managed to
retain its own petty sessions until 1837, meeting (presumably in a
public house) at Tetford, but it was then split and allocated to three
neighbouring divisions. On the petty sessional divisions were based
in their turn the parliamentary polling districts and the police districts. The lieutenancy subdivisions were also based on wapentakes,
but, as we have seen, they had fallen into disuse by the middle of the
century. The areas and also the names of the wapentakes were kept
alive, however, by the rural deaneries, the tax commissioners, and
in some parts of the county by the commissioners of sewers.

The commissioners of sewers were the ancient drainage
authorities of the county. Their constitution derived from an act of
1532, but they had originated in medieval times. They were
appointed by the Crown, through the lord lieutenant, in the same

[2] HQS, records of Elloe statute sessions.
[3] 3 ANC 9/14/323.
[4] *Archivists' Report* 25 (1973–5), p. 69.

way as the county magistrates, although they were a much less influential body, and by the nineteenth century of little political importance. They were composed mainly of farmers, though supported at times by a few of the more active magistrates. The commissioners held courts in each wapentake or group of wapentakes, appointed dikereeves, and empanelled juries who inspected drains and sluices. By the nineteenth century the most active commissioners were those concerned with the drainage of the coastal marshland, with its river outfalls and sea banks. The commissioners met regularly at Spalding (for Elloe), Boston (for Kirton and Skirbeck), Spilsby (for Candleshoe, Hill, and Bolingbroke), Alford (for Calceworth), and Louth (for Ludborough and Louth Eske). Clerkships to these bodies were sought after by attorneys, and in the early nineteenth century the Lindsey courts of sewers were part of the Brackenbury family's portfolio.[5] The courts of sewers mentioned above continued to function until they were superseded by drainage districts in 1930.

Another survival into the twentieth century was the manorial court. Scattered over the county were parishes, mostly in smallholding areas, where the land was not freehold but copyhold. Copyholders held their land from the lord of the manor in which the land was situated, and their title to it was the copy of the court roll on which the purchase or inheritance was recorded. Manors varied in their customs, and in the fines payable to the lord. At North Thoresby, for instance, according to White's 1856 *Directory*, Lord Yarborough held a court leet and baron twice a year for the manor of Thoresby-cum-North Cotes: 'the custom of borough English [descent to the youngest son] prevails here'. At Epworth at this date the court leet still functioned as a unit of local government, regulating the drainage of a considerable area of the Isle of Axholme and preserving the boundaries of the open-field strips. As late as 1900 the lord of the manor of Bourne-cum-membris, the marquis of Exeter, still held his court leet, although it was probably as much an excuse for an annual dinner as a meeting for essential legal business.[6]

THE NEW POOR LAW

Late in 1835 the Poor Law commissioners began their work of revolutionizing local government in Lincolnshire. They started forming poor law unions in the south of the county, and ended at Spilsby in April 1837. The boundaries that they drew cut across the

[5] LINDSEY MISC SEWERS 4.
[6] *Archivists' Report* 22 (1970–1), p. 55; *SM* 29 June 1900.

wapentakes and even overlapped counties and county divisions. The Stamford union included parishes in Rutland and Northamptonshire as well as Lincolnshire. Seven Nottinghamshire parishes fell into the Gainsborough union, and six Leicestershire parishes were attached to Grantham. Crowland became part of the Peterborough union; several Kesteven parishes helped to form the Newark union; and the Isle of Axholme was given not to Brigg but to Goole. Other unions, though entirely within Lincolnshire, crossed divisional boundaries. The large Lincoln union included both Lindsey and Kesteven parishes. The Boston union, although mainly in Holland, embraced part of the fen district of Lindsey and the Kesteven village of Dogdyke.[7]

The commissioners did not have an entirely free hand, since they had to take account of the parishes that had voluntarily formed themselves into unions under Gilbert's Act of 1782. Lincoln was no great problem, since it would in any case have been chosen as the centre of a union. The county benefited from the existence of a house of industry at Claypole, which became the workhouse of the Newark union. But the old Caistor union caused difficulties in arranging the boundaries in Lindsey. Caistor was an unimportant town, not even at this period the centre of a petty sessional division, but the large union based upon it included both Grimsby and Market Rasen, and stretched from Buslingthorpe to Immingham. Grimsby had to give up its large parish workhouse, and its paupers had to tramp twelve miles to be relieved at Caistor.[8] A proposal for the board of guardians to circulate between Caistor, Market Rasen, and Grimsby was negatived because of the inconvenient distance of twenty-one miles that separated the latter two places. It was not until 1890 that the Grimsby relieving district was made into a separate union. The Brigg union, lying to the north of the Caistor union, was also forced into an unsatisfactory shape. Barton, the larger town, had hoped to become its capital, but Brigg was chosen for its more nearly central position.

The new poor law was not universally welcomed in Lincolnshire. Colonel Johnson, though chairman of the Bourne bench, was still radical enough to withhold his approval. Unrest among the labouring classes was especially evident in the Trent valley, a fact which Archdeacon Stonehouse attributed to its 'constant intercourse' with the West Riding.[9] The newly begun workhouse at Gainsborough

[7] See also J. A H. Brocklebank, 'The New Poor Law in Lincolnshire', *Lincs. Historian* vol. 2 no. 9 (1962), pp. 21–33.

[8] *SM* 30 Dec. 1836.

[9] 4 BNL box 3, Stonehouse to Brownlow 1 July 1837.

was razed to the ground in July 1837, and that summer the military were called in to quell a riot at West Butterwick.

The magistrates were made guardians *ex officio*, and in most Lincolnshire unions took the lead at the early meetings. Sheffield became chairman at Brigg, for instance, and the Revd William Dodson chairman at Spilsby. At Lincoln, however, the Hon. A. L. Melville, an elected guardian, took the chair in the hope of instilling some Scotch frugality into the Lincolnshire peasantry; and at Caistor the chairman was George Skipworth, son-in-law of the original founder of the union. But the *ex officio* element, though influential, was not numerically preponderant; and the magistrates found themselves for the first time associated with elected representatives of the ratepayers. The guardians elected by the parishes included a few squires and clergy, but they were mostly farmers and tradesmen. The farmers were in many cases used to poor law business as parish overseers or churchwardens, but they were not used to discussing business round a table with landlords and magistrates. Nor were the elected representatives of urban parishes, but they were less inclined to let the gentry have their way. At Bourne and Gainsborough, for instance, townsmen secured the post of vice-chairman of the union. Even at Stamford, where the Exeter interest was exerted, the guardians rejected the nominee for the clerkship supported by the *ex officio* members. The vigilant parsimony of the ratepayers' representatives was soon revealed at Sleaford, where the workhouse design approved by Chaplin was rejected in favour of a cheaper model.[10]

As time went on the gentry took a less prominent part in the work of the boards of guardians. Even the first elections revealed characteristic patterns of local behaviour that (except in places like Stamford) owed little to landed influence. At Gainsborough wrangling broke out on wholly irrelevant topics. At Spilsby the voters divided on party-political lines. At Holbeach rival contenders for the clerkship dominated the first election, and Richard Mossop failed to be appointed auditor, despite an early canvass and the fact that six of his relatives were among the guardians returned.[11] Despite the injunction of the assistant Poor Law commissioner that 'all family connections and private influence must be put out of the question', there was a scramble everywhere to secure the salaried post of relieving officer.

In one way the boards of guardians prepared the middle classes

[10] POOR LAW UNIONS, guardians' minutes, Stamford (19 Nov. 1835) and Sleaford (17 Nov. 1836).
[11] *SM* 17 Dec. 1835.

for the further extension of their power in local government that was to be won later in the century. But in another way the magistrates lost power not so much to the ratepayers locally as to the authorities in London. The trickle of Home Office circulars received by clerks of the peace was nothing to the steady flow of instructions from the Poor Law Board to the officials in the unions. Even minute matters of diet were rigidly prescribed.

THE COUNTY COUNCILS

The principle of 'no taxation without representation' was not conceded to the county ratepayers until over fifty years after the introduction of the New Poor Law. As already described, there were grumblings over various aspects of county expenditure from the 1830s onwards, and they reached a climax in Lindsey in the 1860s, when the financial burdens of prison improvement coincided with those of the cattle plague. By the late 1880s, however, the régime of the magistrates was somewhat less unpopular. Prisons were no longer a county charge, and much of the routine expenditure sanctioned in quarter sessions was grant-aided by the central government. In 1888 the County Government Act was welcomed not only by reformers but by some magistrates, who hoped that it would revitalize local government and help it to resist dictation from Whitehall.

Their hopes were justified in so far as the old boundaries largely escaped rationalization by the Local Government Board, the bureaucratic successor to the Poor Law Board. There was little enthusiasm for a united Lincolnshire, and some positive opposition from Holland. Canon Moore took a strong 'Home Rule' line, and had no desire to have matters such as the breach of a fen bank referred to Lincoln—'As well keep a fire engine for the county on the top of Lincoln hill.'[12] In any case there was no specific machinery for uniting the county, and Lindsey, Kesteven, and Holland became separate county councils. The boundary commissioners, hoping to make county divisions approximate more closely to Poor Law unions, had the idea of transferring Stamford to Rutland, but Rutland would have none of it.[13] In the end minor adjustments were left to the councils themselves, subject to the approval of the Local Government Board. Nobody had ever known precisely what part of the parish of Misson belonged to Lincolnshire, and it was agreed to transfer it wholly to Nottinghamshire. In 1895

[12] *SM* 27 April 1888.   [13] *SM* 10 Aug. 1888.

that county also acquired part of the parish of Lea that had been stranded on the left bank of the Trent by a change in the course of the river.

In the autumn of 1888 candidates began to issue their addresses for the first county council elections. Magistrates stressed their experience of local government and other aspirants their knowledge of the needs of their localities. In Lindsey twenty-five out of the fifty-seven seats were uncontested, in Kesteven twenty out of forty-eight. But in many divisions there were contests on class and party-political lines. This was particularly the case in Holland, where only ten of the forty-two seats were uncontested. Anti-magisterial feeling was revealed on a scale that surprised the magistrates themselves. In the Uffington division of Kesteven, for instance, Lord Kesteven was opposed by William Cross, who proclaimed himself a 'tenant farmer and labourers' candidate'. Edward Heneage stood for a division of Lindsey that included Binbrook, Ludford, and Donington-on-Bain, and was annoyed to find himself opposed by A. E. Alington of Binbrook, an eccentric member of a local landed family. Heneage consulted his agent Wintringham about what would be necessary in the way of electioneering:

> ... The cost will be limited to £25, and the number of electors will only be about 500. I thought of putting out an address and having about 500 small letter size to distribute to the electors, and to visit Binbrook, Ludford and Donington some evenings in November and make a short business speech also at Hainton. I am the only resident landowner in the district except Mrs Fox, who will do everything she can for me, as will no doubt the non-residents Mr Clayton, Mr Walker and Mr Mason in Withcall and Donington on Bain. Binbrook is the unknown quantity, but the farmers will be right, and of course I shall get hearty support in Ludford, Hainton and S. Willingham, Girsby, etc., etc. I do not expect any opposition except as it is manufactured in Louth and got up in Binbrook and Donington on Bain. ... I shall write a few private letters asking some of the largest ratepayers to act as a committee on my behalf in their respective parishes.[14]

Despite these measures the opposition proved too strong. Yarborough wrote to Oxenbridge about the Lindsey elections: 'It is curious how the J.P.s seem to have been beaten everywhere. I

[14] 2 HEN 5/16.

expect we shall all hear about Heneage being defeated, as he will doubtless write to us all.'[15] In all eight Lindsey magistrates were defeated at the polls, another four in Kesteven (despite free advice from the clerk of the peace), and four in Holland. Some magistrates however, were, voted back in as county aldermen, but the gentry had been given notice that they should no longer expect to govern the county unchallenged.

A major cause of Alington's victory had been the support of the Louth divisional Liberal association, and the contest developed into a party question (Heneage being a Liberal Unionist) as well as a ratepayers' one. Even where party affiliations were not openly declared by the candidates, politics were never far beneath the surface. At Market Rasen, for instance, the canvass was 'not wholly free from a bias of the "pot and kettle" kind'. Allotments and parochial charities were favourite topics of those appealing to the labourers' vote, despite the fact that the new county councils had yet to be granted powers in either matter. In Holland the Liberals made an all-out effort to capture the council, and the *Boston Guardian* adumbrated a full party programme of retrenchment and reform.[16] It was in Holland, indeed, that the Liberals were most successful, and they proceeded to strengthen their position by drafting Liberal aldermen *en bloc*. Only two of the councillors were magistrates, and the first chairman of the Holland County Council, the Spalding wine merchant G. F. Barrell, was a strong Liberal who had yet to be put on the bench. The results of the elections in Holland must be seen partly as a reflection of the strength of Liberal organization in the division, but mainly as a reaction against years of rule by a small, unrepresentative, and predominantly tory bench of magistrates. In Lindsey, by contrast, party politics were much less in evidence, a phenomenon no doubt connected with the fact that the bench had already become less socially exclusive. Oxenbridge, the Liberal chairman of quarter sessions, became the first chairman of the county council. In Kesteven the Liberals were active, especially at Bourne, but the Conservatives secured a comfortable majority. Continuity of leadership was demonstrated by the election to the chair of Sir W. E. Welby-Gregory, the chairman of the Sleaford sessions.[17]

The following table analyses the social composition of the three

[15] MON 25/13/21.

[16] *SM* 18 Jan. 1889; J. P. Dunbabin, 'Expectations of the new County Councils and their realisation', *Hist. Journal* VIII no. 3 (1965), pp. 353 ff.

[17] For the formation of Kesteven County Council see Joan Varley, *The Parts of Kesteven*, 1974, pp. 101 ff.

county councils elected in January 1889, including aldermen as well as councillors.

	Holland	Kesteven	Lindsey
gentry	1	19	17
clergy	0	0	4
farmers	22	17	12
doctors	0	1	2
solicitors	3	4	3
agents and auctioneers	3	3	9
merchants and manufacturers	8	5	15
shopkeepers	10	7	7
others	9	8	7
total	56	64	76

Nearly half the Holland councillors were returned from urban or semi-urban divisions, compared with just over one-third in Lindsey and just under one-third in Kesteven. Townsmen also stood for rural seats: the Spalding journalist Richard Winfrey, for example, was returned for the Whaplode division.[18] At the same time the abstention of the clergy meant that a number of farmers were returned for rural seats. The farmers and shopkeepers between them outweighed the other social groups on the Holland council and were in a good position to influence its tone and policy. Kesteven and Lindsey both returned a sufficient number of the old guard—magistrates and landowners—to exert a strong influence on their new councils. In Kesteven the gentry were joined by a number of farmer candidates, reinforcing the predominantly rural tone. Lindsey on the other hand had a significant manufacturing and trading element, and even the rural seats were sometimes taken by agents or clergymen rather than by farmers. In all three divisions a number of solicitors were returned, men whose expertise had hitherto been available to the county only in an executive capacity. Other men already well-known in the county now came forward as councillors, including politicians such as William Frankish of Limber, Joseph Hardy of Goxhill, Charles Sharpe of Sleaford, and Eli Crabtree of Great Ponton. Nonconformist elements achieved for the first time a kind of county recognition, and prominent farming families—the Howards of Nocton, the Sauls of Wrangle, the Casswells of Gosberton—were also represented. But, especially in Lindsey, the bad times seem to have kept other leading farmers out of local government.

The first task of the newly returned county councils was to draw

[18] See R. Winfrey, *Memories of Forty Years and More Ago,* 1929.

up their own constitutions, in which some latitude was allowed. The election of chairmen, aldermen, and committee-men could give rise to local animosities and party battles within the councils, as could the fixing of meeting places. The Lindsey and Kesteven chairmen tended to be re-elected annually until they retired, but Holland evolved a system of electing a new chairman each year, from the Boston and Spalding sides alternately. Meetings were also held alternately at Spalding and Boston, but this equitable arrangement did not prevent arguments from breaking out. In March 1899 the south Holland members, having failed in their bid to prevent an increase in the north Holland surveyor's salary, rushed away from a Boston meeting before its conclusion to catch their train back to Spalding, leaving Alderman Bedford to comment on their discourtesy.[19] The Spalding men for their part considered that they did more than their fair share of the council's work. In Kesteven the council met alternately at Grantham and Sleaford, although Grantham did not count as part of Kesteven for all purposes. Lindsey County Council met at first alternately at Grimsby and Lincoln, but after the grant of county borough status to Grimsby in 1891 meetings took place at Lincoln only. A movement in favour of Louth as an alternative meeting place was short-lived.

Resentment of the magistrates was not entirely forgotten after the initial campaigns. The Holland Liberal group decided on one-party council representation on the joint police committee, in order to ensure the end of magisterial domination. In Lindsey the Liberal William Taylor Sharpe tried to exclude J.P.s from the fourteen council members of the joint committee, but he was defeated, Oxenbridge pointing out that in any case nine of the fourteen members chosen by the magistrates were also county councillors. In 1893 Alderman Halmshaw of Brigg came out in favour of removing the powers of lord lieutenants to select magistrates and giving county councils a chance to make recommendations instead.[20]

Once procedural matters were settled, the councillors, many of them of limited experience in such matters, had to begin their financial and administrative work: levying and adjusting county rates, arranging polling districts, maintaining the highways, controlling contagious diseases such as cattle plague, and taking their share of police business. Of their powers only those relating to highways had not been enjoyed in full by their predecessors the magistrates. Under an act of 1878 the old turnpike roads had become either 'main' roads or parish roads, and in the former case

[19] *SM* 17 March 1899.   [20] *SM* 5 April 1889; 3 Feb. 1893.

they had come under the superintendence of the county surveyor. The county councils now had power to maintain as well as merely supervise the main roads, but only in Holland was this implemented. Even there the urban authorities (Boston, Spalding, Holbeach, Long Sutton, and Sutton Bridge) elected to maintain their own highways, leaving the county at the outset with only 117 miles of rural main roads.[21] In Kesteven and Holland the actual work of repairing even these roads was delegated to the rural districts. In 1895 an attempt in Kesteven to 'dis-main' all the main roads in the county, on the ground that they were used mainly by townspeople and constituted an unfair burden on the rural ratepayers, was only narrowly defeated.[22] Some of the so-called main roads were in truth scarcely used at all: grass grew down the middle of them while the bulk of the county's traffic went by rail. Many of the newly-classified main roads led to railway stations.

Under an act of 1890 county councils acquired powers to compel the purchase of allotments under the Allotments Act of 1887. As might be expected, Holland was the most active authority, with Lindsey not far behind. Guy's Hospital was obliged to provide allotments at Sutton Bridge, giving in before the case went to court, and there were similar cases in the early 1890s at Winterton and Messingham in Lindsey.

In Kesteven, on the other hand, the main emphasis in the 1890s was on technical education. Under an act of 1890 limited funds deriving from customs and excise duties were made available to county authorities. For Kesteven a strong committee was appointed, chaired by Sir John Thorold. Local committees were set up, teacher training provided, outside lecturers engaged, and classes provided in agricultural science, cookery, dairying, and other similar subjects. Lindsey set up a similar scheme, which included the establishment of a dairy school and the sponsorship of university extension lectures. The county councils were therefore involved in adult education some years before they took over responsibility for elementary education from the school boards under the Education Act of 1902. In the twentieth century education was to become the major concern of every county authority.

DISTRICT AND PARISH AUTHORITIES

Victorian principles of public health were adopted slowly and piecemeal in the towns of Lincolnshire. To this day they have not

[21] T. B. Browne, *The County Council Year Book*, 1892.
[22] *SM* 23 Aug. 1895.

penetrated parts of the countryside. By obtaining improvement acts, towns like Spalding or Horncastle could raise money for lighting, paving, and watching. Later, under the Public Health Act of 1848, towns could apply for the establishment of local boards of health with powers connected with sewage, the removal of nuisances, and lodging houses. In Lincolnshire Holbeach (1850), Sleaford (1851), and Gainsborough (1851) led the way, followed by several others, mainly in Lindsey. Under the Public Health Acts of 1872 and 1875 the boroughs, local board districts, and towns under improvement acts became urban sanitary districts, and the poor law guardians were made the sanitary authorities for the remaining rural areas of their unions. In 1894 these urban and rural sanitary authorities were replaced by urban and rural district councils, elected on the same wide suffrage as the county councils. Apart from sanitary matters the districts also took over from the parishes the maintenance of the highways.

Unlike the unions the new rural districts had to lie within administrative county boundaries, and this created some strange effects in Lincolnshire. The Lincoln and Boston unions had to be split into two rural districts each, lying north and south of the Witham. The Axholme district of the Thorne union and the Claypole district of the Newark union became separate Lincolnshire rural districts. So did the single parishes of Uffington, in the Stamford union, and Crowland, in the Peterborough.

The new urban districts reflected the haphazard distribution of local boards. A market town without a local board, such as Bourne or Spilsby, found itself merely one parish among others in a large rural district.[23] On the other hand there were one or two villages that had been granted local boards and were now raised to urban district status. The growing village of Ruskington near Sleaford was one that justified its existence by showing an interest in council elections; in 1899 the newly formed ratepayers' association won three seats. The urban district of Roxby near Brigg, on the other hand, was something of a farce. In December 1895 a vacancy was contested by John Andrew, a cottager, and George Crowston, a farmer aged ninety-eight. Crowston was fit enough to walk to the poll, but lost by seventeen votes to nineteen.[24]

The pattern of urban districts is well shown by the map accompanying the 1901 census volume for Lincolnshire (see Fig. 6). Of the twenty-four districts sixteen were in Lindsey and only four each in Kesteven and Holland. Of the Lindsey urban districts no less than seven lay within the rural district of Brigg, indicating not just the

[23] Bourne became a UDC in 1899.   [24] *SM* 31 March 1899, 6 Dec. 1895.

urban population but also the urban spirit of that part of the county. The four urban districts of Holland were all in Elloe, of which they covered a considerable portion.

Some of the old leaders of the local boards received chastisement at the first U.D.C. elections, but the new men were of similar social status, at least in the market towns. All those returned at Market Rasen were 'master tradesmen or principals in their several callings', and Wesleyan Methodism was well represented. The strength of Liberalism at Scunthorpe was attested by its capture of twelve out of the fifteen U.D.C. seats.[25] Party feeling and new blood were also in evidence in the rural districts. At Brigg Joseph Hardy of Goxhill, a strong Liberal, was elected chairman, defeating Thomas Tombleson of Barton, the chairman of the board of guardians and a magistrate. Contests also took place on party lines in some unions in the south of the county. But in many rural districts the largely Conservative farming class soon established their control, freed from the admixture of urban interests that had always been present on the boards of guardians. Of the two main concerns of the rural districts, it was natural that the farmers should take a greater interest in the roads that took their corn to market than in the sanitation of the cottages of the poor.

The labourers, however, were given a chance to challenge the hegemony of the farmers at the parochial level. The Local Government Act of 1894 directed that in parishes of three hundred or more people vestries should be superseded by parish councils. The newly conferred as opposed to the inherited powers of these councils turned out not to be of great significance. They could hire and manage land for the purpose of providing allotments, but the Liberals, who had been working up the rural electorate since before the general election of 1892, had hoped for much more. They had advocated parochial control of schools and charities, which they wished to see wrested from the grip of the parsons and farmers. Speaking at North Thoresby in April 1892 R. W. Perks, Liberal parliamentary candidate for the Louth division, said that villagers should have the right to close public houses in their localities, just as landowners had the power to exclude them from their estates.[26]

The Temperance factor may explain why the Primitive Methodists of the Lincoln and Grimsby district decided in May 1894 to take an active part in the approaching parish council elections. In August the Liberals held a conference at Lincoln on the issues of parochial democracy, with Alderman Barrell of Spalding in the chair,

[25] *SM* 28 Dec. 1894, 8 Feb. 1895.   [26] *SM* 15 April 1892.

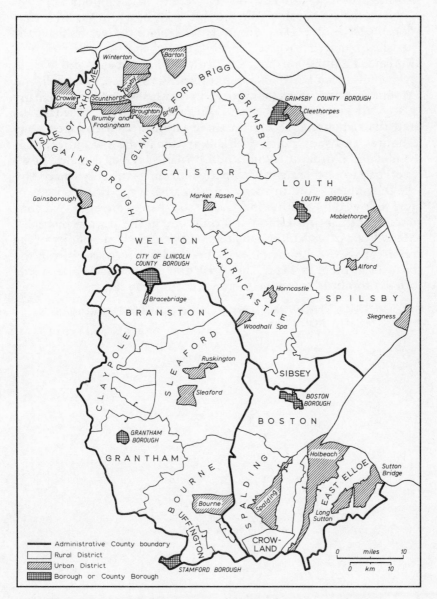

Figure 6   *Lincolnshire in 1900, showing administrative divisions*

although by this time it was known that the more sanguine hopes for the powers of the new bodies were to be disappointed.[27]

Nevertheless considerable interest was shown in the first elections in December 1894. Contests took place in over half the 291 parishes required to· hold elections, a larger proportion than in Rutland, Huntingdonshire, or Norfolk. The Liberals did well in such contrasting parishes as Scunthorpe, Crowland, Bucknall, and Mount Pleasant (near Coningsby). Labourers were elected in many places. At Leasingham the candidates returned were three farmers and two labourers, at Martin three farmers, two cottagers, one labourer, and one saddler. At Blankney the farmers withdrew their candidates in order to avoid a poll.[28] Many smaller parishes, however, had to rest content with parish meetings, usually chaired by the incumbent. And in many larger parishes the first excitement was followed by apathy: in March 1899 there were only two contests in the Lincoln Union and only one in the Boston district.[29] Many years of agricultural depression had sapped the vitality of the rural parishes. Administratively they had not recovered from the blow dealt them in 1834. The legislation of sixty years afterwards offered too little to revive them, and came too late.

[27] *SM* 4 May, 10 Aug. 1894.   [28] *SM* 14 and 21 Dec. 1894.
[29] *SM* 31 March 1899.

CHAPTER VIII

PARTY POLITICS

THE UNDIVIDED COUNTY

LINCOLNSHIRE in 1800 had the appearance of a firmly whig county. Its lord lieutenant, the duke of Ancaster, was a whig. The whole county was one two-member constituency, and both its members, Robert Vyner and Sir Gilbert Heathcote, were whigs. Most of the leading landed families active in local politics in the late eighteenth century—the Pelhams, Monsons, Thorolds, and so on—were likewise whig. The county had not had a tory M.P. since 1727, and the last contested county election had been in 1724, when Robert Vyner had defeated the tory Sir Neville Hickman. That defeat, according to the whigs, deprived their opponents of the power 'ever to chuse another Member for our County'.[1]

Eighteenth-century Lincolnshire was, however, no tame county under the influence of a great magnate, returning M.P.s to vote at the government's behest. The dukes of Ancaster did not in fact have a great pull, although the family interest was partially revived in 1761 after an extensive canvass.[2] For much of the century the members were chosen at meetings of the country gentlemen, and they were expected to act independently at Westminster. The county M.P.s—Vyners, Whichcots, and Thorolds—had to please not only fellow-members of their own class but also a numerous body of small freeholders who were beyond the normal channels of landed influence. The electors of the Isle of Axholme, Holland, and areas of Kesteven such as the wapentake of Loveden had considerable electoral power. The Whichcots owed part of their strength (they were not great proprietors) to family connections in the Isle and in Holland, whilst the Thorolds were popular with the Kesteven freeholders.

Moreover, the fact that the tories were not strong enough to take the whigs to the poll did not mean that their interest was negligible. Certain families, such as the Massingberds, maintained their tory tradition throughout the century, and they were joined by the weightier Custs and Chaplins. When the dominant party at Westminster was whig, independent members would sometimes be

---

[1] ASW 10/27/13.   [2] 3 ANC 8/3.

found consorting and voting with the tories. At the time of the revival of the militia in the late 1750s there were stirrings among the Lincolnshire tories. But they did not come into their own until the 1790s when, in the face of revolutionary dangers from across the Channel, the nobility and gentry became markedly more conservative.

In 1794 Pelham and Heathcote, the two largest and wealthiest whig proprietors in the county, became supporters of Pitt's government. Pelham was elevated to the peerage as baron Yarborough, and was succeeded in the county representation by Robert Vyner junior, who was returned with tory support. Two years later the young Sir Gilbert Heathcote came forward, forcing Sir John Thorold, last of the eighteenth-century style independent members, to retire. In 1802 Charles Chaplin senior, a popular tory country gentleman, succeeded Vyner without a contest. In 1807, following the dismissal of the short-lived whig administration, Heathcote tamely followed Vyner into retirement, and the tories were bold enough to try to capture his seat. Their candidate was Richard Ellison, not a member of that aristocratic class from which the county was accustomed to elect its M.P.s but nevertheless well known as a magistrate and milita officer. His hopes were dashed, however, by the appearance of Charles Anderson Pelham (Lord Yarborough's son) as a contender for Heathcote's vacant seat. After three days' polling Chaplin and Pelham were returned with 1,589 and 1,162 votes respectively, Ellison trailing with 948.

A notable feature of the polling was the number of voters, including leading gentlemen such as Edmund Turnor and Sir Joseph Banks, who gave one of their two votes to Chaplin and the other to Pelham.[3] This way of voting may have made little sense in party terms, but it made sense in terms of *county* politics. The country gentlemen preferred to avoid contests and to keep on good terms with their neighbours. The hustings were a place to demonstrate a consensus of county opinion. Banks, who was conservative in his opinions and who supported the tory interest at Boston, deprecated the introduction of partisan parliamentary politics into county elections.[4] This attitude was reinforced in the Napoleonic war period, when subscriptions were needed for other things and when the upper classes closed their ranks against threats from abroad and discontents at home.

There were stirrings among the independent politicians of Lincolnshire in 1809 and 1812. Between 1814 and 1816 the farmers,

[3] *The Poll for the County of Lincoln* ..., pr. Lincoln (William Brooke) 1807.
[4] 4 BNL box 2, Banks to Brownlow 4 Nov. 1819.

who were suffering from the rapidly falling prices for their produce, began to show interest in the independents' platform of peace, retrenchment, and reform. In 1816 Charles Chaplin died, and the lord lieutenant pushed his brother William Cust into the vacant seat. This replacement of a popular county man by a virtually unknown aristocratic nominee caused anger among tories as well as whigs, and led to a contest at the next general election in 1818. The independents had a good candidate in the whig Sir Robert Heron, who for a dozen years had cut a figure on local political platforms; but Cust retired in favour of Charles Chaplin junior, who set up an election organization that proved superior to Heron's. The result of the three-day poll in June 1818 was Pelham 3,693, Chaplin 3,069, and Heron 2,623.[5]

The contest was one of the great landowners against the small. Among the gentry there was even more cross-party voting than in 1807. Pelham and Chaplin had separate local committees but several gentlemen sat on both. Heron's only enthusiastic supporter among the gentry was Sir John Thorold, and his programme of tax reform was directed mainly at the small owner-occupying farmers—'it is in you, Independent Yeomen, that I have always relied'. It seems that the title of yeoman was adopted in parts of the county as a political as well as an economic label. Voters described as yeomen in the poll book were concentrated in the Isle of Axholme, the east bank of the Trent below Gainsborough, the wapentakes of Loveden and Aveland in Kesteven, and the wapentakes of Kirton and Skirbeck in Holland. Only in Elloe, of those regions where Heron received strong support, does the term yeomen not appear to have been in vogue among the small farmers. The following table contrasts the voting of the yeomen in 1818 with that of the gentry ('baronet', 'esquire', or holder of a military rank) and the clergy (described in the poll book as 'clerk' or 'D.D.').

	Chaplin or Chaplin + Pelham	Heron or Heron + Pelham
gentry	69·3%	19·3%
clergy	81·1%	10·8%
'yeomen'	31·2%	60·6%

Outside Boston very few of the independent voters were consistent reformers, and they were easily swayed by local and personal factors. But the 1818 election revealed a considerable strength of feeling against the ruling class of the county, especially in those areas where few gentlemen lived and none hunted.

[5] *The Poll for the County of Lincoln*, pr. Lincoln (W. Brooke) 1818.

In 1823 Pelham succeeded his father as the second baron Yarborough, and in the absence of a suitable candidate from his own family was obliged to look around for a successor to his seat. After failing to persuade Heathcote to start his son, Yarborough decided to support a candidate who had already declared himself. Sir William Amcotts Ingilby was anything but a whig. Of tory background, he had lately begun to show radical leanings. Yarborough no doubt hoped that Ingilby would split the tory and independent opposition and be returned unopposed. He reckoned without the more radical wing of the independent interest, who put up Sir John Thorold, although neither Heron nor Thorold himself wished to see a contest. The radicals took Ingilby to the poll but were soundly defeated by 3,824 votes to 1,574. Colonel Johnson, who had emerged as the leading reformer among the county's independent politicians, gave an analysis of Ingilby's support at the close of the poll. He ascribed 800 of the baronet's votes to Yarborough influence, 600 to other whig lords and gentry, 1,300 to eating and drinking motives, 500 to clergy and others with a view to patronage, and 500 to 'well paid agents and attorneys, tavern keepers, steam-packet men, publicans and sinners'. The balance of just over 100 votes he attributed to Ingilby's own influence.[6] In fact Ingilby had more personal influence than was ascribed to him by Johnson. He was the last county member, except perhaps Sir Robert Sheffield, to rely in part on a personal connection with the Isle of Axholme. But Johnson was right to stress the absence of issues in Ingilby's campaign and the predominance of personal and mercenary motives among his supporters. What Johnson did not mention was that Thorold's support also owed much to local feeling. The contest in one of its aspects was a battle between Lindsey and Holland on the one hand and Kesteven on the other. Ingilby almost annihilated the independent vote in Lindsey and Holland. In Kesteven, however, Thorold was supported not only by the independent yeomen but also by some of his tory gentry neighbours around Grantham. The voting by county divisions was as follows:[7]

	Ingilby	Thorold
Lindsey	2,984	325
Holland	557	184
Kesteven	225	1,015
out-voters	58	50
total	3,824	1,574

[6] *SM* 12 Dec. 1823.

[7] *The Poll for the County of Lincoln*, Lincoln 1824. A count of votes printed in the poll book gives a slightly different result from the official return (Ingilby 3,816, Thorold 1,575).

Ingilby, making it clear that he felt under no strong obligation to his whig sponsors, set about consolidating his popularity with the independent voters. He was returned unopposed with Chaplin at the general elections of 1826 and 1830.

REFORM AND PROTECTION

In 1831, during the period of excitement over parliamentary reform, the anti-reforming Chaplin retired from the representation of the county. As in 1818 an independent reformer, this time Johnson, was ready to come forward; but as in 1807 the Brocklesby interest supervened, and Charles Anderson Worsley Pelham, later baron Worsley and second earl of Yarborough, was returned unopposed with Ingilby. This represented roughly the current state of feeling in the county: the tories in retreat, the moderate whigs more active with the revival of reforming sentiment, and the radicals gaining ground, especially among the urban voters. The boroughs of Lincoln and Boston, followed by Grantham and Stamford, had the strongest reforming movements, and Bourne and Holbeach, also in the south of the county, took the lead among the market towns. In Lindsey there was less excitement, and over the county as a whole the villages were slow to catch the infection.

The Reform Act as eventually passed in 1832, by giving the vote to fifty-pound tenants, increased the rural and agricultural elements in the Lincolnshire electorate. The smallest tenant farmers still lacked the franchise, but in many parts of the county a rented holding of thirty or forty acres now conferred the parliamentary vote. Even more important in its immediate effect on the life of the county was the division of Lincolnshire into two two-member constituencies. Lindsey was taken as the area for the North Lincolnshire division, whilst Kesteven and Holland were put together to form South Lincolnshire. Each division was further divided into polling districts, so that whereas before 1832 the whole county polled at Lincoln, from 1832 onwards voters could poll (with some exceptions) at their nearest market town.

In terms of landed influence it was the whigs who benefited from the division of the county. Lord Yarborough, with his estates concentrated in the north of the county, could reasonably hope to return one of the two members for North Lincolnshire. Likewise in South Lincolnshire the Heathcotes would have had a strong interest had they been disposed to keep it up: in fact they preferred to concentrate on Rutland. The leading tories on the other hand found their influence reduced. Chaplin's seat was in South Lincolnshire but his Tathwell estate lay in the northern division, and this dissection of his interest was probably one reason why he never re-emerged from his parliamentary retirement after 1832.

Brownlow was in a similar position. In June 1835 he gave a lead at county level by calling a meeting in London at which registration funds were established for both divisions.[8] The parliamentary register was a new feature of post-Reform politics, and the machinery for claims and objections was a great stimulus to party organization. The Conservative association for the whole county, to which these funds were a preliminary, failed to materialize. Gentlemen such as Sheffield, Chaplin, and Trollope, though generally prepared to follow Brownlow's lead in county affairs, disliked his rigid partisanship, and still more any attempt at dictation by a peer. Brownlow's intervention in 1816 had not been welcomed. In 1841 he tried again, starting his grandson C. H. Cust for North Lincolnshire, but that too proved a failure.[9]

By 1841, however, the tide was running strongly for the Conservatives in Lincolnshire. The reforming enthusiasm apparent in small towns such as Holbeach and Spilsby in the early 1830s was beginning to evaporate, and the nonconformists, after numerous local battles on the question of compulsory church rates, were becoming more quiescent. The urban voters were losing interest in rural politics, and the declining influence of the borough of Boston in county politics after 1832 was particularly noticeable. In 1832 reformers had been returned for all four county seats—two whigs (Pelham and G. J. Heathcote) and two independent reformers (Ingilby and Henry Handley). Ingilby was defeated in 1835, Handley in 1841. In the latter year Heathcote retired, leaving Pelham (now Lord Worsley) to share the representation of the county with three Conservatives. Independence was losing its appeal to the small freeholders, and the great landowners were becoming less concerned with the 'peace of the county'. The cross-party voting that had still been in evidence at the general elections of 1832 and 1835 was negligible in 1841.

It is not surprising that in the predominantly agricultural constituencies of North and South Lincolnshire the fortunes of agriculture became an absorbing topic. Parliamentary members and candidates felt obliged to keep in touch with their farming constituents not only at but also between elections; from time to time they made tours of the market towns in their constituencies, dining

[8] 4 BNL box 14.
[9] For a more detailed account of the political movements and issues of the period see R. J. Olney, *Lincolnshire Politics 1832–1885*, 1973.

Electors

OF

LINDSEY

VOTE FOR THE

Hon. C. H. Cust.

You will then have a Representative in Parliament who never saw your faces before and whose face is perfectly unknown to you!!! A Member who knows nothing of your County business and was never in Parliament before!!! A Man who does not reside among you, and is never likely to do so!!! But never mind this when you want to see him on business, you can easily trot over to Belton in the Southern division of the County, and if you dont find him there you can trot on to the *Horse guards*, London, that is the proper place to talk about Turnips and Barley, Seeds and Wheat, at least if you Lincolnshire Farmers dont think so, so think Mr. Christopher and Mr. Chaplin who have introduced this Honorable Gentleman to you as a fit and proper person to represent you in Parliament.

A Pink Farmer.

MARSHALL, PRINTER, MERCER-ROW, LOUTH

Figure 7 *A North Lincolnshire election squib, 1841, issued on behalf of Lord Worsley, the whig candidate* (Lincolnshire Archives Office STUBBS 1/14/3)

with the farmers at their ordinaries and making speeches at the small agricultural shows. Their audiences never tired of three great questions—the need to keep up wheat prices by protective duties on imports of foreign corn, the effect of the malt tax on the barley market, and the grievances of the farmers as ratepayers.

The farmers of Lincolnshire had shown militancy as long ago as the 1780s, when the low price of wool had agitated a county still largely dependent on its sheep. From that period originated the connection of the independent interest with the graziers, for it was independent politicians like Thorold, themselves landowners in pastoral districts of the county, who took the lead in the graziers' movement. This tradition survived longest in the sheep and barley regions of Kesteven, where its last faint echoes could be heard as late as the 1860s.[10] The demand for the abolition of the malt tax became the characteristic cry from this part of the agricultural community, and it was a cry that was easily associated with demands for a more general reduction in government expenditure.

From the 1820s, however, the nature of agricultural politics in Lincolnshire was determined less by the barley growers and graziers than by the wheat growers. The acreage of wheat greatly increased with the drainage of the Fens and the inclosure of wide tracts of wold and heath land. At the same time the price of wheat went through several periods of depression, most notably 1820–2, 1833–6 and 1849–52. Farmers also had to contend with successive political attacks on the corn laws, which were modified in 1815, 1828 and 1842, and finally repealed in 1846. It was the campaigns of the agriculturists to preserve Protection in the period 1815–46 and then to restore it in the period 1849–52 that provided the most spirited aspect of Lincolnshire politics at this period. Local associations were formed to air the farmers' grievances and to circulate petitions to parliament. The Kesteven Agricultural Association and the Lincoln and Lindsey Agricultural Association both sprang up in 1826, the former inspired by independent politicians, the latter tory-influenced and strongly protectionist, its chief supporters being the large farmers of the Wolds and the area around Lincoln.[11] Organizations of this kind, proliferating in times of depression but dying down when times improved, continued to provide an important element in county politics, especially in Lindsey, down to the 1860s.

[10] See also J. A. Perkins, *Sheep Farming in Eighteenth and Nineteenth Century Lincolnshire*, Occasional Papers in Lincolnshire History and Archaeology no. 4, 1977, pp. 22 ff.
[11] *SM* 6 Jan., 17 Feb., 29 Dec. 1826.

Why was the cause of Protection associated with Conservatism? It was partly because the farmers were temperamentally resistant to change. But their natural inclinations were reinforced by the political connotations of agricultural policy. The cry for free trade and a cheap loaf came from the great industrial centres; the farmers were threatened not just (as they thought) with an attack on their means of livelihood but with a radical aggression against the whole social structure of the countryside.

In the wheat-producing division of Lindsey this alignment was hardened by local factors. The whig earls of Yarborough were suspected of equivocation on the issue of Protection; and independent opposition to them, fuelled by agricultural discontents, was bound to acquire a tory colour. In normal times the Brocklesby interest was a strong one, based on a network of connection and influence that spread even beyond the borders of the immense Yarborough estates. Even so, much depended on careful management, and on the maintenance of personal contact between the representatives of the family and the constituency. The first earl, who died in 1846, spent a good proportion of his latter years outside the county. His son, who had sedulously tended his interest while M.P. for North Lincolnshire, was unable to provide a successor from within the family and was forced to put in an incompetent squire, Sir Montague Cholmeley, as a seat warmer. This led to electoral disaster during the depression of 1849–52. The farmers got up a vigorous protectionist movement, and adopted James Banks Stanhope, the tory squire of Revesby, as an independent candidate at the general election of 1852. Despite an expenditure of £10,000, shared by Yarborough and Cholmeley, the latter was defeated at the poll. Stanhope's somewhat reluctant tory partner was R. A. Christopher, who had sat for the division since 1837, and who, partly for financial reasons, still believed in the peace of the county, though at Westminster he was a strong partisan.

THE LAST YEARS OF THE OLD SYSTEM

Although the county returned tory protectionist members in both its divisions and for most of its borough seats in July 1852, it proved useless to struggle against the tide. Lord Derby's ministry accepted the verdict of the country against Protection, and for the next twenty-five years the issue dropped out of practical politics. It was with something like relief that the county entered on a calmer and more conciliatory phase: the Conservatives became less acrimonious, the Liberals less aggressive, and whig landed influence had a final period of revival. Cholmeley got his seat back in 1857 without a contest, and in South Lincolnshire G. H. Packe of Caythorpe, having contested the division in 1857, was allowed an unopposed return two years later. Packe was an active magistrate, a relative by marriage of the Heathcotes, and a very moderate Liberal.

As at the beginning of the century, this appearance of whig strength was deceptive. The Conservative gentlemen were willing for the sake of quietness and economy to allow their Liberal neighbours a share in the representation of the county, and were content with the return of one Liberal and one Conservative in each division at the general elections of 1859 and 1865. When the county was re-divided into three constituencies in 1867 local politicians strove to preserve this balance by securing boundaries that respected territorial spheres of influence. Liberal gentry such as Packe or Weston Cracroft Amcotts (Liberal M.P. for Mid Lincolnshire from 1868 to 1874) were not strong partisans. Their politics were at least partly determined by a respect for whig traditions, a respect that was itself conservative in character. The Pelhams and Heathcotes ceased to give a clear lead. The latter in particular had always been lukewarm politicians, and Lord Aveland showed himself no friend to Reform in 1866. He died in 1867, and his son the second baron (later Lord Willoughby de Eresby and first earl of Ancaster) became a Conservative. The politics of the third earl of Yarborough were uncertain. His son the fourth earl, who came of age in 1880, began as a Liberal but went over to the Conservatives in 1885.

The second Reform Act, passed in 1867, did not add many Liberal voters to the Lincolnshire electorate, and the Ballot Act of 1872 had remarkably little effect on landed influence in the county. The Conservatives, led by new and more partisan politicians such as Henry Chaplin, Edward Stanhope, and Rowland Winn, improved their party organizations after 1868, and in 1874, at the general election which brought Disraeli to power, they took all six Lincolnshire county seats without a struggle. Liberalism was now much stronger in the boroughs, particularly in Lincoln, Grantham, and Grimsby, but borough politicians tended to keep themselves to themselves, indifferent to the eclipse of Liberalism in the countryside.

All this changed in the late 1870s, which saw a dramatic revival of Liberalism in the market towns of the county. In South and Mid Lincolnshire urban interests were not strong enough to challenge effectively the entrenched forces of rural Conservatism; but in North Lincolnshire movements at Louth and Gainsborough in 1874 led to the formation of local Liberal associations, quite independent of the old registration machinery set up by the second earl of Yarborough in the 1850s. In 1879 the enthusiasm spread to the smaller market towns of Market Rasen, Brigg, and Barton. The Grimsby Liberals took an unprecedented initiative in co-ordinating the district associations, and for the general election of 1880 a new type of candidate was adopted. Robert Laycock was not a gentleman of old Lincolnshire family: he lived in Nottinghamshire and owed his wealth to Northumberland coal. His success at the North Lincolnshire poll in April 1880, pushing a local tory squire into third place, owed very little to the support of such landowners as Yarborough and Edward Heneage.

This triumph was short-lived. Laycock died the following year, and at the ensuing by-election an old-fashioned independent Liberal, George Tomline, was defeated by a protectionist Conservative, James Lowther. The farmers of the division had since the later 1870s been suffering from a severe depression, and protectionist sentiments, suppressed since the 1850s though never entirely forgotten, had become increasingly vocal. The Liberals had little to say to the farmers, but concentrated instead on a section of the rural community that might soon be given the vote—the agricultural labourers. The Conservatives were left to enjoy their last years of dominance. The labourers, with their recent (if ultimately discouraging) experience of trades unionism and their attachment to Primitive Methodism, were bound to change the terms of reference of county politics. And so it proved in 1885.

POPULAR POLITICS

The Reform Act of 1884, giving the vote to male householders in county constituencies, more than doubled the Lincolnshire electorate. Whereas in 1871 only 34 per cent of its adult male population had the vote, in 1891 the figure was 85 per cent. As part of a redistribution of seats in 1885 Lincolnshire's electorate of 72,000 was divided into seven single-member constituencies. In Lindsey there were four divisions, centred on Gainsborough, Brigg, Louth, and Horncastle. In the south of the county were three divisions, Sleaford, Stamford, and Spalding, whose boundaries did not entirely keep to the administrative boundary between Kesteven and Holland. The abolition of double-member constituencies, together with this further political fragmentation of the county, finally put an end to the gentry's traditional concern with the peace of the county and the arrangement of compromises. After enjoying a near monopoly of the representation of Lincolnshire in parliament for centuries the great landowners were forced to give way to new men. Henry Chaplin, it is true, continued to sit for the Sleaford division until defeated in 1906. Edward Stanhope and later Lord Willoughby de Eresby had no great trouble in holding the Horncastle seat, but elsewhere candidates appeared that the old farming electorate would have scorned as foreigners and carpet-baggers. This was particularly the case in the three divisions with the largest urban electorates—Gainsborough, Brigg, and Louth.

Whether carpet-baggers or local candidates, those aspiring to be members for Lincolnshire divisions had to do more than merely attend a few markets and speak at a few ploughing meetings. Local politics were now a matter of village meetings, of travelling the length and breadth of an awkwardly shaped constituency to make full-length speeches to tiny audiences, or to open fête after village fête, whilst one's wife chatted amiably to the Liberal Women or the Primrose Dames. During the 1892 election campaign the Liberal candidate for the Louth division, R. W. Perks, drove nearly three hundred miles in ten days and spoke in nearly seventy villages.[12] Between March and November 1893 Herbert Torr held sixty-one meetings in the Horncastle division after his adoption as Liberal candidate, and this was followed by two months of concentrated activity leading up to a by-election in January 1894. It was a bitterly cold winter, and journeys by railway, carriage, and butcher's cart, interspersed by long walks through the snow, required considerable stamina. On 3 January he drove to Bratoft, 'where we had three electors and a dozen boys in a barn, the latter following us for half a mile with "Vote for Willoughby" as we drove on to Burgh'. A week later, after a wearisome journey from Horncastle via Sibsey, there was no carriage to meet the Torrs at Willoughby station and they had to walk to the meeting. But this time their reception was enthusiastic—'one of the few satisfactory village meetings'. 'From there we drove on to Alford and found a really grand meeting in full swing . . ., heat tremendous and every inch packed.' The pace was maintained until the disappointing end. The first day of the polling found them being dug out of the snow near Hagworthingham, Mrs Torr's hat having already been ruined by a tory snowball.[13]

Of the seven Lincolnshire divisions only Brigg returned a Liberal at every general election between 1885 and 1906, and even there the record was broken by a by-election in 1894. Gainsborough and Louth were usually Liberal, although both returned Conservatives in 1886, and Gainsborough again, under somewhat peculiar local

[12] Denis Crane, *The Life-Story of Sir Robert W. Perks*, 1909, p. 180.
[13] Diaries of H. J. Torr, in the possession of Mrs H. N. Nevile.

circumstances, in 1900. The Spalding division was marginal, and the three most rural and unwieldy divisions, Horncastle, Sleaford, and Stamford, were formidably though not hopelessly Conservative.

Even in the three seats which normally produced Liberal majorities, much depended on the personalities of the candidates. The Conservative victor at Brigg in 1894 was John Maunsell Richardson, the popular sporting husband of the dowager countess of Yarborough. He was assisted, it is true, by an old register and by the temporary collapse of the Liberal organization.[14] It was partly because the Liberal member for the Gainsborough division was under a cloud that he lost his seat in 1900. Perks held the Louth division from 1892 to 1910, but it is very doubtful whether any other Liberal could have done so. A Methodist, an assiduous worker in the constituency, and a rich man generous with subscriptions, he was also that rare thing among rural politicians—a speaker who could appeal simply and directly to his rural audiences. Even Perks came perilously close to losing his seat in 1895, and had to trim his sails. Previously a firm Gladstonian, even radical in tone, he became much more moderate in the later 1890s. He began voting with the tories on agricultural questions, and dropped Home Rule in 1898.[15]

The numerical weakness and at times the uncertain tone of Liberalism in Lincolnshire at this period may at first sight seem surprising. After all, that great ally of Liberalism, nonconformity, was especially strong among the newly enfranchised rural electors. The Liberal programme, with its concentration on the land question, education, and temperance, had much in it to appeal to the farm workers. In village politics the labourers might find themselves ranged against squire, parson, and large farmers on such matters as the administration of charities, the provision of allotments, and the management of the village school. There was no doubt which of the two great parties was more in sympathy with the labourers on all these issues. Furthermore the great free trade principles of the Liberal party were firmly embedded in the minds of many farm workers, especially those old enough to remember the days of the 'dear loaf' before 1846. The National Agricultural Union, led by Lord Winchilsea, a Lincolnshire landowner and former M.P. for the Spalding division, attempted to unite landlords, farmers, and labourers in a common policy for the revival of agriculture; but despite Winchilsea's local influence Lincolnshire labourers looked

[14] *The Tory*, no. 23, Dec. 1894. I owe this reference to Mr G. D. M. Block.
[15] Denis Crane, *op. cit.*, p. 199.

askance at the idea of a wage regulated according to the price of corn. At a Working Men's Liberal Association demonstration at Heckington in February 1893 it was roundly declared that the farm worker was now 'too independent to fear either the coercion of the landlord, the tyranny of the farmer, or the canting hypocrisy of the parson'.[16]

Against what might be called these natural advantages the Liberals had to contend with many less favourable aspects of rural politics. Perhaps their chief weakness was one of leadership. Local candidates were hard to find. Liberalism had all but disappeared among the squirearchy; one or two small country gentlemen such as Francis Otter of Ranby and Herbert Torr of Riseholme came forward, but neither was a very effective politician, and both lacked the popularity of a Chaplin or a Richardson. They were not outstandingly rich men, and wealth was still a prerequisite for a rural candidate. A contested election could cost £1,500, which in a period of shrinking incomes meant that few could afford to fight more than one election, let alone nurse a constituency over a number of years. Between elections there was a continuing need for organization and a constant demand for subscriptions to every flower show, sports club, and Methodist chapel in the division.

Behind each Conservative member or candidate there was in most divisions a phalanx of landed supporters still able to subscribe handsomely to the local party association. When the Hon. Murray Finch-Hatton (later Lord Winchilsea) stood for the Spalding division in 1885 his funds came largely from leading south Lincolnshire noblemen and gentlemen, mostly Kesteven residents. Lord Aveland and Earl Brownlow subscribed £250 each, followed by the marquis of Bristol with £200 and other well-known tories with £50 or £100 each.[17] No Lincolnshire Liberal candidate after 1880 could hope to draw on this kind of wealth. The lack of influential supporters was felt when it came to bringing in the out-voters, that is, people with property qualifications in a Lincolnshire division but resident elsewhere. The polling of several hundred out-voters was alleged to have played a large part in Conservative victories at several elections in this period. The conveyance of resident voters was also a problem: many of the available traps and gigs belonged to Conservative farmers.

There were a few Liberal farmers such as John Taylor Sharpe of Bardney, a prominent Lindsey politician, and W. S. Fox of Potter

[16] *SM* 10 Feb. 1893.
[17] Sir Richard Winfrey, *Memories of Forty Years and More Ago*, 1929, p. 38. I owe this reference to Mr N. Leveritt.

Hanworth, who stood for the Sleaford division in 1892. But the Liberal party continued to have little appeal for agriculturists in the throes of depression. Low prices were blamed on free trade in the 1890s, just as they had been in 1849–52, and the attempts of the Liberals to work on the grievances of tenants against their landlords were largely irrelevant. Feeling against landlords did emerge from time to time, but it subsided as rents were reduced. During the 1890s the Liberals were increasingly deprived of another traditional source of support and leadership, the middle classes in the smaller market towns. These towns were in decline like the countryside around them, and they no longer harboured many radical shopkeepers or Liberal merchants. In 1892 Otter found that in the Horncastle division it was the towns—Horncastle, Alford, and Spilsby—which failed to pull their weight: 'the villages were all right'.[18]

But were the villages all right? Local influences on the labourers remained strong, and farmers sometimes coerced their work-people. The rural population was in decline, and it was often the most active and outspoken labourers who moved away. By the mid-1890s the excitement of the period 1885–92 was evaporating, and there was less in Liberal programmes to appeal directly to the farm workers. The politics of rural nonconformity were not straightforward, especially when it came to Home Rule. The Wesleyans in particular were concerned about the religious implications of Irish self-government, and on this issue many of them were said to have abandoned their Liberal allegiance in 1892. For the more radical of the labourers, on the other hand, some Liberal candidates did not come up to scratch on religious matters. At the Horncastle by-election of January 1894 Torr was said to have 'fouled his nest by one mistake', his failure to support Welsh disestablishment.[19] Torr was not the first Liberal candidate to lose through his moderation more votes than he gained. The same had happened to the Sleaford seedsman Charles Sharpe in the South Lincolnshire election of 1880 and to Tomline in North Lincolnshire in 1881. Nevertheless there was considerable Liberal potential waiting to be exploited in more favourable circumstances. The rural successes of the Lincolnshire Liberals in 1906 revealed what they could do when they exerted themselves to the full.

POLITICS IN THE LIFE OF THE COUNTY
How deeply did party politics affect the life of the county? How far were politics important *between* parliamentary elections, and were

[18] *SM* 24 March 1893.   [19] *SM* 17 Jan. 1894.

those who took an active part in them ever more than a small
minority of the county's population? From reading the speeches of
M.P.s and other leaders of the local community one might assume
that partisanship was alien to the habits of country people, and that
only in periods of great excitement or when their livelihoods were
involved did party spirit flourish. In the summer of 1853 Cholmeley
visited the farmers of the Market Rasen district and, adverting to
Protection, hoped that 'that unfortunate question, which set father
against son and brother against brother, had been set at rest for
ever'.[20] The gentry's concern with the peace of the county has been
mentioned. Farmers took little active interest in other than bread
and butter questions; tradesmen did not like to risk displeasing their
customers; and labourers, until the last two decades of the century,
saw politics mostly in terms of parish affairs. They could not attend
political meetings during the day, and before the middle of the
century many of them could not read a newspaper, let alone afford
to buy one.[21]

It is nevertheless true that party politics affected the county at
many points, and were even an integral part of its public life. In the
days before 1832 a parliamentary election was one of the few
occasions when the county met together. In the eighteenth century
gentlemen used to come into Lincoln to stay in their town houses,
the candidates rode in at the head of their retainers, and dancing and
feasting followed the declaration of the result. The division of the
county in 1832 brought that era to an end, both socially and politically. But the county meeting, a vehicle for the expression of county
opinion on public and political subjects, was slow to die. In January
1850 a county meeting was held on the subject of Protection, and
Burton wrote to Brownlow during the proceedings that he had
never seen such a large crowd in the castle yard at Lincoln. The
magistrates, alarmed by reports of contingents from adjoining
counties and by the presence of boatmen idling in the city because of
the frost, took the precaution of enrolling three hundred special
constables.[22] The spirit of the meeting, however, was different to
that of earlier county meetings. It was a challenge by the rural
interests of Lincolnshire to the free traders of Lincoln, and had more
to do with party battles than with the old concept of independence
in county politics. Later gatherings attended by delegates from all
over Lincolnshire were not county meetings in the strict sense but
party demonstrations, engineered by the constituency organiza-

[20] *SM* 5 Aug. 1853.
[21] Newspapers were, however, read out in public houses.
[22] CoC 4/2/3, ff. 56–61.

tions. Such were the meetings on Reform in 1884 and on agricultural depression in 1886.

After 1832 party politics took its place in the seasonal round of Lincolnshire affairs. Until 1880 the county members were all large Lincolnshire landowners, and nearly all Lincolnshire residents. They visited their constituencies at the autumn ploughing meetings, and later in the century winter evenings were enlivened by lectures and debates on political subjects. The annual progress of the revising barrister to hear claims and objections in connection with the electoral register provided a focus for party workers in the constituencies, and associations were formed on a divisional and later on a more local basis.

All these activities were reported in the county press, which became more partisan after 1832. The *Stamford Mercury*, with its wide county coverage and lukewarm Liberalism, remained the most important Lincolnshire newspaper. From 1833, however, it had a strongly tory rival in the *Lincolnshire Chronicle*, founded by a body of gentry, clergy, lawyers, and others avowedly to uphold the Conservative party, the Church of England, and the agricultural interest.[23] Newspaper production was confined almost entirely to Lincoln, Boston, and Stamford in the first half of the century. After the abolition of the newspaper stamp duty in 1855 other market towns began to have their own weekly journals, but they often had too small a circulation to be partisan. By 1880, however, there were several local newspapers of pronounced party views, with the Liberal press strong especially in the north of the county.

Nineteenth-century local newspapers carried much more national news, with an emphasis on detailed parliamentary reporting, than they do today. To some extent the habit of taking sides in issues of national politics was imported into Lincolnshire, as railway communication improved and as the press spread its influence into the countryside. But the middle and lower classes of the county also caught the habit of partisanship from the gentry, who whatever their attitudes to factious behaviour in local politics had long divided themselves into whig and tory. In their minds party allegiance was closely involved with family tradition and influence. When the Revd F.C. Massingberd was dabbling in Lincoln politics in 1830 he was warned by his relative C. J. Mundy: 'Remember you are now among whigs, a subtle race, so be cautious.'[24] When the young fourth earl of Yarborough addressed his first public political meeting in 1881 he cited the tradition of his family as the chief reason for his support of the Liberal party, although that tradition

[23] *Newspaper Press Directory*, 1846, p. 192.   [24] MASS 1/61.

had been much weakened, and was to be broken by the earl himself only four years later.

The fact that there were gentlemen of various political persuasions in the commission of the peace prevented the county bench from becoming wholly partisan. It is noteworthy how often magistrates of Liberal views—W. A. Johnson, G. H. Packe, Edward Heneage, and others—rose to prominence in county affairs; but there is no denying the weight of toryism on the Lincolnshire bench, especially in the first half of the century. At times resentment came to the surface, for instance over the proceedings of the magistrates in gaol sessions against the radical Philip Ball in the 1830s or in the first elections for the Holland county council. As long as the lord lieutenant was the principal channel through which magistrates were appointed, and as long as the lord lieutenancy itself was a political appointment, party politics were bound to tincture county business. The lord lieutenant did not have an automatic influence at elections beyond that of other great landowners, but the office gave him an excuse to take the lead in co-ordinating party movements. Brownlow, as we have seen, acted in this way in 1835, and in 1857 the second earl of Yarborough received an appeal to stimulate the Liberals in South Lincolnshire. More important, by excluding troublesome politicians from the bench, by appointing politically useful and loyal clerks of the peace, and by encouraging a favourable climate at quarter sessions, a lord lieutenant could do much over the years to supplement and enlarge his personal and landed influence in the county. Brownlow did not hesitate to exploit all these means. In 1821, during a period of political disturbance, he orchestrated the signing of three almost identical 'Loyal Declarations' by the magistrates in quarter sessions.[25]

The success of Brownlow's system can be demonstrated by the comparatively minor rôle played by the Pelhams of Brocklesby in county affairs in the earlier part of the nineteenth century. The first earl of Yarborough and his son had immense landed wealth and political influence, but they had great difficulty while Brownlow held the county reins in establishing a corresponding whig influence in local government. Their candidates for the bench were consistently regarded as light-weight, and their attempts to lead county opinion were suppressed where possible. In 1834 Pelham wrote to Brownlow suggesting a county meeting to promote a wool fair at Lincoln, but received a very dampening reply.[26]

There were other channels, however, through which whig influence could flow, and other aspects of county life that, though

[25] 4 BNL box 2.   [26] 4 BNL box 3.

ostensibly non-political, could be used in consolidating a political interest. The Brocklesby hounds were an asset that Brownlow could not match. A county agricultural society had been founded under Brownlow's patronage in 1819, but the first earl of Yarborough countered with the more successful North Lincolnshire Agricultural Society in 1836. Only in the declining days of the Yarborough interest, in 1869, was one society again established for the whole county. The second earl of Yarborough, who succeeded his father in 1846, paid attention to the commercial as well as the agricultural interests of north Lincolnshire, becoming chairman of the Manchester, Sheffield, and Lincolnshire Railway. He was also a keen freemason, joining the Witham Lodge at Lincoln in 1846 and becoming Provincial Grand Master for Lincolnshire three years later.[27] Both the railway and the masonic connection gave Yarborough ample opportunities for patronage, thus creating ties of obligation that could be brought into play at election times.

Patronage of a more directly political kind was also of much importance. For middle-class people, especially lawyers and clergymen, it often supplemented political conviction as a motive for engaging in constituency work. Many posts at the disposal of nineteenth-century governments were filled not by public competition but through private influence. Lincolnshire lacked a naval dockyard, but there were plenty of excise and post office appointments tenable within the county. These situations were 'as a matter of course, given to the Member least opposed to the ministry of the day'.[28] Other opportunities to recommend candidates for appointments arose less regularly. In 1847 Yarborough, though no longer member for North Lincolnshire, obtained the valuable new post of county court judge for a farming tenant, J. G. Stapylton Smith of Melton Ross.[29] In 1852 R. A. Christopher, having been given office in Lord Derby's government, secured the receivership of the northern division of the crown estates for his agent, John Higgins of Alford.[30] As late as 1898 Henry Chaplin as President of the Poor Law Board made J. A. Cole of Roxholme poor law auditor for Lincolnshire. Cole was a leading Conservative in Chaplin's constituency. Living off a dwindling agricultural rent roll, he was no doubt glad of a salary of about £1,000 a year.[31]

[27] William Dixon, *A History of Freemasonry in Lincolnshire*, Lincoln 1894, pp. 138–9. The Liberal connections of Lincolnshire masons were strong down to the 1860s.

[28] Uppleby papers, in the possession of Professor and Mrs J. Barron, Charles Chaplin to G. C. Uppleby 10 Jan. 1830.

[29] YARB 9, letter books.   [30] *Archivists' Report* 25 (1973–5), p. 68.

[31] *SM* 14 Oct. 1898.

Although solicitors were often successful in obtaining local posts they did less well from government patronage. There were few appointments which could be held concurrently with their legal practices, and for even those few a solicitor was not always the best choice. Yarborough did not choose one of the several solicitors in his pay for the county court judgeship in 1847 because it would have caused rancour and disappointment among the rest.[32] Clergy frequently failed in their efforts to secure preferment. One had to be exceptionally well connected or exceptionally lucky in one's timing to obtain one of the really good livings in the prime minister's gift. When the Revd James Morton was offered Holbeach in 1832 through the influence of his old pupil Lord Grey, he hesitated about accepting a living in such a dreary part of the country. But, mindful of the proverb about the bird in the hand, he decided it would be unwise to wait for something better.[33] The Revd E. R. Larken had been presented to the rectory of Burton-by-Lincoln by his brother-in-law the sixth Lord Monson, but he lived in hope that his political work for the Liberal party in North Lincolnshire would be rewarded with something better. His great white hope was Waddingham, whose wealthy pluralist incumbent, the Revd William Cooper, died in 1856. Larken arranged that as soon as news of Cooper's demise reached him he would telegraph 'Waddingham is vacant' to Yarborough, who was then to exert his charm on the prime minister.[34] But it was no use. Yarborough wrote consolingly to Larken, 'When such good livings . . . become vacant one cannot be surprised at Ministers wishing to oblige their friends irrespective of politics.'[35]

The patronage system was thus of limited efficacy. It did not always work, and it could cause more disappointment than gratification. There were, moreover, those who chose to stand apart from the net of mutual influence and obligation. Sir Charles Anderson wished to obtain a Treasury post for a connection in 1854, but, as he explained to his friend Bishop Samuel Wilberforce, he preferred to avoid the obvious local channel. 'I do not like to put myself under any obligation to Lord Yarborough,' he wrote, 'because I don't at all know if I should support his man at the next election.'[36] Others objected to the whole patronage system. At the beginning of the century a demand for the reduction of government pensions and places had been a chief plank of the independents' platform. As late as 1855 the issue was revived by the expense and

[32] YARB 9, letter book 1847–8.   [33] MISC DEP 306.
[34] MON 25/13/10/8.   [35] YARB 9, letter book 1856–7.
[36] Bodl. MS. Dep. c.·190.

mismanagement of the Crimean War. Speaking at Boston at a
meeting on administrative reform, the veteran Liberal Alderman
Noble called for army and civilian officials to be selected on merit
and not through party or family interest.[37]

THE TOWNS

In the early nineteenth century the politics of patronage and influence were as familiar in the parliamentary boroughs of Lincolnshire
as they were in the county. There was an Ancaster interest at
Boston, a Monson interest at Lincoln, and a Yarborough interest at
Grimsby. The families of Cust and Manners had power at
Grantham, and at Stamford, the nearest Lincolnshire approxi-
mation to a pocket borough, the Cecils, marquises of Exeter, held
almost undisputed sway. By the 1850s, however, county and
borough politics were diverging. In 1852 the Lincolnshire boroughs
returned protectionist members in sympathy with their rural hin-
terlands, but in all except Stamford industrial interests were coming
to the fore, and with them a new type of politics. At Lincoln the old
whig interest was forced into an unholy alliance with the tories
against the more progressive politicians. At Grimsby the railway
interest became an independent force in the borough. Even Grantham shook off aristocratic leadership and returned two Liberals in
1868. At Boston the whig or orange interest, never very strong,
became simply a means of attracting wealthy candidates to spend
money in the town. The growing independence of the boroughs fed
on urban resentment of rural interests. In the eyes of many townsmen it was the landowners who wished to hold down commerce
by maintaining the corn laws, and whose privileges were represented most gallingly by gross inequalities in rating.

Seen from within, however, urban politics took on a different
aspect, with class and religious rivalries destroying the appearance
of unanimity. A Liberal canvass of Lincoln in 1855 secured promises
from no solicitor or Anglican clergyman and from only one doctor.
'If this', said the ironmaster Nathaniel Clayton, 'did not show a war
with the professional interest against the commercial and mercan-
tile interest, he did not know what did.'[38] Here was one form of
property and social position pitted against another. Later in the
century Lincoln politics became more a battle of the propertied
against the propertyless. As early as 1836 a poll of the parish of
Horncastle on the church rate question had shown alarming symp-
toms of democracy. The rate was defeated by 270 votes to 242,

[37] *SM* 18 May 1855.   [38] *SM* 28 Dec. 1855.

although two-thirds of the town in terms of rateable value had been on the side of the Church.[39]

Church rates were also a lively issue in Louth, which was a municipal though not a parliamentary borough; there religion fuelled the fires of many a party battle. If Louth babies were not actually born little Liberals or Conservatives, their whole lives could declare their religious if not their political allegiance. As children they would be sent either to the National (Church) or British (non-sectarian) school. Later they would vote for councillors on party lines and take a political stand on such matters as charities or Temperance. (In 1853 1,000 people were said to have signed a petition against Sunday drinking, in a town of only 10,000 inhabitants.) And when they died they would lie in the burial ground either among the churchmen or across the road among the dissenters. The Liberals of Louth, stimulated by the Municipal Reform Act of 1835, made great headway in the 1830s against the old clerical and corporation interests. They lost ground in the 1840s but staged a revival in the mid-1850s, a time of exceptional activity among the nonconformists. In 1862 the Liberals made an effort to recapture the burial board, and a meeting was held at which John Booth Sharpley, a merchant and a leading Wesleyan Reformer, reviewed the progress of the dissenting cause. 'Of course some would be ready to say this was a party meeting: he unhesitatingly avowed that it was; it would be folly to deny it. It was well known that there were two great parties in the town, Conservative and Liberal.' At the ensuing municipal election, however, some of the Wesleyans, who did not regard themselves as political dissenters, broke ranks and voted with the Conservative and Church party.[40]

In a small market town, even more than in a fair-sized parliamentary borough, it was almost impossible to conceal one's political actions. Poll books were occasionally published after municipal and even parish as well as parliamentary contests, and word soon got round of any change in allegiance. Tradesmen, especially when dependent on a few wealthy customers, were vulnerable to pressure. When the Market Rasen coach builder Lawrence Dawson died in 1889 it was thought worthy of public record that he had managed to build up a good business 'without in the least concerning himself with party affairs'.[41] Political action and political opinion (if the latter existed) were not always the same thing. In

[39] *An Account of Persons Assessed to the Poor Rate, in the Parish of Horncastle, and of the manner in which they voted at the poll for a Church Rate* . . . , pr. Horncastle (Jas. Babington) 1836.
[40] *SM* 7 and 21 Nov. 1862.   [41] *SM* 10 May 1889.

1855 Clayton remarked not only on the class divisions in Lincoln but on the prevalence of 'breeches-pocket feeling'. 'Most men seemed to make the election a personal question,' he lamented, and their main concern was to gauge the effect on their businesses of voting one way or another.

If the eastern side of the county was more politically alive than the inland districts, it also contained the two most corrupt boroughs in the county, Grimsby and Boston. In 1876 a royal commission on corrupt practices at Boston reported that 'the views of the electors on political subjects are not enlarged, a speech from a candidate on such a topic is the last thing they care to listen to; and the cherished wish of all classes is to see the navigation of the Witham restored, and the town reinstated in its ancient commercial prosperity'. About 600 of the voters were among the victims of this commercial decay, and of these the fishermen were said to be the most corrupt. The Conservatives spent over £2,000 at the general election of 1868, and ten years later Thomas Garfit managed to spend £600 on an uncontested by-election. At the general election of 1880 'the system of corruption adopted was that of making a number of gifts of money and of giving corrupt employment in the hopes of votes being given'. Direct bribery was less common than indiscriminate largesse. Neither side, however, could calculate accurately the effect of its largesse, and the result was to heighten rather than diminish excitement. 'The name of whig and tory has merged into that of Liberal and Conservative, but the blue and pink parties still regard each other with the same jealousy as of old.'[42]

WIDER ISSUES

As the nineteenth century progressed more and more of Lincoln-shire's population engaged in party-political activity, and did so more and more regularly. The constituency associations, the demonstrations, the speechmaking, and the amount of political news carried by the local press in the 1890s must have been a source of amazement to the older inhabitants of the county; for them in their youth politics had been a sporadic and more spontaneous phenomenon.

Yet the politics of the 1810s and 1820s were more truly an expression of Lincolnshire's county consciousness than were the politics of the 1890s. With the decline in landed influence went the decline of political arrangements and compromised elections designed to preserve the peace of the county. The last time this was

[42] *Parl. Papers*, 1876 XXVIII, 1881 XXXVIII.

attempted was in 1868, and then, in South Lincolnshire, it broke down before the election took place. The real blow was the division of the county into two constituencies in 1832. Gradually the regional features of county politics—the orbit of the Yarborough interest, the independent Isle of Axholme, the grazing districts of Kesteven—became blurred. Local divisions were increasingly replaced by class distinctions, a process much accelerated by the decline of the whigs and the emergence of Liberalism among the farm workers in the 1870s and 1880s. Increasingly too the subjects discussed at political meetings were not of local or county but of national and imperial interest. Ireland and the foreign policy of successive governments were matters of more lively concern in the Lincolnshire of the 1890s than similar topics could have been fifty years before. In 1888 a working man in the Brigg division made a walking stick entirely of leather for Mr Gladstone, and was taken to present it in person to the Grand Old Man.[43] His tribute was symbolic of the de-localization of Lincolnshire politics.

[43] *SM* 27 April 1888.

CHAPTER IX

THE COUNTY IN 1900

POPULATION AND OCCUPATIONS

I N three inter-connected ways the Lincolnshire of 1900 was strikingly different from that of 1800. The ancient county had more than doubled its population, from 208,625 in 1801 to 498,847 in 1901; the population of 1901 was to a much greater extent concentrated in the larger towns; and communications between town and town, village and village, had been revolutionized.

The most startling change was the growth of Great Grimsby, which had 63,138 inhabitants by 1901. With its railway, docks, and fishing industry, it was something of a foreign body in the north Lindsey landscape: many of its immigrants had come from outside the county rather than from the surrounding villages. Lincoln, with 48,784 people in 1901, came second to Grimsby in size as it had come second to Boston a hundred years before. But no other town in Lincolnshire could now rival Lincoln and Grimsby. The borough of Grantham had 17,593 inhabitants, the borough of Boston 15,667, Gainsborough 17,660, and Louth only 9,158. Now that Grimsby was a county borough in its own right, Lincoln was the undisputed capital of Lindsey, and exerted more influence over the county as a whole than it had in 1800. The railway system of the county, as nearly complete by 1900 as it ever would be, meant that most Lincolnshire residents could get to Lincoln, transact their business, and be home again the same day.

The railways may have strengthened the position of Lincoln as a centre of communications in the county, but in other respects the old patterns were confirmed by the new mode of transport. East–west routes still carried more trade than the north–south routes. Grimsby was connected with Doncaster, Sheffield, and Manchester, and Lincoln with the Midlands through Newark and Nottingham. The Great Northern Railway had many more miles of track in the county than the Midland or the Manchester, Sheffield, and Lincolnshire (by 1900 renamed the Great Central), but the G.N.R. main line followed a route similar to that of the Great North Road, whilst the East Lincolnshire line, from Peterborough through Spalding and Boston to Louth and Grimsby, never carried as much traffic as had been expected.

Lincoln, Grimsby, Grantham, and Gainsborough had been greatly affected by the coming of the railways and by the growth of new industries. A few other towns were entirely a product of the nineteenth century. Iron ore quarrying and smelting were transforming the small heathland settlements of Frodingham, Scunthorpe, Brumby, and Crosby into a dramatically industrial corner of the county, although their total population in 1900 was still under 10,000. Cleethorpes had burgeoned from a group of cottages inhabited by Methodist fishermen into a resort of 12,500 people. Woodhall Spa, known as 'the English Kreuznach' on account of its bromo-iodine waters, was developed in the late 1880s by 'a syndicate of Lincolnshire gentlemen', and the railway brought it 47,000 visitors in 1889.[1] Its permanent population, however, was under 1,000 in 1901.

On the other hand there were several small market towns and many villages whose population declined during the second half of the century. Horncastle had 4,921 inhabitants in 1851 and 4,374 forty years later. Caistor declined from 2,166 people to 1,788 over the same period. Folkingham by 1900 had lost its coach service, its market, its sessions, and its prison, and its population had sunk from 820 in 1841 to 502 in 1901. Binbrook, a populous agricultural village of over 1,300 people in 1860, was by 1900 sinking towards the 1,000 mark and was to sink further in the early twentieth century. Such places were already losing population by emigration in the 1860s and 1870s, and the agricultural depression of the 1880s and 1890s did nothing to stop the flow. Henry Winn (1816–1914) of Fulletby near Horncastle attributed the exodus from the villages to two factors above all, the railways and education. 'I taught in a village school myself several years,' he recorded, 'and nearly all the boys passing through that school were lost to agriculture.' One went to London to be a policeman; one family of four boys entered the Lincoln foundries; whilst 'the smartest and best of the young men found employment upon the railways, a few in the post office, and many in the rural police'.[2] This exodus is borne out by the occupational tables in the census returns; between 1861 and 1891 the number of people working directly in agriculture fell from about 60,000 to 54,000, whilst the number involved in crafts, trades, and industry rose from 30,000 to 39,000. By 1891 there were in addition nearly 19,000 engaged in occupations connected with railways, docks, fishing, ironstone working, and general labouring, thus turning the

[1] *SM* 30 May and 31 Oct. 1890.
[2] Henry Winn, 'Some Reasons for the depopulation of Lincolnshire Villages in the nineteenth century', written *c*.1900, *Lincs. Historian* no. 6 (autumn 1950) p. 232.

agriculturists into a minority of the county's productive population.

The agriculturists were not the only dwindling group. Publicans were reduced from 1,247 in 1861 to 859 in 1891. (In 1890, however, Caistor still had thirteen licensed houses—one for every 143 inhabitants.) Millers shrank from 1,503 to 1,001, a measure of the growth of steam milling and the decline of village windmills. The most rapidly expanding occupations, besides engineering, fishing and ironstone mining, were those connected with road and rail transport, administration, and services. Railways and docks have already been mentioned; but it is also interesting to note the increase in the number of carters and carriers (from 439 in 1861 to 1,153 in 1891) and the growth in coach making (from 247 coach makers in 1861 to 376 in 1891). Those employed by central or local government including the police rose from 641 to 1,370, and with them rose the supply of teachers to educate them, clerks to copy their letters, and printers, messengers, and postmen to reproduce and distribute their official notices.

More than many counties, Lincolnshire in 1900 was visually and architecturally a product of the preceding hundred years. The 'great rebuilding' that had begun centuries earlier in counties nearer London affected Lincolnshire mainly after 1800. New farmhouses were built for the new-style farmers, and new sheds and yards for their improved livestock. Cottages were run up for the rapidly growing rural population, and village brickyards multiplied to keep pace with demand, for brick and tile was the universal fashion, rapidly superseding stone, mud, and thatch. By 1900, however, the old materials had not entirely vanished. A report of a fire at Sausthorpe in 1888 described the house involved as 'a roomy old-fashioned one, being thatched and composed of mud and stud, with brick facings and walls in part, and massive timber beams'.[3] Once an inn, it was now occupied by a farm foreman.

Many churches in the county had been restored or completely rebuilt in the middle years of the century. The money came partly from wealthy benefactors, but large sums were raised by often small and poor congregations. The parish of Harrington had only 114 souls in 1851, but, led by the squire and the parson, it raised £1,000 towards a new church by S. S. Teulon in 1854–5. At the same time the rector acquired a new parsonage house by the same architect. In many other Lincolnshire villages the rebuilt parsonage, usually next door to the church, gave a local dignity to the Establishment that had been lacking fifty years before. In 1800 schools

[3] *SM* 16 Nov. 1888.

and prayer meetings had been held in private houses in many Lincolnshire villages, but by 1850 most parishes had a neat low school-room and a small box-like Methodist chapel. After the middle of the century chapels grew in size and architectural pretension as building mania seized village societies. According to White's *Directory* the Free Methodists of Normanby-by-Spital spent £1,000 on their new chapel in 1864, and that, needless to say, was without the aid of squire or parson. In some places it was the chapel, not the church, that became the dominant architectural feature of the village.

In the last quarter of the century local brickmaking declined, but the railways supplied the expanding building industry of the county with London brick and Welsh slate. Most towns and large villages could by 1900 boast a few smart new villas, inhabited by professional men and tradesmen who fifty years before would have been found living in the market place or over their shops. Where there was a railway station there would also be a Station Road, comparatively well-surfaced and lined with respectable artisans' terraces or semi-detached cottages. The towns of Lincolnshire in 1900 looked cleaner and less 'rural' than they had thirty years before. They were better drained and more brightly lit. Spilsby might be slow to understand the importance of main drainage or Lincoln the necessity of a pure water supply, but Sleaford at the end of the century had an active district council which believed not only in drains but in asphalt pavements and electricity.

All these demographic and economic changes affected Lincolnshire's regional balance, which during the century tipped away from the south of the county and towards the north. In the 1820s much of the county's activity and prosperity was concentrated in Kesteven, Holland and south-eastern Lindsey: by the 1880s the most rapidly improving areas were mostly in north and west Lindsey. There was a corresponding shift in social, administrative, and political life. From the 1840s the politics of North Lincolnshire became more vital than those of the South, and from the 1860s the nobility and gentry of Kesteven ceased to dominate county affairs. In the mid-Victorian period the nearness of southern Lincolnshire to London became of less significance than the strengthened links of other parts of the county with the industrial Midlands, Yorkshire and Lancashire.

COUNTY INSTITUTIONS

Apart from the innovations of the county councils the uppermost social and administrative layer of the county looked superficially in

1900 much as it had in 1800. The high sheriff and the grand jury still assembled to meet the judges of assize; the lord lieutenant apparently retained many of his old functions; Brocklesby and Belton were still the arbiters of county society; and Lincoln still had its races and its stuff ball. But much had changed beneath external appearances. At the highest social level fashion had altered and restricted the appointed seasons for county gatherings. The autumn was now spent on the Scottish moors, not in the English countryside, and continental excursions often followed the end of the London season. During the season, it is true, the formation (or revival) of the London Lincolnshire Society in 1886 gave those with county connections the chance to come together at one of the big London restaurants or hotels. But the only regular time for residence in Lincolnshire for such magnates as Lord Brownlow was the Christmas and new year season. The stuff ball was moved from November to January in about 1890, and by 1900 was well-established in its new position in the calendar, drawing parties from all the big houses within ten or fifteen miles of the city. The equivalent at Grantham was the hospital ball, where a party from Belton generally set the tone. It became common in the 1890s for the local papers to carry reports of the company and the ladies' dresses on such occasions. At the Grantham Hospital ball in January 1891 as readers of the *Stamford Mercury* were informed, Lady Henrietta Turnor 'looked exceedingly well in salmon brocade, trimmed with maroon velvet'.[4] Despite improved communications Lincoln balls and assemblies drew on a smaller area of the county than they had in the early nineteenth century. The Lincoln races, now held in March and October, were numerously rather than fashionably attended.

The assizes, too, had lost their social importance. The social composition of the grand jury was remarkably unchanged, but it now had little to do. The last entry in the grand jury book records the death in 1891 of Sir Charles Anderson, its foreman on many occasions.[5] Taking the high shrievalty signified the arrival in county society of the newly rich, but so it had since the 1860s. If Lincolnshire's industrialists took their turn more frequently in the 1890s, that was partly because they had more money to spare for entertainment. The loss in real power suffered by the lord lieutenancy has already been described. In the case of the third earl Brownlow his position in the county was not helped by the fact that he was so seldom in it. His largest estates were in Shropshire, and his grandest country house was Ashridge in Hertfordshire.

[4] *SM* 9 Jan. 1891.   [5] CoC 2/1, p. 383.

By 1900 hunting, still the principal organized amusement of the countryside, was recovering from the worst effects of the agricultural depression, but it was inevitably affected by changed social conditions. The subscriptions of the gentry were less forthcoming, the large farmers less prosperous, and the number of urban objectors to cruel sports more numerous and vocal. At a social evening of the Louth Liberal Club in April 1897 Perks noted that the temporary absence of a Conservative candidate for the division had left the South Wold hunt £50 per annum the poorer: Perks himself had no intention of making up the deficit.[6] Unsympathetic attitudes were not confined to townspeople. As early as 1888 the master of the South Wold, E. P. Rawnsley of Raithby, made a public appeal to farmers to remove barbed wire during the winter months.[7] If hunting was less than flourishing, however, shooting was more popular in the county in 1900 than perhaps it had ever been before. Game preservation increased especially in southern Kesteven, where the poor soils had been particularly hardly hit by the depression.

In the sphere of more typically middle-class institutions, activity on a county scale was much greater than it had been a century before. The Lincolnshire Agricultural Society was formed by a junction of societies for the north and south of the county in 1869, and its annual show soon became the major county event that it remains to this day. In the 1890s it was joined by two successful specialist bodies, to promote the breeding of long-wool sheep and red short-horn cattle respectively. To hear Sir John Thorold, chairman of the sheep-breeders' association, urging ladies to wear wool was to appreciate one thread of Lincolnshire life that went back unbroken to the late eighteenth century. The county Chamber of Agriculture, more avowedly political in its objects and connected with a Central Chamber in London, was never a great success. From its inception in 1867 it fluctuated uneasily between outspokenness and deference to the landlords. By 1900 it had less than 200 members.

Meanwhile other middle-class groups—the lawyers, the doctors, the land agents—had all formed county bodies. The Church, too, was more in evidence in 1900 than it had been in 1800. Since the loss of Nottingham in 1884 the diocese had been co-terminous with the county. Bishop King was too ritualistic for some shades of clerical and lay opinion, but his persecution brought him as much sympathy as hostility, and his simple sermons to country congregations

[6] *SM* 16 April 1897. [7] *SM* 9 Nov. 1888.

won him many hearts. The Diocesan Conference, first held in 1872, was a forum in which leading laymen such as Edward Heneage and William Garfit could express their views on Church affairs.[8] Education, meaning the defence of the National schools, was one of the favoured topics. Indeed, schools and hospitals were as much a matter of concern in the 1890s as they had been in the 1810s. The county hospital was rebuilt on a new site in 1878 and enlarged through the generosity of Joseph Ruston in 1891. In 1893 Lord and Lady Winchilsea helped to form the Lincolnshire Nursing Association to provide district nurses.

In contrast with the established Church, the Methodists, who since 1800 had transformed the cultural life of Lincolnshire, had no respect for ancient boundaries. The circuits that the Wesleyans established around Lincoln and Grantham, for instance, took in villages in Nottinghamshire and Leicestershire respectively. Moreover, with its centralized administrative structure and its itinerant ministry, Wesleyanism was a powerful solvent of local attitudes.

THE COUNTRY CALENDAR

The characteristic institutions of the market towns and villages of Lincolnshire showed the same mixture of continuity and change. Even in those towns which had become dependent mainly on industry for their prosperity, the major events of the year were still in 1900 connected with the farming calendar. Fairs, markets, and agricultural societies did not escape the effects of the great depression, but after a low period at the end of the 1880s those that survived regained part of their vitality in the 1890s.

The great Horncastle horse fair had shrunk from three weeks to three days by 1888, and by the end of the century Boston sheep fair was a quarter of its former size. Holland was no longer a grazing region, and most of the 7,000 or 8,000 sheep that were penned were brought by dealers from Louth or Lincoln, but the activity of the fair still lasted three days—sheep on the Thursday, beasts on the Friday, and amusements on the Saturday. In 1899 the Great Northern Railway ran fifteen special trains to bring visitors to the town. Smaller fairs in remoter towns had dwindled to one-day affairs of not much greater commercial or social importance than an ordinary market. The Lincoln April fair, however, continued to thrive, filling the city's hotels and lodging houses with dealers, attracting

[8] See J. H. Overton and E. Wordsworth, *Christopher Wordsworth, Bishop of Lincoln*, 1888, p. 236.

stock and sheep breeders from all over the country and gaining a continental reputation for riding and driving horses.[9]

By 1900 little or no hiring was done at the May statutes in the smaller towns such as Kirton-in-Lindsey, Holbeach, or Market Deeping. At other places the days specially assigned for holding statutes went out of favour, although the weekly market following leaving or 'pag-rag' day still saw some hiring of farm servants—generally unmarried men and boys: married men were by 1900 more frequently hired from Lady Day to Lady Day, and were increasingly advertised for in the newspapers. For female domestic servants the registry office was gaining in popularity as a more refined alternative to market-place bargaining, and it was reported in 1896 that girls for milking were 'almost extinct'. In 1888 the decline of the statutes was attributed comprehensively to 'increased education, greater facilities of communication, migration to towns and emigration to our young and vigorous colonies, political agitation, and a growing disinclination to any system of labour contract that limits individual independence'.[10]

But the statute had life in it still. Hiring fairs flourished at Lincoln and Grimsby, and there were even movements to institute new statute sessions at Grantham and Stamford, in 1888 and 1889 respectively. In 1900 farm servants were still being hired at Spilsby, Market Rasen, Brigg, and elsewhere, whilst Scunthorpe that year saw its biggest statute yet, with farmers attending from Nottinghamshire and Yorkshire. Even when little hiring took place the statute fair remained popular with the labouring class as a social occasion; a week's holiday was taken following May Day, and servants were reluctant to re-engage themselves until they had enjoyed their spree. There was less drunkenness and violence than earlier in the century, but a steam roundabout, various stalls, and a dance in the evening were expected, after which the young people would part 'seldom with tears, often with kisses' for the coming year of labour.[11]

By the 1880s the autumn ploughing meetings were decidedly less of an attraction than the spring fairs. 'The men do not care to excel in ploughing as they used to do,' it was said at the Long Sutton Agricultural Society shortly before it broke up in 1888. 'If boys would love the plough more than their bicycles they would be sure to get on,' a Bourne audience was told in 1900.[12] Only the Alford ploughing meeting, still a useful platform for the local M.P., was still in a flourishing state in 1900, although the Bourne meeting had

[9] SM 12 May 1899, 23 April 1897.   [10] SM 22 May 1896, 18 May 1888.
[11] SM 24 May 1889.   [12] SM 17 Feb. 1888, 19 Oct. 1900.

been revived in 1898 by amalgamating it with Edenham. But to replace these autumn events, the weeks after harvest being particularly depressing ones at this period, there was a great increase in summertime activities. Flower shows and foal shows became the rage in every market town and many villages.

In the winter months there was a growth in the number and range of evening entertainments. The professional theatre had declined in the market towns; but the railways brought speakers, some of them distinguished, to address meetings on every conceivable subject. 'The inhabitants of Spalding,' it was said in January 1888, 'can never be at a loss for amusement on winter evenings. ... A meat tea for twopence and a grand concert for a penny are certainly prices which even the poorest or the most penurious need not grudge; and these luxuries of modern times are provided every Saturday evening at the Corn-exchange.' At Caistor the growing demand for such entertainments, harmless though they seem to have been, was attributed to a 'decided relaxation of religious discipline'.[13]

In the villages the churches and chapels were still important centres of social activity: indeed, compared with a hundred years before, the existence of hundreds of Methodist chapels all over the county and the flourishing activities associated with them were the most remarkable feature of Lincolnshire village life. The celebration of the Wesleyan Sunday School anniversary at Castle Bytham in May 1889 provides a not untypical example. At the chapel service on the Sunday there were special hymns and recitations and a preacher from Peterborough. The next day the children processed through the village, with band, flags, and hymn singing, to Alfred Gordon's farm, where they sat down to tea at four o'clock, followed by 130 grown-ups at five o'clock. Games and more music concluded the festivities, and £4 was raised for the funds—'a small advance on last year'.[14] The only secular events to rival the chapel red-letter days were the annual celebrations of the friendly societies. Although there were still local independent sick clubs in the 1890s, most village benefit societies were branches of the Foresters or some other large organization. The strength of these societies at the end of the century may be connected with the fact that the labourer could now save a little more than formerly. The thrift of villagers is also indicated by the number of village pig clubs active in the 1890s. One such club at Ashby near Scunthorpe had 102 members in January 1896, insuring 141 pigs.[15]

[13] SM 13 Jan. 1888.   [14] SM 24 May 1889.
[15] SM 10 Jan. 1896. See also F. W. Brooks, 'A Village Pig Club', Lincs. Mag. vol. 2 (1934–6), p. 241.

At all levels of society women played a greater part in the life of the county in the 1890s than they had ever done before. They still had no vote at a parliamentary election, but they could participate in county, district, and parish elections. They were better educated, they had views of their own, and were beginning to express them. Both political parties formed their local female supporters into associations, and excellent canvassers and leaflet distributors they proved to be. The established Church gave little scope for female activists, but the case was different among the Methodists, where women often held local office. The day was not far distant when women's institutes were to become a power in Lincolnshire, and when ladies were to be admitted even to the magistrates' bench.

THE GREAT DEPRESSION

'Father has been to a sale at Hainton walk', noted Fanny Fieldsend of Orford in her diary on 31 October 1887. 'Mr Hibbitts has made an assignment. There are many farms given up, we don't know who to hear of leaving next. How long will this agricultural depression last?'[16]

Over such a predominantly agricultural county as Lincolnshire the depression in farm prices and the poor seasons that set in in the late 1870s were bound to cast a long shadow. Lincolnshire did not suffer as badly as Suffolk, where the heavy clays became almost unworkable and the very light sandy soils went partially out of cultivation, but the fall in the price of wheat meant that Lincolnshire suffered more than the pastoral counties of the north and west of England. Some parts of the county, notably the Wolds, did not markedly deteriorate. But then the traditional way was the only way they could be farmed. Few parts of Lincolnshire, or so it was maintained at the time, were suitable for conversion to pasture, which was in any case an expensive business, requiring heavy capital outlay on stock and buildings; and many farms were too far from centres of population and too poorly served by railways to make a change to market gardening practicable. In Holland some of the small farmers led the way in bulb growing from the mid-1880s, and the potato was an invaluable stand-by. New crops were also experimented with, less vigorously, in the Isle of Axholme. Elsewhere farmers struggled on with an increasing sense of hopelessness.

The effect on the great landowners can be fairly accurately gauged. Between 1879 and 1892 rents fell 20 per cent on some

[16] MISC DEP 265/7.

estates and as much as 60 per cent on others. Net income fell even more sharply, because landlords were not able to cut back their expenditure in proportion. To attract new tenants or to keep old ones repairs had to be undertaken that the tenants had formerly done themselves, and it became usual for landlords to take over the payment of tithes. Edmund Turnor, tenant for life of 21,000 acres in Lindsey and Kesteven, experienced a drop in net annual income from £28,000 in 1878 to £16,000 in 1893. The latter figure seems enough to be going on with, but it represented a very small return on the capital that had been poured into the estate over many years. Lord Ancaster, with his Kesteven estate on relatively poor land and his Lindsey coast estate heavily encumbered, was especially hardly hit; his net income in 1893 was £14,394, a return of only 2·2 per cent on the £1,039,551 he had spent on improvements since 1872. He told a royal commission in 1894: 'I thought that by expending large sums of money on my property, keeping it in good repair, and getting really good tenants, my son would one day be able to reap the advantage of it, and pay off the charges made for the benefit of members of the family.' But the recent introduction of estate duty coming on top of his other problems had caused him to abandon hope.[17]

The depression exaggerated differences that had always been significant in landed society—the difference between those owners solely dependent on landed income and those with other resources, and among the purely agricultural landlords the difference between those with clear incomes and those with encumbrances. Mortgage payments and jointures remained constant while incomes fell, so that in some cases squires were forced either to retrench and live quietly on their estates or to let their large houses and go to live cheaply on the south coast or even abroad. In 1890, for instance, F. W. Allix let West Willoughby Hall to a Captain Rennie and retired to Brussels, where he died in 1894.[18] Country house letting particularly affected Kesteven, where attractive seats were thicker on the ground than elsewhere in the county. It was rare, however, for a large estate to be sold. Owners hung on rather than lose a large proportion of their capital, and buyers willing to sink *their* capital in estates that would yield only two or three per cent on their outlay were now hard to find. The declining value of agricultural land is illustrated by the East Firsby estate, of 534 acres, which changed hands around 1852 at £17,000 but which in 1899 fetched only £6,700.[19]

[17] *Parl. Papers*, 1895 XVI, pp. 176, 230.   [18] *SM* 12 Sept. 1890, 19 Oct. 1894.
[19] *SM* 25 Aug. 1899.

Among the farmers it was perhaps the occupiers of land under the largest and most generous landlords who weathered the storm best, assisted by rent reductions and interest-free improvements, though in the worst times they were forced to eat into their capital. Even on the Yarborough estate, however, famed in former times for the stability of its tenantry, there had been many changes by 1900. The larger farms required considerable capital to maintain them in a good state of cultivation, and sons became increasingly unable or unwilling to follow their fathers. The larger owner-occupiers were badly hit, especially if they had heavy mortgages. When J. W. Dixon of Gravel Hill Farm, Thornton-le-Moor, became insolvent in 1890 the failure was attributed mainly to the fall in the value of land. He had incurred a debt of £18,000 to buy his farm (worth about £6,000 by 1890), and his interest payments had reached the equivalent of a double rent.[20] The large farmers who managed to hold their own and even to thrive during the depression were of three main types. There were the successful graziers like Henry Dudding of Riby or J. E. Casswell of Laughton, whose reputations as sheep breeders spread far beyond the county. There were the land-skinning farmers who took a number of scattered holdings at low rents and put foremen into the farmhouses.[21] And there were the engrossers who, especially in south Holland and the Lindsey Marsh, bought out smallholders and amassed holdings of 1,000, 2,000 or even 3,000 acres.

The smallholders were not all swept away. Many small owners failed through an inability to keep up their mortgage payments, some having originally borrowed as much as three-quarters of the purchase price of their farms. But in the Isle of Axholme, despite reports of the utmost gloom in the 1890s, many small farmers won through, and there continued to be a demand for small tenancies if not for small freehold farms. One early twentieth-century recorder of the agricultural scene referred to the reluctance of mortgagees to foreclose, and remarked on the 'solidarity of local interests' in the 'compact and somewhat isolated' farming community of the Isle.[22]

The labourers—those who remained on the land—were generally held to have suffered least of all the classes involved in agriculture. Real wages, as we have seen, rose in the late 1890s. But farmers cut down on casual labour, and seasonal unemployment persisted. Prices fell, benefiting the labourer as a consumer. But irregular work meant that cheap bread, though now in the labour-

[20] *SM* 24 Jan. 1890.
[21] See H. Rider Haggard, *Rural England*, new edn. (1906), ii. 166.
[22] A. D. Hall, *A Pilgrimage of British Farming*, 1913, p. 106.

ers' view, was not always on their tables. The winter of 1888–9, with its soup kitchens in the market towns, its vagrancy problem, and even the occasional incendiary fire, was reminiscent of forty years before, but winter conditions did improve in the 1890s.

One class connected with agriculture which could not easily emigrate or become absentee was the clergy. Tithes were revised downwards, glebe tenants got into arrears, and bills for repairs became more burdensome. Even a living such as Waddingham was by no means as desirable a plum as it had been a few decades earlier. Summoned for non-payment of rates in 1897, its incumbent explained that its value had dropped by a third, and that he had to spend half his income on educating his five children away from home. The incumbent of Rowston, whose problems were exacerbated by drink, left his creditors only three shillings in the pound when he died in 1900.[23]

With rent revisions, farms falling vacant, insolvencies, and foreclosings, there was no shortage of work for agents and attorneys. But it was not work of the highly remunerative kind that had made fortunes earlier in the century, and professional men had generally ceased to have the means or indeed the inclination to set up as landed proprietors in the county. Their largest clients were less able than formerly to lavish local patronage, and this had its inevitable effect on the economies of the market towns. It had always been the complaint in many parts of Lincolnshire that money made locally was spent elsewhere, but never was there more justification for that view than at the end of the nineteenth century. Those with dwindling incomes resented the growing burden of local and imperial taxation, and despite the measure of rate relief passed by the Conservative government in 1896 there were many members of the agricultural community who considered that they were a neglected interest. Mr Tindall, a land agent at Wainfleet, told Rider Haggard that the farmers wanted justice, not merely a dole. 'The whole question is: Is agriculture to be kept subservient to all other interests in the State?'[24]

Describing the effects of the agricultural depression, a recent historian concluded that 'In general the structure of agricultural society was severely shaken and the landowners' power much weakened'.[25] For Lincolnshire it is certainly true that, though the structure still stood in 1900, the process of dilapidation had been

[23] *SM* 17 Sept. 1897; *Archivists' Report* 24 (1972–3), p. 16.

[24] Rider Haggard, *op. cit.*, ii. 204.

[25] F. M. L. Thompson, *English Landed Society in the Nineteenth Century*, 1963, p. 316.

going on for nearly twenty-five years, and the mortar holding it together was visibly crumbling. Tenants had things much their own way, and farmed without regard to restrictive covenants; old tenants were not restrained by deferential attitudes from bargaining for rent reductions, and new tenants, some of them from outside the county, knew not the old estate traditions. The strengthened position of the farmers was demonstrated in 1904 by the formation of the Lincolnshire Farmers' Union, a body that led to the creation of the National Farmers' Union four years later.

Deference was in any case connected closely with the landlord's power of spending money in his locality; when that power shrank so did his sphere of influence. When country houses were let, their new occupants were to some extent accepted into rural society and were even put on the bench, but they lacked the historical roots and family connections of the indigenous gentry. The great owners survived in most cases, but their contribution to the day-to-day running of the county had always been limited. It was the impoverishment of the small gentry class and the lack of recruitment into it that in the long run had the most important effect on the society and administration of the county. Nevertheless it is easy to exaggerate the decline of the old county society, and to attribute that decline too sweepingly to the effects of the depression. Few large estates, as we have seen, changed hands, and landlord-tenant relations were in general preserved by a sense of mutual dependence from becoming openly strained. An exception was the Nocton estate, where its new owner, George Hodgson, tried in 1890 to impose stringent agreements on his tenants. It was said that he wanted 5 per cent on his investment, plus all the sport the estate could afford.[26] By contrast the Lincoln ironmaster Nathaniel Clayton treated his Withcall estate not as a way to make money but as an experiment in highly capitalized and mechanized farming. He created four farms where before there had been one, and since he continued to live in Lincoln he was not likely to harass his new tenants by over-preserving his game. The grievances of the farmers with regard to rates and foreign competition were shared by their landlords, who were mostly of the same political persuasion. Those landowners who had taken farms into their own hands, moreover, were well aware of the difficulties that their tenants were up against. In the mid-1890s Turnor had 3,600 acres in hand and Ancaster about 7,000.[27]

The most striking effects of the depression were in fact delayed until after the depression was over. Only in the early twentieth

[26] SM 4 July 1890.
[27] Parl. Papers, 1894 XVI (part 2), p. 17; 1895 XVI, p. 176.

century was Lincolnshire, more particularly Lindsey, transformed from a county of landlords and tenants into a county of owner-occupying farmers. Large sales occurred in the period 1906–14, but the biggest turnover was after the first world war, during the years 1919 to 1921. Even then, however, the old resident aristocracy of the county showed an impressive durability. The Pelhams, the Willoughbys, the Custs, and the Monsons survived: the Hornsbys, the Hodgsons, the Garfits, and the Clayton-Cockburns, as landed families, did not.

THE DECLINE OF COUNTY FEELING

In the Lincolnshire of 1900 old met new at many points. If courts leet and plough jacks were reminders of the past, motor cars and professional football were portents of the future. In 1900 the Automobile Club visited Lincoln, and four years earlier Grimsby Town had sold its goalkeeper to Aston Villa for the record transfer fee of £200.[28] Farm workers still stood in the market place to be hired, but trades unionism of a modern type had already become powerful in Lincolnshire's industrial centres. Grimsby formed a Trades Council in 1888, Lincoln in 1892. Tom Mann visited Lincoln in 1890 to address the local branch of the Amalgamated Society of Engineers. Two years later Ben Tillett was in the Scunthorpe area in connection with a strike of blast furnacemen.[29]

Education was free and compulsory, but enlightenment had not spread far in a county where a pauper girl convicted of attempted suicide could be given three months' hard labour, as happened at the Holland midsummer sessions of 1890. Workhouses were still miserable places in which to end one's days, although efforts were being made to brighten them up. In 1888 the aged male inmates of Spalding workhouse were allowed an ounce of tobacco a week, and provided with 'darker and less conspicuous clothing', while the women were allowed tea cups and saucers instead of mugs.[30]

Despite these variations in the pace of social change, many factors had combined by 1900 to produce one change that affected the life of the county as a whole. The social and administrative unity of Lincolnshire, never very strong, was weaker in 1900 than seventy years before, and county consciousness was in decline. Under the first earl Brownlow the gaol sessions had provided a forum for

[28] *SM* 27 March 1896.
[29] Hill, *Victorian Lincoln*, p. 209; Edward Dodd, *The Quibell Story*, pr. Scunthorpe, n.d., p. 14.
[30] *SM* 13 April 1888.

county business, and had undertaken important improvements in the public buildings of the county. The lord lieutenant himself had exercised a central guidance in militia and magistracy matters. The magistrates of the three divisions had not always worked together in amity, but they had shared a common social if not political outlook, and the quarter sessions chairmen were often men with a strong county sense. All that had changed by the end of the century. The county lost its gaol, and the functions of the lord lieutenant and gaol sessions were circumscribed. Local government was more vigorous in the 1890s than ever before, but the battles were no longer fought on a county scale. The county councils were less inclined to co-operate with each other than their quarter sessions predecessors, and the collapse of the agreement over the lunatic asylum was symptomatic of this new spirit in local affairs. Now that county councillors had to study the ratepayers there was less eagerness to embody county pride in public buildings, and the new councils were reluctant to build administrative headquarters.

Politically too there had been fragmentation. The division of the county in 1832 had been followed by the demise of the county meeting, and later by the disappearance of the 'peace of the county' as a factor influencing electoral arrangements. By 1900 class feeling had triumphed over local feeling, and there was a barbed wire fence down the middle of county politics over which Conservative farmers and Liberal labourers eyed each other with hostility.

For much of the nineteenth century the leaders of the county had been the greater gentry—Chaplins, Sheffields, Heneages, Trollopes and the like. Through their social dominance, their wealth locally acquired and locally spent, and their leadership in politics and on the bench they had set the tone of the county more effectually than the titled aristocracy. But in the last quarter of the century their position had been challenged by new elements in local society, and at the same time their wealth had been sapped by declining agricultural rents. Equally significant was the shrinkage of the class immediately below them, the small gentry and the rural upper middle class. These men may never have been strongly attached to the county as a concept, but they had provided the solid structure on which the upper ranks of county society rested. From the 1870s both economic depression and administrative change contributed to their social eclipse.

In view of its close connection with rural culture, it is not surprising that county feeling was sapped by the partial urbanization of Lincolnshire in the later nineteenth century. Townsmen found their way on to the bench, and the introduction of the county councils increased their importance. Urban ways of thought were carried into the countryside by newspapers, nonconformist preachers, trade union emissaries, political organizers, and town workers returning to their native villages for the annual feast. During the Boer War national and world events were more closely studied in Lincolnshire than for many years previously. With education came broader horizons, and increased mobility meant that the county was becoming ever less self-contained.

In 1800 Lincolnshire had been too big to make a coherent social and administrative unit. By 1900, due above all to the railways, it was in some ways too small. Nevertheless the ancient county survived the threat of boundary-mongering in 1888, just as it had survived the Wisbech assize proposals fifty years previously. It remains to be seen how much county spirit will survive the more drastic administrative 'reform' of the 1970s.

SELECT BIBLIOGRAPHY

Note: all manuscript sources cited are in LAO unless otherwise stated. The most common sources used are as follows:

Manuscript Sources, Lincolnshire Archives Office (LAO)

Holland Quarter Sessions (HQS): minutes, clerk's papers (including papers relating to Boston quarter sessions 1843–8), records of Elloe statute sessions 1767–1867.

Kesteven Quarter Sessions (KQS): minutes, clerk's papers from 1824, papers relating to sessions and sessions houses, papers relating to the commission of the peace 1855–6, militia papers 1793–1854, Bracebridge Asylum papers 1844–55, county police papers 1856–9.

Lindsey Quarter Sessions (LQS): minutes, clerk's papers, papers relating to prisons and sessions 1866–75.

Kesteven County Council (KCC): minutes, clerk's papers, Rauceby Asylum papers.

Lindsey County Council (LCC): clerk's papers.

County Committee (CoC): grand jury book 1741–1891, 'minutes of county meetings' 1792–1823, county hall commissioners' minutes 1822–30, gaol sessions papers (from 1824) and minutes (from 1842), county committee records from 1889, county gaol records.

Poor Law Unions: guardians' minutes and accounts.

Lindsey Sewers: miscellaneous papers.

Ancaster MSS (ANC): Grimsthorpe and Lindsey Coast estate correspondence, Heathcote family correspondence.

Anderson MSS (AND): papers of Sir C. H. J. Anderson.

Brownlow MSS (BNL): papers of the first earl Brownlow as lord lieutenant 1809–52.

Dixon MSS (DIXON): family papers.

Heneage MSS (HEN): estate papers, including letters to Edward, first baron Heneage.

Monson MSS (MON): correspondence of the sixth baron Monson and the seventh baron Monson (later viscount Oxenbridge).

Tennyson D'Eyncourt MSS (TDE): papers of George Tennyson and Charles Tennyson D'Eyncourt.

Yarborough MSS (YARB): estate papers, letter books of the second earl of Yarborough.

Manuscripts in Private Custody

Anderson (Helmsley) MSS, in the possession of the Rt Hon. the Earl of Feversham.

Diary of Catherine Rawnsley, in the possession of R. Fenwick Owen, Esq.

Diaries of H. J. Torr, in the possession of Mrs H. N. Nevile.

Uppleby family papers, in the possession of Professor and Mrs J. Barron.

Printed Works

Bateman, John, *The Great Landowners of Great Britain and Ireland*, 4th edn. 1883.
Collins, G. E., *History of the Brocklesby Hounds 1700–1901*, 1902.
Directories of Lincolnshire, especially those published by William White, Sheffield, 1826, 1842, 1856, 1872, 1882 and 1892.
Haggard, H. Rider, *Rural England*, new edn. 1906, 2 vols.
Hill, Sir Francis, *Georgian Lincoln*, Cambridge, 1966.
——, *Victorian Lincoln*, Cambridge, 1975.
Hobsbawm, E. J., and Rudé, George, *Captain Swing*, 1969.
Lincoln, Rutland, and Stamford Mercury (SM).
Lincolnshire Archives Committee, *Archivists' Reports* 1–25 (1950–75).
Lincolnshire Constabulary 1857–1957, Lincoln, 1957.
Lincolnshire Magazine (1932–9).
Malcolmson, R. W., *Popular Recreations in English Society 1700–1850*, 1973.
Mather, F. C., *Public Order in the Age of the Chartists*, 1959.
Mingay, G. E., *Rural Life in Victorian England*, 1977.
Moir, Esther, *The Justice of the Peace*, 1969.
Obelkevich, James, *Religion and Rural Society: South Lindsey 1825–1875*, Oxford, 1976.
Olney, R. J., *Lincolnshire Politics 1832–1885*, Oxford, 1973.
——, ed., *Labouring Life on the Lincolnshire Wolds: A Study of Binbrook in the Mid-Nineteenth Century*, Occasional Papers in Lincolnshire History and Archaeology no. 2, 1975.
Parliamentary Papers. Reports and statistics: agriculture, Boston elections, endowed schools, justices of the peace, municipal corporations, owners of land (1873), poor laws, population censuses, prisons, etc.
Pevsner, N., and Harris, J., *The Buildings of England: Lincolnshire*, 1964.
Poll books, especially those for the County of Lincol 1807, 1818, and 1824.
Rogers, A., ed., *Stability and Change: Some Aspects of North and South Rauceby*, University of Nottingham Department of Adult Education, 1969.
Rudkin, Ethel H., *Lincolnshire Folklore*, repr. 1973.
Russell, Rex C., *The 'Revolt of the Field' in Lincolnshire*, Lincolnshire Committee of the National Union of Agricultural Workers, 1956.
——, *A History of Schools and Education in Lindsey, Lincolnshire, 1800–1902*, 4 parts, Lindsey County Council Education Committee, 1965–7.
Thompson, F. M. L., *English Landed Society in the Nineteenth Century*, 1963.
Varley, Joan, *The Parts of Kesteven*, Kesteven County Council, 1974.
Webb, Sidney, and Webb, Beatrice, *The Parish and the County (English Local Government vol. 1)*, repr. 1963.
——, *English Prisons under Local Government (English Local Government, vol. 6)*, repr. 1963.
Young, Arthur, *General View of the Agriculture of the County of Lincoln, 1799*.

INDEX

INDEX

Places are in the ancient county of Lincoln unless otherwise specified.

202 RURAL SOCIETY IN NINETEENTH-CENTURY LINCOLNSHIRE